The Complete

Instant Pot

Pressure Cooker Cookbook

999 Quick and Delicious Instant Pot Recipes for the Smart

People on a Budget

By Jessica Johnston

Legal & Disclaimer

The information and contents herein are not designed to replace or take the place of any form of medical or professional advice and are not meant to replace the need for independent medical, financial, legal or other professional advice or services, as may be required. The content and information in this book have been provided for educational and entertainment purposes only.

The content and information in this book have been compiled from reliable sources and are accurate to the author's best knowledge, information, and belief. The author cannot guarantee this book's accuracy and validity and cannot be held liable for any errors and/or omissions. Further, changes will be periodically made to this book when needed. It is recommended that you consult with a health professional who is familiar with your personal medical history before using any of the suggested remedies, techniques, or information in this book.

Upon using the contents in this book, you agree to hold harmless the author from and against any damages, costs, and expenses, including any legal fees potentially resulting from the application of the information provided You agree to accept all risks associated with using the information presented inside this book.

Table of Content

Introduction

- Will instant pot really reduce my time in the kitchen?
- Would it really make my life easier?
- Surely, instant pot cannot be that brilliant as said, can it?
- What is it unique about instant pots that is making it so popular?
- Are the foods cooked in an instant pot healthy?
- What makes it different from the regular pressure cooker?

The instant pot is revolutionary equipment that I can say it has changed my life. I know how this sounds when you say it, but after using it to make some of the top recipe dishes, you will confirm to me that instant pots are awesome. Thanks to this revolutionary kitchen item, you will not have to keep compromising your diet values because you are sure that you cannot serve your family junk food anymore.

We have created a book with a hundred instant pot recipes, and you can cook them at the comfort of your house. The book covers all types of foods from poultry, beef, seafood, desserts, breakfast, entrees, among others. The book is the ultimate solution for someone who is looking for the best way to eat healthy and prepare meals within a short period. Some of the outstanding features of the book include:

- You will learn how to prepare vegetable and beans recipes
- You will learn how to combine different recipes to create a wonderful meal
- You will know how to measure liquids when cooking
- You will be familiarized with the technicalities about instant pot and how you can change it to different set modes.
- We will give you information on how to maintain your food warm for a long time without affecting its taste or nutrients

Instant pots are simply amazing, and you can use it to make any dish in our 100 instant pot recipes at any time.

Chapter 1 Understanding the Instant Pot Basics

What Is Instant Pot?

An instant pot is a multi-functional countertop cooker that is revolutionized cooking. It is a multi-functional component rolled into one, all rolled into one. You have an electric pressure cooker, a steamer, a rice cooker, a slow cooker, a yogurt maker, a sauté pan, and a warming pot too.

The instant pot will allow you to start making steel cut oats overnight, and you can have all your house smelling exceptionally good. You can make any rich, satisfying soups, stews, or sauces within a short period. You do not have to wait for a long time for the meat to be extra tender because when you have an instant pot, you will achieve the tenderness that you want within no time. Besides, you can make indulgent desserts within a fraction of the time that you usually spent making them. I have to repeat what I said earlier; the instant pot is a revolutionary kitchen item that will change your life!

A few notes that you should understand from us is that we have made everything as simple as possible to ensure that you understand all the dynamics before you get the instant pot. We try to keep exotic ingredients to the minimum throughout the recipes in the book. All the ingredients can be found at your local grocery store. You can use regularly available items and make an amazing meal that you have been yearning for. Before we delve into nitty-gritty into the benefits of instant pots and then we will guide you on the buttons you will find on the instant pot so that you can hit the ground running as soon as possible. Finally, I will share with you over 100 instant pot recipes that are mouth-watering. These include poultry, vegan dishes, breakfasts, appetizers, entrees, meat, fish, soups and stews, seafood, and we will round off the boom with scrumptious desserts. Let us get started.

The Advantages of Using An Instant Pot

Nearly all top chefs, food bloggers, and home cooks have been raving for the ingenious kitchen appliance to be available in the market. When it was first launched in the market a few years ago, many people were pessimistic. However, they have maintained their reputation, and they kept the benefits that were indicated as earlier indicated. To be frank, I cannot remember what I cooked with my instant pot the first time I purchased it. However, since these days, I do most of my cooking, it has become a part of my daily kitchen appliances. So, what are the benefits of an instant pot?

❖ Saves Time

The major advantage is that the instant pot will save you a lot of cooking time. You do not have to spend hours to cook that hearty meal your loved ones adore. In the modern era, everyone is busy, and we do not have time to spent in the kitchen. The instant pot will save you 70% of the time you would have used in cooking. Most of the time, you take cooking roast meats, lentils, beans, and other foods which usually take time. However, with the instant pot, you can cook your amazing dishes within no time.

❖ Saves Money

It is not just time that you will save with an instant pot; you will save plenty of food that would have otherwise gone to waste. Besides, the pot is made with the latest technology, and power consumption is at its lowest. Therefore, you will save fuel bills. Since the instant pot is a sealed device, the water used in cooking will not evaporate, leaving your food sumptuous and succulent. Besides, it helps to cook the meal faster and make healthier choices too.

❖ **You Will Have More Nutritious Foods**

When you boil your vegetables, a lot of the nutrition is lost during the cooking. However, the instant pot allows you to steam the veggies and retain all the ingredients while retaining water to make it succulent.

❖ **Eliminates Bacteria And Other Microorganisms**

It is important to note that instant pots will cook the food beyond their boiling points; therefore, you will be able to kill all the bacteria that can cause diseases and infection. This is especially important if you are cooking corn, wheat, beef, or foods that are known to harbor toxins.

❖ **You Will Require Less Kitchen Equipment**

You do not need to have multiple types of equipment anymore because the instant pot can do activities for all the equipment that you may need. You will have a cleaner, tidier kitchen and less wash up to when you are done cooking because you are using only one equipment.

❖ **It Is a Safer Option Than a Pressure Cooker**

While I can attest that I own a pressure cooker and I have used one for the past decade, it is imperative to note that the instant pot is on a league of its own. The instant pot has many self-regulating features that will allow you to monitor pressure and temperature; therefore, you can stay safer throughout your cooking. Instant pots will not only save time in the kitchen, enhance the nutrition of your foods, but you will discover that you can also make hearty meals at the comfort of your house.

❖ **Features of Instant Pot**

If you are lucky enough to get an instant pot or own an instant pot currently, you will realize that there are so many buttons on the side, and if you are not a tech-savvy individual, it can be quite challenging. However, you should not fret because we have a detailed description of how you can get acquainted with using an instant pot. In this section, we will run you through all the essential buttons and how you can use them as effectively as possible.

The Main Functions

➢ Sauté

You can use this button to sauté garlic, onions, meat, and vegetables in the same way you can utilize any stove. You can also simmer using the heat setting or reduce the heat by adjusting the button to the 'less' option. Besides, you can brown or increase heat by pressing 'more.'

➢ Keep Warm/ Cancel Button

It does exactly what is indicated. You can use this feature to cancel a function or keep your food warm. On some models, you can use the option to increase or decrease the temperature.

➢ Manual/ Pressure Cook Button

This is one of those magic buttons that will keep your food as long as you want. You can use the +

Pre-Set Buttons

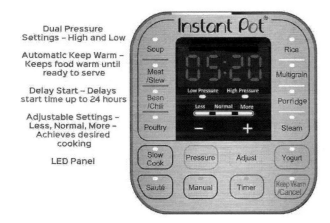

✧ Soup

This feature allows you to cook at high pressure for 30 minutes and adjust time with + and – buttons.

and – buttons to adjust the cooking time that you want.

➢ Slow Cooker

This is a feature of the instant pot that gives you 4 hours cooking period. You can use the + and – button to adjust the cooking time. This allows you to cook the food as long or as short as you want.

➢ Pressure

This is a feature of the instant pot that allows you to interchange between low and high pressure.

➢ Yogurt

You can use this button to make yogurt! this can be done in the comfort of your home.

✧ Meat/Stew

This is a feature that allows you to cook at high pressure for 35 minutes. Besides, you can use + and – buttons to adjust your cooking time.

✧ Beans/Chili

This setting will cook your food at high pressure for 30 minutes. You can adjust time with + and – buttons.

✧ Poultry

This setting allows you to cook the food on high for 15 minutes. As usual, use + and – buttons to adjust the cooking time.

✧ Rice

This setting allows you to automatically cook the rice at low pressure as long as it takes.

✧ Multi-Grain

This setting allows you to cook the grains at high pressure for 40 minutes. Besides, you can use the + and – buttons to adjust the cooking time.

5

✧ **Porridge**

This setting will cook your porridge on high pressure for 20 minutes. Also, you can use the + and – buttons to adjust the cooking time.

✧ **Steam**

This setting allows you to cook on high for 10 minutes and you can use the + and – buttons to adjust the cooking time. You will need to use a steamer basket or a rack to get the best results.

✧ **Cake**

It is imperative to know that not all models have this button. But if you have a model that has this feature, then you can count yourself lucky. You can select 'more,' 'less,' and 'normal' to cook a wide array of sweet treats.

✧ **Egg**

Some new models have an egg setting, and you can select 'more' or 'less' to cook eggs to a level you like.

✧ **Sterilize**

It is important to understand that you can even sterilize your utensils and jars in some models. You can adjust the time required on the setting option and ensure that you get the best results. Understandably, you have never used an instant pot before, and the list of the buttons might seem too many. However, you can get started immediately, as you progress to more complex food varieties.

Start Using The Instant Pot

The instant pot is a multipurpose appliance that can be programmed to make a wide array of dishes. It cooks meals faster, and you can customize the food varieties. Here is how to use the instant pot for the first time.

1. Connect the power cord. The LED display will indicate 'OFF' which means it is on a standby mode.
2. Select any cooking function you want, for example, soup, meat/stew, etc. ensure that the steam release handle should be in 'sealing' position. Once you have pressed the function key, the indicator will light up, and you can select any other cooking option.
3. Choose the cooking pressure. All functions except 'RICE' are default to high pressure. It is essential to note that for rice, you will have to choose low pressure for fluffy and tasty rice.
4. Choose a cooking time. You can adjust the cooking time using + and – to ensure that you can get and fine-tune your cooking time to minutes specified as per the recipes. You can change to default settings in case you unplug your instant pot.
5. Cooking starts immediately after 10 seconds after the last key that you pressed. Three audible beeps will indicate that the cooking process has just begun. The LED display will indicate 'ON,' and the preheating will be in progress. Once the cooker has reached the required pressure, the display will change to 'ON.'
6. When the cooking cycle ends, the cooker will beep and automatically shift to 'keep warm' mode, also called Auto 'Keep warm' mode. You can deactivate this by pressing the cancel button twice.

Slow Cooking In An Instant Pot

1. Connect your cooker to the power outlet. The LED will indicate 'OFF,' and this will indicate a standby mode.
2. Press the 'Slow cook' option. It is important to note that the steam release handle should be in the venting position.
3. Change the cooking time to 0.5 hours to 20 hours by adjusting the + and – keys.
4. You can select the desired cooking mode by pressing the 'Adjust' key to select temperature from 'more' for high, 'normal' for medium, and 'less' for low.
5. Cooking will begin exactly after 10 seconds of pressing your last button.
6. Once you have completed cooking, the instant pot will beep and go into auto 'keep warm' mode for 10 hours.

Sautéing

It is important to note that the lid muse is off when using the sautéing option. Press 'sauté' function and for safety purposes, the maximum operation time for one sauté cycle should be 30 minutes. You can select cooking temperature from high to low using the + and – buttons.

How To Release Pressure

Turn the steam release handle to the venting position and let out the steam until the float valve begins to the dropdown. You mustn't do a quick release if you are cooking food with a large liquid volume. Alternatively, you can use natural release by cooling the cooker down slowly, and this may take up to 10 minutes.

Cooking Preparations

1. Open the lid: grasp the handle and rotate it about 30 degrees in a counterclockwise manner until it reaches the direction of 'open.'
2. Remove the inner pot from cooker: this option is only applicable to all options except when you are sautéing. Clean and wipe the cooker before returning it to the inner part of the cooker.
3. Add liquid and food to the inner pot: for all the pressure cooking options, the amount of precooked food and liquid should NEVER exceed two thirds the inner pot capacity. For starchy foods such as porridge do not fill the inner pot past halfway.
4. Close the lid and place the steam handle release button to the exact position. When running any of the programs except 'sauté,' 'keep warm,' and 'slow cook' align it to 'sealing position. The sauté option must be done without the lid.

Instant Pot Cook Time Table

Meat: raw meat is perishable, and it should not be left at room temperature for more than 2 hours. When you are using the delayed cooking, do not set it for more than 1 to 2 hours.

Veggies: when you choose to steam your vegetables, you are required to use at least 2 cups of water and a free-standing vegetable steamer or wire mesh basket — quick pressure release to stop cooking.

Fruits: when steaming fruits, you should use at least 2 cups of water and free-standing vegetable steamer — quick pressure release once you are done the cooking.

Meat	Cooking time
Beef, steak, pot roast, chuck, brisket, large, rump, and round	35-40 minutes
Beef, ribs	25-30 minutes
Chicken, breasts	8 -10 minutes
Chicken cut up with bones	10-15 minutes
Chicken, dark meat	10 – 15 minutes
Chicken, whole	20-25 minutes
Ham slice	9-12 minutes
Lamb, leg	35-45 minutes
Pork, butt roast	45-50 minutes
Pork, ribs	20-25 minutes
Turkey, breasts, boneless	15-20 minutes
Turkey, breast, whole with bones	25- 30 minutes

Fruits

Fruits	Fresh cooking time (minutes)	Frozen cooking time(minutes)
Apples, in pieces or slices	2-3	3-4
Apples, whole	3-4	4-6
Apricots, whole or halves	2-3	3-4
peaches	2-3	4-5
Pears, slices or halves	2-3	4-5
Pears, whole	3-4	4-6

Rice And Grain

Rice and grain	Water quantity	Cooking time(minutes)
Barley, pearl	1:4	25-30
Couscous	1:2	5-8
Oats, quick-cooking	1:1 1/2	6
Oats, steel-cut	1: 1 2/3	10
Porridge, thin	1:6	15-20
Quinoa, quick-cooking	1:2	8
Rice, basmati	1:1.5	4-8
Brown rice	1:1 ¼	22-28
Jasmine rice	1:1	4-10
White rice	1:1.5	8
Wild rice	1:3	25-30

Chapter 2 Breakfast

Cinnamon & Coconut Porridge

Serves: 6, Prep+ Cook time: 21 minutes

Ingredients

- Cinnamon sticks, 2 ½.
- Sweetened condensed milk, ¾ cup.
- Vanilla extract, 1 ¼ tsps.
- Coconut flakes, ¾ tsp.
- Water, 6 cups
- Fine yellow cornmeal, 1 ¼ cups.
- Coconut milk, 1 ¼ cups.

Directions:

1. Put the instant pot on fire then add coconut milk and 5 cups of water.
2. In a small bowl, combine 1cup of water and cornmeal then add to the pot.
3. Mix in coconut flakes, cinnamon sticks, and vanilla extract.
4. With the lid sealed, press manual function key.
5. Cook on high pressure for six minutes
6. Once the timer clicks, Release the pressure naturally then open the lid.
7. Mix in sweetened and condensed milk then serve.

Nutritional Information:
Calories: 253, Carbs: 46.2g, Protein: 6.9g, Fat: 3.1g, Sugar: 17.2g, Sodium: 179mg

Creamy Strawberry Oatmeal

Serves: 4 , Prep+ Cook time: 11 minutes

Ingredients

- Milk, 2 ¼ cups.
- Ground cinnamon, ½ tsp.
- Chopped strawberries, 8.
- Salt, ½ tsp.
- Sugar, ¼ cup.
- Old-fashioned oats, 2 cups.
- Water, 2 ¼ cups.

Directions:

1. Transfer all the ingredients in your instant pot but reserve some sliced strawberries for garnishing.
2. With the lid in position, select multigrain option.
3. Allow to cook for six minutes
4. Release the pressure naturally once the timer beeps and remove the lid.
5. Serve topped with the strawberries.

Nutritional Information:
Calories: 436, Carbs: 75g, Protein: 14.7g, Fat: 8g, Sugar: 22g, Sodium: 360mg

Orange Flavored Strawberry Compote

Serves: 4 , Prep+ Cook time: 25 minutes

Ingredients

- Chopped vanilla bean, 1.
- Fresh orange juice, 2 oz.
- Sugar, ¼ cup.
- Trimmed and halved fresh strawberries, 2 lbs.
- Toast.
- Ground ginger, ½ tsp.

Directions:

1. In an instant pot, combine all the ingredients.
2. With the lid closed, press manual function key.
3. Let it cook for 15 minutes at a high pressure.
4. Naturally release the pressure and open the lid after the beep.
5. Mix in the prepared compote and allow to thicken before cooling.
6. Serve on toast.

Nutritional Information:
Calories: 152, Carbs: 35.5g, Protein: 2.4g, Fat: 1.6g, Sugar: 27.6g, Sodium: 14mg

Instant pot Rice Pudding

Serves: 2 , Prep+ Cook time: 15 minutes

Ingredients

- Short grain basmati rice, ½ cup.
- Whipped cream.
- Water, ¾ cup.
- Coconut cream, ½ cup.
- Sea salt, ¼ tsp.
- Coconut flakes.
- Coconut milk, 1 cup.
- Maple syrup, 2 tbsps.

Directions:

1. In an instant cooking pot, combine coconut milk, maple syrup, water, coconut cream, basmati rice, and sea salt.
2. With the lid in position, press the manual function on the cooker
3. Set the cooker at a high pressure to cook for 10 minutes.
4. Release the pressure naturally once the timer clicks then open the lid.
5. Give the pudding a gentle stir then serve in a bowl
6. Top with coconut flakes and whipped cream.
7. Enjoy.

Nutritional Information:
Calories: 476, Carbs: 36.5g, Protein: 18.6g, Fat: 27.9g, Sugar: 9.8g, Sodium: 747mg

Apricot Raisins Steel-Cut Oats

Serves: 4 , Prep+ Cook time: 15 minutes

Ingredients

- Ground cinnamon, ½ tsp.
- Dried cranberries, 2 tbsps.
- Water, 3 cups.
- Pure maple syrup, 2 tbsps.
- Freshly squeezed orange juice, 2 cups.
- Chopped dried apricots, 2 tbsps.
- Butter, 4 tbsps.
- Salt, ¼ tsp.
- Chopped strawberries, ¼ tsp.
- Steel-cut oats, 2 cups.
- Raisins, 2 tbsps.
- Chopped pecans, 4 tbsps.

Directions:

1. In an instant pot, combine all the ingredients.
2. Tap the Manual function key after sealing the lid on the cooker.
3. Set the cooker at high pressure to cook for 10 minutes.
4. Release the pressure naturally then open the lid after the timer beeps.
5. Give the meal a gentle stir and serve in a bowl.
6. Top with fresh strawberries to garnish.
7. Enjoy.

Nutritional Information:
Calories: 351, Carbs: 45.3g, Protein: 6.4g, Fat: 16.8g, Sugar: 14.5g, Sodium: 238mg

Bell Pepper Stuffed with Eggs

Serves: 4 , Prep+ Cook time: 11 minutes

Ingredients

- Refrigerated fresh eggs, 4.
- Mozzarella slices, slices
- Bell peppers, 4.
- Aluminum foil.
- Toasted whole wheat bread slices, 4.
- Arugula small bunches, 2.

For the Mock Hollandaise Sauce:

- White wine vinegar, 2 tbsps.
- Dijon mustard, 3 tsps.
- Salt, 1 tsp.
- Fresh lemon juice, 2 tsps.
- Turmeric, 2 tsps.
- Mayonnaise, 1 ½ cup.
- Orange juice, 6 tbsps.

Directions:

1. Whisk together lemon juice, mayonnaise, turmeric, Dijon mustard, orange juice, white

wine vinegar and salt in a medium bowl and reserve.

2. In a pot, add water then put the steamer trivet inside.
3. Arrange the bell pepper cups over the trivet then break an egg into each cup then cover with aluminum foil.
4. Press the "manual" function key on the cooker after sealing the lid.
5. Allow to cook on low pressure for 6 minutes.

6. Release the pressure naturally then open the lid once the timer clicks.
7. Remove the bell peppers
8. Stack the bread slices with slices mozzarella, arugula, and pepper cups.
9. Pour the reserved sauce slowly over the stacks.
10. Serve and enjoy.

Nutritional Information:
Calories: 614, Carbs: 46.4g, Protein: 19.6g, Fat: 40.4g, Sugar: 15.6g, Sodium: 1119mg

Creamy Latte Cut Oats

Serves: 6 , Prep+ Cook time: 20 minutes

Ingredients
- Steel-cut oats, 2 cups.
- Espresso powder, 2 tsps.
- Vanilla extract, 4 tsps.
- Finely grated chocolate
- Sugar, 4 tbsps.
- Milk, 2 cups.
- Freshly whipped cream
- Water, 5 cups.
- Salt, ½ tsp.

Directions:
1. In your instant pot, combine milk, vanilla extract, sugar, salt, water, espresso powder, and oats.

2. With the lid in position, press the manual function key on the cooker.
3. Set the cooker at high pressure to cook for 10 minutes.
4. Release the pressure naturally once the timer beeps then open the lid.
5. Give the meal a gentle stir then serve in the bowl.
6. Top with grated chocolate and whipped cream for garnishing.

Nutritional Information
Calories: 274, Carbs: 46.6g, Protein: 9.4g, Fat: 5.2g, Sugar: 18.4g, Sodium: 360mg

Tasty Mixed Peppers Morning Hash

Serves: 3 , Prep+ Cook time: 35 minutes

Ingredients
- Cheddar cheese, ½ cup.
- Chopped green bell pepper, ½.
- Black pepper, ¼ tsp.
- Chopped bacon slices, 2.
- Milk, 1 tbsp.
- Chopped red bell pepper, ½.
- Aluminum foil.
- Salt, ¼ tsp.
- Eggs, 6.
- Chopped yellow bell pepper, ½.
- Spring form pan, 6-inch

Directions:
1. In an instant pot, add bacon and press the "Sauté" function to cook for 3 minutes.
2. Put the cooked bacon on a greased spring pan.
3. Top bell pepper on the bacon.

4. Crash together the eggs and milk in a mixing bowl.
5. Transfer the egg mixture over the bell peppers in the spring pan.
6. Add some seasonings on top then cover with aluminum foil.
7. Add water to the instant pot and set the trivet inside. Place the spring pan over the trivet.
8. Press the Manual key to cook for 15 minutes at high pressure.
9. Release the steam naturally once the timer is over.
10. Open the lid and transfer the meal to a plate.
11. Top with cheddar cheese to serve.

Nutritional Information:
Calories: 406, Carbs: 23.1g, Protein: 27.9g, Fat: 19.2g, Sugar: 2.9g, Sodium: 512mg

Cornmeal & Cinnamon Porridge

Serves: 6 , **Prep+ Cook time:** 16 minutes

Ingredients

- Milk, 1 ¼ cups.
- Pimento berries, 5.
- Sweetened condensed milk, ¾ cup.
- Fine yellow cornmeal, 1 ¼ cups.
- Vanilla extract, 1 ¼ tsps.
- Cinnamon sticks, 2 ½.
- Water, 6 cups.
- Ground nutmeg, ¾ tsp.

Directions:

1. Combine milk and 5 cups of water in an instant pot.
2. Combine one cup of water with corn meal then add to the pot.
3. In the pot add cinnamon sticks, pimento berries, vanilla extract and nutmeg then stir.
4. With the lid in its position, press the manual function.
5. Let it cook for 6 minutes at a high pressure.
6. Release the pressure naturally once the timer beeps and remove the lid.
7. Gently stir in sweetened condensed milk then serve
8. Enjoy.

Nutritional Information:

Calories: 247, Carbs: 43.5g, Protein: 6.9g, Fat: 5.4g, Sugar: 23.7g, Sodium: 90mg

Cinnamon Bread Pudding

Serves: 4 , **Prep+ Cook time:** 16 minutes

Ingredients

- Cinnamon, ½ tsp.
- Egg, 1.
- Sweetened condensed milk, ¼ cup.
- Milk, ¼ cup.
- Baking pan, 6-inch.
- Chopped and cubed challah bread, 2 cups.
- Semi-sweet chocolate chunks, 1/3 cup.
- Aluminum foil
- Water, 1 cup.

Directions:

1. Mix all the wet ingredients and the egg in a mixing bowl.
2. Grease the baking pan before pouring egg mixture into it.
3. Top the chocolate chunks and challah bread to the pan.
4. Pour one cup of water to the pot before placing the trivet inside.
5. Put the spring pan over the trivet then cover with aluminum foil.
6. With the lid closed, press the manual function key.
7. Let it cook for 11 minutes at high pressure.
8. Once the timer clicks, Release the pressure naturally then remove the lid.
9. Allow the pudding to cool before serving.
10. Enjoy.

Nutritional Information:

Calories: 305, Carbs: 48.1g, Protein: 8.7g, Fat: 10.3g, Sugar: 22.2g, Sodium: 229mg

Egg & Black Bean Casserole

Serves: 3 , **Prep+ Cook time:** 30 minutes

Ingredients

- Mozzarella cheese, ½ cup.
- Chopped large red onion, ¼.
- Green onions, ¼ cup.
- Chopped red bell pepper, ½.
- Cotija cheese, ½ cup.
- Cilantro.
- Rinsed black beans, ½ can.
- Well-beaten large eggs, 4.
- Mild ground sausage, ½ lb.
- Sour cream.
- Flour, ¼ cup.

Directions:

1. Add onion and sausage to the instant pot and tap the Sauté function to cook for 3 minutes.

2. Mix eggs and flour then add to the sausage mixture.
3. Top with beans, all the vegetables, and cheese
4. With the lid in position, select manual function
5. Let it cook for 20 minutes at high pressure.
6. When the timer clicks, let the pressure to release naturally and remove the pressure.

7. Remove the inner pot and place a plate on top.
8. Flip the pot and place the casserole to the plate.
9. Serve while warm and enjoy.

Nutritional Information:
Calories: 564, Carbs: 33.4g, Protein: 36.2g, Fat: 30.7g, Sugar: 4.3g, Sodium: 1050mg

Red Bell pepper Frittatas

Serves: 2 , Prep+ Cook time: 15 minutes

Ingredients
- Water, 1 cup.
- Salt.
- Silicon baking molds, 3.
- Cheddar cheese, ¼ cup.
- Chopped onion, ¼ cup.
- Eggs, 3.
- Almond milk, 2 tbsps.
- Pepper.
- Chopped red bell pepper, ¼ cup.
- Oil, 1 tbsp.

Directions:
1. In an instant pot, add a cup of water put the trivet inside.

2. Mix all the vegetables, cheese, spices, eggs and milk in a small dish.
3. Grease the silicon baking molds then pour the veggie mixture in each mold.
4. Set the silicon baking molds over the trivet.
5. With the lid in place, press the manual function key.
6. Allow to cook on high pressure for 5 minutes
7. Once the timer clicks, Release the pressure naturally then open the lid.
8. Serve the meal while still warm and enjoy.

Nutritional Information:
Calories: 196, Carbs: 4g, Protein: 12.5g, Fat: 14.9g, Sugar: 2.4g, Sodium: 183mg

Instant pot Orange Oatmeal

Serves: 4 , Prep+ Cook time: 11 minutes

Ingredients
- Orange marmalade, 2 tbsps.
- Milk, 2 ¼ cups.
- Salt, ½ tsp.
- Plain low-fat Greek yogurt, 2 tbsps.
- Water, 2 ¼ cups.
- Orange slices.
- Old-fashioned oats, 2 cups.
- Kiwi slices
- Ground cinnamon, ½ tsp.
- Sugar, ¼ cup.

Directions:

1. Set all the ingredients in your instant pot except kiwi and orange slices.
2. Seal the pressure cooker lid and select manual function key.
3. Allow to cook on high pressure for 6 minutes
4. Immediately the timer clicks, allow the pressure to naturally release then remove the lid.
5. Give the meal a gentle stir then serve in a bowl garnished with kiwi and orange slices.

Nutritional Information:
Calories: 523, Carbs: 84.8g, Protein: 26.5g, Fat: 8.2g, Sugar: 31.3g, Sodium: 423mg

Simple Garlic & Turmeric Eggs

Serves: 4 , **Prep+ Cook time:** 25 minutes

Ingredients

- Chopped green onion, 1.
- Salt.
- Eggs, 4.
- Minced garlic, 1 tsp.
- Small tomatoes, 6.
- Olive oil, 1 tbsp.
- Turmeric powder, 1 tsp.
- Pepper.

Directions:

1. Before anything else, slice the tomatoes into four slices then reserve.
2. Put one tbsp. of oil in the instant pot then select sauté.
3. Add the tomato slices to sauté with the cut side down.
4. Mix in powdered turmeric and minced garlic.
5. Stir in eggs and scramble using a spatula.
6. Mix in turmeric, garlic, and seasoning.
7. Allow the egg scramble to cook on sauté mode for 15 minutes.
8. Once the timer clicks, select cancel.
9. Serve the eggs topped with green onions.

Coconut & veggies Rice Mix

Serves: 4 , **Prep+ Cook time:** 27 minutes

Ingredients

- Turmeric powder, ½ tsp.
- Sea salt, ½ tsp.
- Chopped cilantro, 1 bunch.
- Sliced cremini mushrooms, ½ cup.
- Shredded coconut, 3 tsps.
- White basmati rice, 1 cup.
- Whole mung beans, 1 cup.
- Water, 6 cups.
- Grated ginger, 2 inches.

Directions:

1. In your instant pot, add all the ingredients.
2. With the lid in position, select the manual function on the instant pot.
3. Allow the meal to cook at high pressure for 15 minutes.
4. Immediately the timer clicks, Release the pressure naturally and remove the lid.
5. Give the meal a gentle stir and serve in the bowl.

Chia Carrot Oatmeal

Servings: 6, **Prep + Cook time:** 25 minutes

Ingredients:

- Steel cut oats -1 cup
- Grated carrots -1 cup
- Chia seeds -1/4 cup
- Butter -1 tbsp.
- Maple syrup -3 tbsp.
- Water -4 cups
- Cinnamon -2 tsp.
- Raisins -3/4 cup
- Pie spice-1 tsp.
- Salt - a pinch

Directions:

1. Set your Instant Pot on the Sauté mode.
2. Add butter to its insert and let it melt.
3. Toss in oats and sauté for 3 minutes.
4. Stir in water, carrots, cinnamon, spices, maple syrup and a pinch of salt.
5. Mix well then seal the lid of the Instant Pot.
6. Select Manual mode for 10 minutes at High pressure.
7. Once done, released the pressure naturally for 10 minutes.
8. Add raisins and chia seeds to the cooked oatmeal.
9. Mix gently then keep it aside for 10 minutes.
10. Serve fresh.

Dill Pickle Potato Salad

Servings: 4 , **Prep + Cook time:** 15 minutes

Ingredients:
- Potatoes, peeled and cubed -6
- water -1 ½ cups
- Homemade mayonnaise -1 cup
- Cup onion; finely chopped -1/4
- Dill pickle juice -1 tbsp.
- Parsley; finely chopped -2 tbsp.
- Mustard -1 tbsp.
- Eggs -4
- Salt and black pepper -to the taste

Directions:
1. Add one cup of water to the insert of the Instant Pot.
2. Place the steamer basket in the Instant Pot.
3. Add potatoes and eggs to the basket then seal the lid.
4. Select the manual mode for 4 minutes on High settings.
5. Release the pressure by turning the pressure release handle to the venting position.
6. Transfer the steamed eggs to an ice bath then leave them to cool.
7. Mix mayonnaise with onion, pickle juice, mustard and parsley in a bowl.
8. Add potatoes to the mayo mixture and mix well to coat.
9. Peel the cooled eggs and chop them.
10. Add the eggs to the potato mayo salad.
11. Mix gently then add salt and pepper.
12. Serve with bread slices.
13. Enjoy.

Maple Glazed Potatoes

Servings: 8 , **Prep + Cook time:** 20 minutes

Ingredients:
- Pecans chopped -1 cup
- Water -1 cup
- Cup butter -1/4
- Cup maple syrup -1/4
- Lemon peel -1 tbsp.
- Cup brown sugar -1/2
- Cornstarch -1 tbsp.
- Salt -1/4 tsp.
- Sweet potatoes peeled and sliced -3
- Whole pecans for garnish

Directions:
1. Add water to the Instant pot insert.
2. Stir in brown sugar, salt, and lemon peel.
3. Add potatoes then seal the lid.
4. Select Manual mode for 15 minutes with High settings.
5. Once done, release the pressure quickly, then transfer the potatoes to a plate.
6. Empty the Instant Pot and switch it to the Sauté mode.
7. Add butter, pecans, cornstarch, and maple syrup.
8. Sauté for a minute then add them to the potatoes.
9. Mix well and garnish with pecans.
10. Enjoy.

Plum Cinnamon Cobbler

Servings: 4 , **Prep + Cook time:** 25 minutes

Ingredients:
- Plum; chopped -1
- Cup coconut; shredded -1/4
- Cinnamon; ground -1/2 tsp.
- Coconut oil -3 tbsp.
- Sunflower seeds -2 tbsp.
- Pecans; chopped -1/4 cup
- Pear; chopped -1
- Apple chopped -1
- Honey -2 tbsp.

Directions:
1. Toss all the fruits with coconut oil, honey, and cinnamon in a heatproof dish.
2. Place steamer basket in the insert of Instant pot then set the fruits dish in the basket.
3. Seal the lid and select Manual mode for 10 minutes at High setting.

16

4. Allow the steam to release naturally, then remove the dish.
5. Add the fruits to a bowl then add pecans and sunflower seeds.

6. Mix well then add the mixture to an insert of the Instant Pot.
7. Switch the pot to the Sauté mode and stir cook for 5 minutes.
8. Serve fresh.

Cinnamon Oats Granola

Servings: 6, Prep + Cook time: 35 minutes

Ingredients:
- Cup steel cut oats -1
- Cups water -3
- Cup pumpkin puree -1
- Soft butter -1 tbsp.
- Maple syrup -1/4 cup
- Cinnamon -2 tsp.
- Pumpkin pie spice -1 tsp.
- Salt - a pinch

Directions:

1. Set the Instant Pot on Sauté mode then add butter to melt.
2. Toss in oats and stir cook for 3 minutes.
3. Stir in water, cinnamon, pumpkin puree, salt, pumpkin spice, and maple syrup.
4. Seal the lid and cook on Manual mode for 10 minutes at High.
5. Allow the pressure to release naturally in 10 minutes.
6. Serve fresh.

Tapioca Milk Pudding

Servings: 4 , Prep + Cook time: 15 minutes

Ingredients:
- Tapioca pearls -1/3 cup
- sugar -1/2 cup
- Whole milk -1 ¼ cup
- Water -1 ½ cups
- Zest from the lemon -1/2

Directions:
1. Add a cup of water to the base of Instant Pot.

2. Add tapioca pearls, milk, lemon zest, sugar and ½ cup water to a bowl and mix well.
3. Set the steamer basket in the Instant Pot, then set the tapioca bowl in the basket.
4. Seal the lid then cook for 10 minutes on Manual mode at High.
5. Release the pressure quickly by turning the pressure valve to the venting position.
6. Serve fresh.

Cherry Apple Risotto

Servings: 4 , Prep + Cook time: 25 minutes

Ingredients:
- Arborio rice -1 ½ cups
- Butter -2 tbsp.
- Cinnamon powder -1 ½ tsp.
- Brown sugar -1/3 cup
- Cherries; dried -1/2 cup
- Apples; cored and sliced -2
- Apple juice -1 cup
- Milk -3 cups
- Salt – a pinch

Directions:
1. Choose Sauté mode on your Instant Pot and add butter to its insert.

2. Once melted, add rice and stir cook for 5 minutes.
3. Toss in apples, sugar, milk, a pinch of salt, cinnamon and apple juice.
4. Mix well then seal the lid and cook on Manual mode for 6 minutes at High.
5. Once done, release the pressure naturally in 6 minutes.
6. Remove the lid then add cherries and seal the lid again.
7. Let it sit for 5 minutes.
8. Serve fresh.

Poached Eggs with Rucola

Servings: 2 , Prep + Cook time: 20 minutes

Ingredients:
- Bell peppers; ends cut off -2
- Mozzarella cheese -2 slices
- Eggs -2
- Rucola leaves -1 bunch
- Water -1 cup
- Whole wheat bread; toasted -2 slices

For the sauce:
- Mustard -1 ½ tsp.
- Orange juice -3 tbsp.
- Turmeric powder -1 tsp.
- Lemon juice -1 tsp.
- White wine vinegar -1 tbsp.
- Homemade mayonnaise -2/3 cup
- Salt - desired taste

Directions:

1. Mix mayonnaise with salt, mustard, turmeric, lemon juice, vinegar and orange juice in a suitable bowl.
2. Use a plastic wrap to cover it then place it in the refrigerator for 30 minutes or more.
3. Add a cup of water to the base of Instant Pot and place the steamer basket in the pot.
4. Place the bell pepper in the basket and break one egg into each pepper.
5. Cover this basket with tin foil and seal the lid.
6. Select Manual mode and cook for 5 minutes on Low.
7. Allow the steam to release naturally from the pot then remove the lid.
8. Divide the toasted bread into 2 serving plates and top them with cheese and rucola leaves.
9. Place the pepper cups over the bread and drizzle the prepared sauce on top.

Sweet Lemon Marmalade

Servings: 8 , Prep + Cook time: 25 minutes

Ingredients:
- Lemons; washed and sliced with a mandolin -2 lbs.
- Vinegar -1 tbsp.
- Sugar -4 lb.

Directions:
1. Place the lemon slices in the insert of the Instant Pot and seal the lid.
2. Cook for 10 minutes on Manual mode at High.
3. Once done, release the pressure quickly then add sugar.
4. Seal the lid again and cook again for 4 minutes at High.
5. Once done, release the pressure again then add cooked marmalade to a mason jar.
6. Allow it to cool then seal the jar then refrigerate.

Lemon Pepper Egg Muffins

Servings: 4 , Prep + Cook time: 20 minutes

Ingredients:
- Eggs -4
- Bacon slices; cooked and crumbled -4
- Green onion; chopped -1
- Water -1 ½ cups
- Cheddar cheese; shredded -4 tbsp.
- Lemon pepper -1/4 tsp.
- Salt – a pinch

Directions:
1. Whisk eggs with lemon pepper and a pinch of salt in a bowl.
2. Divide bacon, green onion, and cheese into the muffin trays.
3. Pour the eggs into each muffin cup and keep it aside.
4. Add 1 cup water to the insert of Instant Pot and place a steamer basket in it.
5. Place the muffin tray in the basket and seal the lid.
6. Cook on Manual mode for 10 minutes at High.
7. Once done, release the pressure quickly.
8. Serve fresh.

Chapter 3 Beans And Grains

Tangy Chorizo with Black Beans

Servings: 6, Prep + Cook time: 55 minutes

Ingredients:

- Black beans – 1 lb. soaked for 8 hours and drained
- Chorizo - 6 oz. chopped
- Yellow onion 1 piece cut into half
- Garlic - 6 cloves, minced
- Vegetable oil - 1 tbsp.
- Bay leaves – 2 pieces
- Orange – 1 piece, cut into half
- Chicken stock - 2 quarts'
- Seasoning - salt
- For toppings - chopped cilantro

Directions:

1. Select Sauté in your instant pot then add oil to heat.
2. Once the oil is hot, cook the chorizo for 2 minutes while stirring gradually.
3. Put the beans, onions, bay leaves, garlic, salt, stock, orange. Mix well, secure the lid then cook it at high for about 40 minutes.
4. Let the pressure release naturally, then gently remove the lid. Remove the onion, bay leaves, and orange. Season with salt and top up with cilantro. Mix well then serve in separate bowls.

Spicy Kidney Beans Stew

Servings: 4, Prep + Cook time: 40 minutes

Ingredients:

- Red kidney beans - 1 cup soaked for 12 hours and drained
- Vegetable oil - 1 tbsp.
- Bell pepper - 2 cups, chopped
- Bay leaves – 3 pieces
- Smoked paprika - 2 tsp.
- Thyme - 1 ½ tsp. dried
- Yellow onion - 1 cup, chopped
- Marjoram - 2 Tsp. dried
- Oregano - 1 tsp. dried
- Canned tomatoes - 14 oz. crushed
- Liquid smoke - 1/2 Tsp.
- Garlic - 2 tsp. chopped
- Water - 1 cup
- Cayenne pepper - a pinch only
- Seasoning - salt and black pepper
- Cooked rice

Directions:

1. Select Sauté in your instant pot then add oil to heat.
2. Place the onions and sauté for 5 minutes.
3. Put the garlic and bell pepper and sauté for another 5 minutes.
4. Put the bay leaves, water, thyme, paprika, cayenne, marjoram, and beans. Mix well. Secure the pot's lid and let it cook at high for 15 minutes.
5. Press quick release, then gently remove the lid. Remove the bay leaves and mix the liquid smoke, salt, pepper, tomatoes, and oregano in the pot. Close the pot and cook for 3 minutes at high pressure.
6. After cooking, let the pressure release naturally. Gently open up the pot, then gather the beans and mix with the cooked rice on separate bowls or plates.

Hot and Spicy Kidney Beans

Servings: 8, Prep + Cook time: 1 hour and 10 minutes

Ingredients:

- Red kidney beans - 2 cups, soaked for 8 hours and drained
- Ginger - 1-inch piece chopped
- Turmeric - 1 tsp. ground.
- Vegetable oil - 2 tbsp.
- Ghee - 2 tsp.
- Red chili peppers – 2 pieces, dried and crushed
- Seasoning - salt and black pepper
- Cloves – 6 pieces
- Cumin -1 tsp. ground
- Coriander - 1 tsp. ground
- Yellow onion – 1 piece, chopped
- Water - 2 cups
- Sugar - 1 Tsp.
- Red pepper - 1 tsp. ground
- Garam masala - 2 tsp.
- Garlic – 4 cloves chopped
- Cumin seeds - 1 tsp.
- Tomatoes – 2 pieces, chopped
- Cilantro - 1/4 cup, chopped

Directions:

1. Crush the garlic, onion, and ginger with a mortar and pestle then put the crushed mixture in a bowl.
2. Select Sauté in your instant pot then put the oil and ghee to heat. Add the cloves, cumin seeds, and red chili pepper. Fry for 3 minutes while stirring.
3. For another 3 minutes cook the onion paste with the other recent ingredients inside the instant pot. Put the cumin, coriander, and turmeric. Mix well and cook for 30 seconds. Right after cooking it, immediately add the tomatoes then cook for another 5 minutes.
4. Pour the water then add the beans, salt, sugar, and pepper. Mix well and secure the lid. Cook for 40 minutes at high pressure.
5. After 40 minutes switch to low pressure and cook for another 10 minutes.
6. Do a quick release, open up the lid of the pot. Top up with masala, cilantro, and garam. Mix well and serve.

Spicy Special Black Beans

Servings: 8, Prep + Cook time: 45 minutes

Ingredients:

- Black beans - 16 oz., soaked overnight and drained
- Yellow onion – 1 piece, chopped
- Garlic - 4 cloves, minced
- Cumin - 2 tsp. ground
- Tomato paste - 8 oz.
- Water - 2 quarts'
- Chili powder - 2 tbsp.
- Chipotle powder - 1 tsp.
- Oregano - 2 tsp. dried
- Sunflower oil - 4 tbsp.
- Seasoning – salt

Directions:

1. Mix up the beans, chili powder, chipotle powder, tomato paste, oregano, garlic, oil, salt, water, cumin, and onion. Secure the pot's lid and cook it for 30 minutes at high pressure.
2. Do a quick release, open up the lid of the pot then select Simmer.
3. Cook for another 3 minutes then serve on separate bowls.

Oyster Mushrooms and Millet

Servings: 4, Prep + Cook time: 25 minutes

Ingredients:

- Onion - 1 cup, chopped.
- Veggie stock - 2 ¼ cups
- Bok Choy - 1/2 cup, sliced
- Snow peas - 1 cup
- Lemon juice - 1 tbsp.
- Garlic - 2 cloves, minced.

- Oyster mushrooms - 1/2 cup, sliced
- Parsley and chives - 1/4 cup, chopped
- Asparagus - 1 cup, chopped
- Green lentils - 1/2 cup, rinsed
- Seasoning - salt and black pepper

Directions:
1. Select Sauté on your instant pot then put the garlic, mushrooms, and onions. Mix well and cook for 2 minutes.
2. Put the lentils and millet, mix them well and then cook for a minute. Pour down the stock. Mix well.
3. Secure the pot's lid and then cook for 10 minutes at high pressure.
4. Do a natural release, open up the lid of the pot. Place the Bok Choy, peas, and asparagus. Mix well then close again the lid and cook it again for another 3 minutes at high pressure.
5. After cooking, release the pressure and gently open up the lid. Put the salt, pepper, mixed parsley, and lemon juice. Mix well and serve.

Hot and Spicy Cranberry Bean Dish

Servings: 8, Prep + Cook time: 50 minutes

Ingredients:
- Cranberry beans - 1 lb. soaked in water for 7 hours and drained
- Canned tomatoes and green chilies - 14 oz. chopped.
- Water - 5 cups
- Cumin - 1 ½ tsp. ground
- Tomato paste - 2 tbsp.
- Chili powder - 1 tsp.
- Ancho chili powder - 1/2 tsp.
- Millet - 1/4 cup
- Bulgur - 1/2 cup
- Garlic- 1 tsp. minced.
- Liquid smoke - 1/2 Tsp.
- Oregano - 1 tsp. dried
- Seasoning - salt and black pepper
- Hot sauce
- Pickled jalapenos

Directions:
1. Place the beans in your instant pot then pour over 3 cups of water. Secure the pot's lid and cook for 25 minutes at high pressure.
2. Do a quick release, then pour the remaining cups of water. Put all the remaining ingredients aside from the hot sauce and pickled jalapenos. Mix well, and again close the lid of the pot. Cook for another 10 minutes at high pressure.
3. Let the pressure out then gently open up the lid of the pot. Put hot sauce and the pickled jalapenos. Serve hot and enjoy!

Italian Chicken and Lentils

Servings: 4, Prep + Cook time: 25 minutes

Ingredients:
- Green lentils - 3/4 cup, soaked overnight and drained
- Brown rice - 1/2 cup, soaked overnight and drained
- Mozzarella cheese - 1 cup, shredded
- Green and red bell pepper - 1 cup, chopped
- Chicken - 2 cups, already cooked and shredded
- Carrots - 3 pieces, chopped
- Chicken stock - 2 ½ cups
- Tomato sauce - 1 cup
- Onion - 3/4 cup, chopped
- Italian seasoning - 3 tsp.
- Garlic - 2 cloves, crushed
- Greens - a handful
- Seasoning - salt and black pepper

Directions:
1. Mix up the lentils, rice, salt, pepper, stock, tomato sauce, onion, red and green pepper, chicken, carrots, greens, Italian seasoning and garlic inside your instant pot. Secure the lid and then cook for 15 minutes at high pressure.
2. Do a quick release, gently open up the lid of the pot. Put cheese and mix well. Serve in bowls.

Marrow Beans Stew

Servings: 4, Prep + Cook time: 55 minutes

Ingredients:

- Marrow beans - 2 cups, soaked for 8 hours and drained
- Rosemary - 1 tbsp. chopped.
- Garlic - 4 cloves, minced
- Carrot – 1 piece, chopped
- Water - 4 cups
- Bay leaf - 1 piece
- Lemon juice - 2 tbsp.
- Yellow onion - 1 cup, chopped
- Extra-virgin olive oil - 1 tbsp.
- Seasoning - salt and black pepper
- Cooked quinoa

Directions:

1. Select Sauté in your instant pot and then pour the oil to heat.
2. Put the carrot, onion, rosemary, and garlic. Mix well and sauté for 3 minutes.
3. Pour down the water then add the beans, bay leaf, and salt. Mix well. Secure the lid of the pot and then cook for 45 minutes at high pressure.
4. Do a natural release, then gently open up the lid of the pot. Remove the bay leaf. Season with salt and pepper then pour down the lemon juice. Mix well and then serve.

Savory Mung Beans

Servings: 4, Prep + Cook time: 1hour and 10 minutes

Ingredients:

- Mung beans - 1 cup, soaked for 6 hours and drained
- Cumin seeds - 1 tsp.
- Cumin - 1 tsp. ground
- Water - 1 ½ cups
- Jalapeno peppers – 4 pieces, chopped
- Cilantro - 1/4 cup, chopped
- Ginger - 1 tbsp. grated
- Yellow onion – 1 piece, chopped
- Tomato – 1 piece, chopped
- Ghee - 2 tsp.
- Cayenne pepper - a pinch only
- Turmeric - 2 tsp.
- Coriander - 1/2 tbsp. ground
- Seasoning - salt and black pepper

Directions:

1. Select Sauté in your instant pot then put the ghee to heat.
2. Put the cumin seeds in the pot once it's hot then cook it for 1 minute. After cooking, put the turmeric, coriander, ginger, cumin, and cayenne. Mix well and cook for another 2 minutes.
3. Put the jalapenos and onion in the pot then cook for 4minutes. Pour down the water then add the beans, salt, and pepper. Mix well, secure the lid of the pot then cook it for 20 minutes at high pressure.
4. After cooking, do a quick release. Gently open up the lid of the pot then put the tomatoes. Select Simmer in the instant pot.
5. Simmer for 20 minutes while stirring gradually. After simmering, put cilantro then serve in separate bowls.

Red Bell Pepper Couscous

Servings: 4, Prep + Cook time: 18 minutes

Ingredients:

- Couscous - 1 cup, rinsed
- Cinnamon - 1/2 tsp. ground
- Coriander - 1/4 tsp. ground
- Red bell pepper - 1/4 cup, chopped
- Veggie stock - 1 ½ cups
- Red onion - 1/2 cup, chopped
- Sesame oil - 1/2 tsp.
- Red wine vinegar - 2 tbsp.
- Seasoning - salt and black pepper

Directions:

1. Press Sauté in your instant pot then add the oil to heat it.

2. When the oil is already hot, put the onion and pepper. Mix well and cook for 5 minutes.
3. Put the couscous, coriander, stock, cinnamon, salt, pepper, and vinegar. Mix well then secure the lid of the pot. Cook it for 3 minutes at high pressure.
4. Do a quick release, then gently open up the lid of the pot. Serve the couscous in separate bowls.

Stewed Three-Bean

Serves: 3 , **Prep+ Cook time:** 30 minutes

Ingredients

- Cumin powder, ¾ tsp.
- Diced medium carrot, ½.
- Paprika powder, ½ tsp.
- Chili powder, ⅛ tsp.
- Finely diced garlic cloves, 3.
- Diced celery stick, ½.
- Cinnamon powder, ⅛ tsp.
- Salt, ¼ tsp.
- Soaked and rinsed white beans, ¼ cup.
- Bay leaf, 1.
- Soaked and rinsed black beans, ¼ cup.
- Lemon juice, 2 tbsps.
- Soaked and rinsed red beans, ¼ cup.
- Vegetable stock, 2 cups.
- Olive oil, ½ tbsp.
- Diced medium white onion, ½.
- Chopped tinned tomatoes, ¼ cup.

Directions:

1. Put the oil to the instant pot to fry the garlic, onion, and celery for 5 minutes on sauté mode.
2. Stir in the rest of ingredients then seal the lid.
3. Switch its pressure release handle to the sealing position.
4. Allow to cook for 15 minutes at high pressure on manual function.
5. Perform a natural release once the timer clicks and open the lid.
6. Give the meal a gentle stir then serve right away.

Nutritional Information:
Calories: 213, Carbs: 35.6g, Protein: 12g, Fat: 3.3g, Sugar: 3.6g, Sodium: 251mg

Simple Lentil & Corn Stew

Serves: 3 , **Prep+ Cook time:** 30 minutes

Ingredients

- Cooked brown rice, ½ cup.
- Water, 3 ½ cups.
- Sliced medium carrot, 1.
- Tamari sauce, 1 tbsp.
- Salt.
- Fresh corn, ½ cup.
- Dried lentils, ⅓ cup.
- Chopped medium onion, ½.
- Olive oil, ½ tbsp.
- Medium tomato, 1.
- Pepper.

Directions:

1. Put the oil to the instant pot to fry the carrots and onion on sauté mode for 5 minutes.
2. Stir in the corn, lentils, water, and tomatoes then seal the lid.
3. Change its pressure release handle to the sealing point.
4. Press the manual function on the pressure cooker to cook for 15 minutes at high pressure.
5. Perform a natural release once the timer beeps and remove the lid.
6. Mix in cooked rice, seasonings, and tamari sauce.
7. Enjoy the meal while still warm.

Nutritional Information:
Calories: 239, Carbs: 47.4g, Protein: 10.1g, Fat: 1.5g, Sugar: 4.2g, Sodium: 367mg

Instant pot Spice Black Bean

Serves: 6 , **Prep+ Cook time:** 30 minutes

Ingredients

- Bay leaf, 1.
- Ground turmeric, ½ tsp.
- Garlic powder, 2 tsps.
- Unsalted vegetable broth, 6 cups.
- Onion powder, 1 tbsp.
- Salt, 1 tsp.
- Sorted and rinsed black beans, 1 lb.
- Red pepper, ½ tsp.
- Cooked white rice.

Directions:

1. In your instant pot, put all the ingredients.
2. With the lid in its position, turn the pressure release handle to sealing position.
3. Select the beans/chili function on the default setting.
4. Immediately the timer is over, perform a natural release for 25 minutes.
5. Gently stir the meal and serve with white rice.

Nutritional Information:
Calories: 289, Carbs: 53.7g, Protein: 18 .7g, Fat: 1.1g, Sugar: 5.8g, Sodium: 633mg

Flavored Pinto Beans with Chorizo

Serves: 3 , **Prep+ Cook time:** 52 minutes

Ingredients

- Diced tomatoes, 7.1 oz.
- Bay leaf, 1.
- Garlic cloves, 1 ½.
- Freshly cracked pepper, ½ tsp.
- Yellow onion, ½.
- Dry Spanish chorizo, 2 oz.
- Chicken broth, 1 ½ cups.
- Boiled white rice.
- Cooking oil, ½ tbsp.
- Dry pinto beans, 1 cup.

Directions:

1. Put oil in the instant pot to sauté garlic, chorizo, and onion for 5 minutes.
2. Mix in bay leaf, beans, and pepper to cook for 1 minute then add the broth.
3. With the lid in its position, set the pressure release handle to the sealing position. Select the manual function key to cook for 35 minutes at high pressure
4. When the timer is over, perform a natural release for 20 minutes.
5. Mix in the diced tomatoes to cook for 7 minutes on sauté mode
6. Enjoy the meal while still hot with boiled white rice or tortilla chips.

Nutritional Information:
Calories: 337, Carbs: 50.5g, Protein: 21.3g, Fat: 5.7g, Sugar: 5.4g, Sodium: 671mg

Garlic Chickpea Curry & Spinach

Serves: 4 , **Prep+ Cook time:** 34 minutes

Ingredients

- Finely chopped green chili, ½.
- Grated garlic, ½ tbsp.
- Cooking oil, 1 ½ tbsps.
- Water, ¾ cup.
- Fresh tomato puree, 1 cup.
- Boiled white rice.
- Coriander powder, ½ tsp.
- Chopped baby spinach, 1 cup.
- Bay leaf, 1.
- Chopped onions, ½ cup.
- Chili powder, 1 tsp.
- Turmeric, ¼ tsp.
- Raw chickpeas, ½ cup.
- Grated ginger, ¼ tbsp.
- Salt.

Directions:

1. Put oil in the instant pot to sauté onions for 5 minutes.
2. Mix in garlic paste, bay leaf, ginger, and green chili to cook for 1minute the mix in all the spices.

3. Stir in tomato puree, water, and chickpeas.
4. With the lid secured, turn its pressure release handle to the sealing position.
5. Select the manual function key to cook for 15 minutes at high pressure.
6. Perform a natural release or 20 minutes once the timer is over.

7. Stir in the spinach to cook for 3 minutes on sauté mode
8. Serve the meal while still hot with white rice.

Nutritional Information:
Calories: 180, Carbs: 25.3g, Protein: 6.7g, Fat: 7g, Sugar: 6.9g, Sodium: 79mg

Almond Flavored Risotto

Serves: 3 , Prep+ Cook time: 15 minutes

Ingredients
- Vanilla extract, 1 tsp.
- Arborio rice, ½ cup.
- Toasted almond flakes, ¼ cup.
- Agave syrup, 2 tbsps.
- Vanilla almond milk, 2 cups.

Directions:
1. In your instant pot, add all the ingredients.
2. With the lid sealed, turn its pressure release handle to sealing position.
3. Select the manual function key and cook for 5 minutes at high pressure.
4. Perform a natural release for 20 minutes once the timer is over.
5. Serve the meal topped with almond flakes

Nutritional Information:
Calories: 116, Carbs: 22.5g, Protein: 2g, Fat: 2.1g, Sugar: 0.2g, Sodium: 82mg

Lentils with Spinach Stew

Serves: 4 , Prep+ Cook time: 34 minutes

Ingredients
- Turmeric, ¼ tsp.
- Water, ¾ cup.
- Fresh tomato puree, 1 cup.
- Coriander powder, ½ tsp.
- Bay leaf, 1.
- Finely chopped green chili, ½.
- Salt.
- Grated garlic, ½ tbsp.
- Chopped baby spinach, 1 cup.
- Chopped onions, ½ cup.
- Chili powder, 1 tsp.
- Raw lentils, ½ cup.
- Cooking oil, 1 ½ tbsps.
- Grated ginger, ¼ tbsp.
- Boiled white rice.

Directions:
1. Put oil in the instant pot to sauté the onions for 5 minutes.

2. Mix in garlic paste, bay leaf, ginger, and green chili to cook for 1 minute then mix in all the spices.
3. Add tomato puree, lentils, and water.
4. With the lid secured, turn its pressure release handle to sealing position.
5. Select manual function key to cook for 15 minutes at high pressure
6. Perform a natural release for 20 minutes after the timer beeps.
7. Mix in the spinach to cook for 3 minutes on sauté mode.
8. Serve the meal while still hot with boiled white rice or quinoa.

Nutritional Information:
Calories: 169, Carbs: 23.2g, Protein: 7.9g, Fat: 5.7g, Sugar: 4.4g, Sodium: 75mg

One Pot Red Bean Curry

Serves: 4 , **Prep+ Cook time:** 34 minutes

Ingredients

- Turmeric, ¼ tsp.
- Fresh tomato puree, 1 cup.
- Cooking oil, 1 ½ tbsps.
- Grated ginger, ¼ tbsp.
- Coriander powder, ½ tsp.
- Grated garlic, ½ tbsp.
- Bay leaf, 1.
- Salt.
- Finely chopped green chili, ½.
- Water, ¾ cup.
- Boiled white.
- Chopped baby spinach, 1 cup.
- Raw red beans, ½ cup.
- Chopped onions, ½ cup.
- Chili powder, 1 tsp.

Directions:

1. Put the oil in the instant pot to sauté the onions for 5 minutes
2. Mix in green chili, ginger, and garlic paste to cook for one minute then add all the spices.
3. Stir in tomato puree and red beans.
4. With the lid secured, turn the pressure release handle to the sealing position.
5. Allow to cook on manual for 15 minutes at high pressure
6. When the timer beeps, perform a natural release for 20 minutes.
7. Add the spinach to cook on sauté mode for 3 minutes.
8. Enjoy the meal with quinoa or white rice.

Nutritional Information:
Calories: 163, Carbs: 22.8g, Protein: 7g, Fat: 5.7g, Sugar: 4.4g, Sodium: 78mg

Squash Veggie Risotto

Serves: 3 , **Prep+ Cook time:** 22 minutes

Ingredients

- White wine, 2 tbsps.
- Sprig sage, 1.
- Olive oil, 1 tbsp.
- Sea salt, 1 tsp.
- Arborio rice, 1 cup.
- Whole garlic cloves, 2.
- Fresh nutmeg, ½ tsp.
- Diced butternut squash, 2 lbs.
- Water, 2 cups.

Directions:

1. Put the oil in the instant pot to sauté garlic and sage for 2 minutes.
2. Mix in the squash to fry for 5 minutes
3. Stir in the remaining ingredients.
4. With the lid secured, turn its pressure release handle to the sealing position.
5. Allow to cook on manual function for 5 minutes at high pressure
6. Perform a natural release when the timer clicks and open the lid.
7. Give the risotto a gentle stir and serve immediately.

Nutritional Information:
Calories: 323, Carbs: 62.4g, Protein: 5.3g, Fat: 5.2g, Sugar: 2.3g, Sodium: 638mg

Spiced Split Pea Curry

Serves: 3 , **Prep+ Cook time:** 24 minutes

Ingredients

- Vegetable stock, 2 cups.
- Diced celery stick, ½.
- Bay leaf, 1.
- Salt, ¼ tsp.
- Diced medium white onion, ½.
- Paprika powder, ½ tsp.
- Cinnamon powder, ⅛ tsp.
- Cumin powder, ¾ tsp.
- Rinsed split yellow peas, 1 cup.
- Chili powder, ⅛ tsp.
- Finely diced garlic cloves, 3.
- Olive oil, ½ tbsp.
- Diced medium carrot, ½.
- Chopped tinned tomatoes, ¼ cup.

- Lemon juice, 2 tbsps.

Directions:
1. Put the oil in the instant pot to sauté garlic, onion, and celery for 4 minutes.
2. Mix in the remaining ingredients.
3. With the lid secured, turn its pressure release handle to the sealing position.
4. Allow to cook on manual for 10 minutes at high pressure.
5. Perform a natural release once the timer clicks and remove the lid.
6. Give the meal a gentle stir and serve immediately.

Nutritional Information:
Calories: 206, Carbs: 33.5g, Protein: 11g, Fat: 3.4g, Sugar: 3.4g, Sodium: 246mg

One Pot Fried Beans Mix

Serves: 6 , Prep+ Cook time: 1 hour

Ingredients
- Vegetable broth, 2 cups.
- Roughly chopped garlic cloves, 2.
- Dried oregano, 1 tsp.
- Ground black pepper, ¼ tsp.
- Lard, 1 ½ tbsps.
- Water, 2 cups.
- Ground cumin, ¾ tsp.
- Seeded and sliced jalapeno, ½.
- Sea salt, ½ tsp.
- Soaked and rinsed pinto beans, 1 lb.
- Chopped onion, ¾ cup.

Directions:
1. In your instant pot, put all the ingredients.
2. With the lid secured, turn its pressure release handle to the sealing position.
3. Select bean/chili function on the cooker to cook for 45 minutes
4. Perform a natural release for 20 minutes once the timer clicks.
5. Allow the mixture to cool before transferring to an immersion blender to process.
6. Stir the pureed beans and serve right away.

Nutritional Information:
Calories: 314, Carbs: 49.6g, Protein: 18.1g, Fat: 4.7g, Sugar: 2.5g, Sodium: 423mg

Lemony Fennel Risotto

Serves: 3 , Prep+ Cook time: 29 minutes

Ingredients
- Lemon zest, ¼ lemon.
- Chopped garlic clove, 1.
- Diced medium fennel, ¼.
- Vegetable stock, 1 cup.
- White wine, 3 tbsps.
- Diced asparagus bunch, ¼.
- Arborio risotto rice, 1 cup.
- Olive oil, 1 tbsp.
- Grated parmesan cheese, ¼ cup.
- Butter, 1 tbsp.
- Finely sliced medium brown onion, ½.
- Salt, ¼ tsp.
- Chicken stock, 1 cup.

Directions:
1. Put the oil in the instant pot to sauté the fennel, asparagus, and onion for 4 minutes.
2. Mix in the remaining ingredients with exception of cheese
3. With the lid secured, turn its pressure release handle to the sealing position.
4. Select the manual function key on the cooker to cook for 10minutes at high pressure.
5. Perform a natural release once the timer clicks and remove the lid.
6. Gently stir in the cheese and serve right away.

Nutritional Information:
Calories: 238, Carbs: 24.1g, Protein: 6.9g, Fat: 17.5g, Sugar: 1.8g, Sodium: 528mg

Cumin Mung Bean Risotto

Serves: 6 , Prep+ Cook time: 50 minutes

Ingredients

- Turmeric, 2 tsps.
- Garlic cloves, 3.
- Cumin seeds, 1 tsp.
- Coconut oil, 1 tsp.
- Ground coriander, 2 tsps.
- Chopped red onion, 1.
- Peeled and chopped ginger, 2-inch.
- Salt, 2 tsps.
- Crushed tomatoes, 2 cans.
- Brown basmati rice, 1 cup.
- Water
- Green mung beans, 1 ½ cup.
- Cayenne, 1 tsp.
- Black pepper, ½ tsp.

Directions:

1. In the food processor, combine garlic, tomatoes, onions, ginger, 2 tablespoons of water, and spices to process until done
2. Heat some oil in the instant pot on sauté mode
3. Add cumin seeds and the tomato puree to cook for 15 minutes
4. Mix in rice and mung beans then close the lid
5. Select the manual function to cook at high pressure for 15 minutes.
6. Perform a natural release when the timer beeps and open the lid.
7. Gently stir the beans and serve with crackers.

Nutritional Information:
Calories: 205, Carbs: 41g, Protein: 7.2g, Fat: 1.4g, Sugar: 4.3g, Sodium: 214mg

Barley & Bean Stew

Serves: 4 , Prep+ Cook time: 30 minutes

Ingredients

- Coriander seeds, 3.
- Soaked and rinsed cannellini beans, ½ cup.
- Olive oil, ½ tbsp.
- Clove, 1.
- Pepper.
- Soaked and rinsed barley, ¼ cup.
- Pepper kernels, 4.
- Water, 2 cups.
- Tea infuser.
- Chopped garlic clove, 1.
- Soaked and rinsed chickpeas, ½ cup.
- Salt.

Directions:

1. In the instant pot, combine the oil, salt, barley, garlic, water, chickpeas, and the tea infuser.
2. Place a steamer trivet above it and set the cannellini beans into it.
3. Select the manual function to cook for 15 minutes at high pressure with the lid sealed.
4. Perform a natural release when the timer beeps and open the lid
5. Carefully take out the steamer trivet and put the beans in the pot.
6. Discard the tea infuser and cook for 5 minutes on sauté mode stirring gently.
7. Serve the meal while still hot.

Nutritional Information:
Calories: 196, Carbs: 32.1g, Protein: 10.5g, Fat: 3.5g, Sugar: 3.2g, Sodium: 161mg

Coconut Vanilla Risotto

Serves: 3 , Prep+ Cook time: 15 minutes

Ingredients

- Vanilla extract, 1 tsp.
- Arborio rice, ½ cup.
- Coconut sugar, 2 tbsps.
- Toasted coconut flakes, ¼ cup.
- Coconut milk, 2 cups.

Directions:

1. Set all the listed items to the Instant Pot.
2. With the lid in its position, turn its pressure release handle to the sealing position.

3. Select manual function to cook for 5 minutes at high pressure.
4. Perform a natural release for 20 minutes once the timer clicks.

5. Serve the meal topped with coconut flakes.

Nutritional Information:
Calories: 532, Carbs: 42.1g, Protein: 5.9g, Fat: 40.4g, Sugar: 13.9g, Sodium: 25mg

Cilantro Black Bean Burrito

Serves: 4 , Prep+ Cook time: 22 minutes

Ingredients

- Chopped cilantro, 2 tbsps.
- De-boned, skinless and sliced chicken thighs, ¾ lb.
- Diced small onion, ½.
- Kosher salt, ¼ tsp.
- Uncooked long-grain white rice, ½ cup.
- Chili powder, ½ tsp.
- Chicken broth, 1 cup.
- Minced garlic clove, ½.
- Shredded cheddar cheese, 2 tbsps.
- Salsa, ½ cup.
- Olive oil, ½ tbsp.
- Rinsed black beans, ½ can.

Directions:

1. Put some oil in the instant pot to sauté garlic and onion for 2 minutes
2. Mix in the rest of ingredients with exception of shredded cheddar cheese and cilantro then seal the lid.
3. Select manual function to cook at high pressure for 10 minutes.
4. Perform a quick release of the remaining steam.
5. Serve the meal topped with shredded cheddar cheese and chopped cilantro.

Nutritional Information:
Calories: 320, Carbs: 23.5g, Protein: 33.1g, Fat: 33.1g, Sugar: 2.1g, Sodium: 633mg

Cheesy Lentil Curry

Serves: 3 , Prep+ Cook time: 20 minutes

Ingredients

- Rinsed and picked over brown lentils, 1 cup.
- Chopped medium green bell pepper, ½.
- Chili powder, 1 ½ tbsps.
- Diced tomatoes, ¼ oz.
- Seeded and chopped chipotle in adobo sauce, 1.
- Chopped garlic clove, 1.
- Canola oil, ½ tbsp.
- Chopped cilantro, 2 tbsps.
- Vegetable broth, 2 cups.
- Chopped sun-dried tomatoes, ¼ cup.
- Shredded cheddar cheese, 2 tbsps.
- Chopped medium onion, ½.
- Ground cumin, ½ tsp.
- Salt.

Directions:

1. Put some oil in the instant pot to sauté the bell peppers and onion for 2 minutes.
2. Stir in chili powder and garlic to cook for 1 minute.
3. Mix in the rest of ingredients and seal the lid.
4. Select manual function to cook at high pressure for 12 minutes.
5. Immediately the timer clicks, perform a natural release for 10 minutes then do a quick release of the remaining steam.
6. Serve the meal topped with shredded cheese and cilantro.

Nutritional Information:
Calories: 204, Carbs: 29.8g, Protein: 13.4g, Fat: 5.2g, Sugar: 10.8g, Sodium: 687mg

Parsley Lentil Risotto

Serves: 2 , Prep+ Cook time: 30 minutes

Ingredients

- Lightly mashed garlic clove, 1.
- Olive oil, ½ tbsp.
- Chopped celery stalk, ½.
- Vegetable stock, 2 cups.
- Chopped medium onion, ½.
- Arborio rice, ½ cup.
- Soaked dry lentils, ½ cup.
- Chopped sprig parsley, 1.

Directions:

1. Put some oil in the instant pot to sauté the onions for 5 minutes

2. Mix in the remaining ingredients and cover the lid.
3. Switch the pressure release handle to the sealing point.
4. Select manual function to cook for 15 minutes at high pressure.Perform a natural release for 20 minutes once the timer clicks.
5. Give the meal a gentle stir and serve while still hot.

Nutritional Information:
Calories: 260, Carbs: 47.2g, Protein: 10.7g, Fat: 3.5g, Sugar: 2.2g, Sodium: 247mg

Mustard Bean& Bacon Curry

Serves: 4 , Prep+ Cook time: 24 minutes

Ingredients

- Apple cider vinegar, 1 tsp.
- Molasses, 2 tbsps.
- Chopped bacon slices, 1½.
- Mustard powder, 2 tsps.
- Chopped medium onion, ½.
- Rinsed and drained navy beans, 1½ cans.
- Olive oil, ½ tbsp.
- Chopped small green bell pepper, ½.
- Ground black pepper, ¼ tsp.
- Ketchup, ½ cup.
- Chopped cilantro, 2 tbsps.

Directions:

1. Set the instant pot on sauté mode then add oil to fry the bell pepper, onion, and bacon for 6 minutes.
2. Mix in the remaining ingredients and seal the lid.Select the manual function to cook on high pressure for 8 minutes.
3. Perform a natural release for 10 minutes once the timer beeps.
4. Perform a quick release to release the remaining steam.
5. Enjoy the meal topped with chopped cilantro.

Nutritional Information:
Calories: 373, Carbs: 64.5g, Protein: 21.2g, Fat: 4.7g, Sugar: 16.1g, Sodium: 507mg

Spiced White Bean Stew

Serves: 4 , Prep+ Cook time: 35 minutes

Ingredients

- Bay leaf, 1.
- Red pepper, ½ tsp.
- Garlic powder, 2 tsps.
- Salt, 2 tsps.
- Boiled white rice.
- Ground turmeric, ½ tsp.
- Onion powder, 1 tsp.
- Soaked and rinsed white beans, 1 lb.
- Unsalted vegetable broth, 6 cups.

Directions:

1. In the instant pot, add all the ingredients with exception of white rice the seal the lid.
2. Switch its pressure release handle to sealing point.
3. Select bean/chili function on default setting.
4. Once the timer beeps, perform natural release for 20 minutes.
5. Give the meal gentle stir and serve with boiled white rice.

Nutritional Information:
Calories: 286, Carbs: 54.1g, Protein: 19.1g, Fat: 1.2g, Sugar: 5.2g, Sodium: 612mg

Turmeric Rice with Corn& pea mix

Serves: 3 , **Prep+ Cook time:** 13 minutes

Ingredients

- Frozen sweet corn kernels, ½ cup.
- Olive oil, 1 ½ tbsps.
- Chopped cilantro stalks, 1 ½ tbsps.
- Finely diced large garlic clove, 1.
- Diced large onion, ½.
- Chicken stock, ¾ cup.
- Salt.
- Frozen garden peas, ½ cup.
- Butter, 1 dollop.
- Turmeric powder, ½ tsp.
- Rinsed basmati rice, 1 cup.

Directions:

1. Put some oil in the instant pot to cook the onions for 5 minutes on sauté mode.
2. Mix in the remaining ingredients with exception of butter then seal the lid.
3. Shift its pressure release handle to the sealing position.
4. Select the manual function to cook for 3 minutes at high pressure
5. Perform a natural release for 7 minutes once the timer beeps.
6. Mix in the butter to dissolve into the rice.
7. Enjoy the meal while still warm.

Nutritional Information:
Calories: 356, Carbs: 61.3g, Protein: 7.1g, Fat: 9.2g, Sugar: 3.6g, Sodium: 363mg

Saffron Shrimp with Rice Paella

Serves: 8 , **Prep+ Cook time:** 20 minutes

Ingredients

- Juiced medium lemons, 2.
- Butter, 4 oz.
- Black pepper, ½ tsp.
- Saffron, ½ tsp.
- Minced garlic cloves, 8.
- Chopped fresh parsley, 4 oz.
- Jasmine rice, 16 oz.
- Chicken broth, 24 oz.
- Crushed red pepper, ½ tsp.
- Frozen wild-caught shrimp, 32 oz.
- Sea salt, 2 tsps.

Directions:

1. In the instant pot, add all the ingredients with the shrimp on top then cover the lid.
2. Change its pressure release handle to the sealing position.
3. Select the manual function to cook for 10 minutes at high pressure
4. Do a natural release for 7 minutes immediately the timer clicks.
5. Remove the shells from shrimp and return to the rice.
6. Gently stir the meal and serve warm.

Nutritional Information:
Calories: 437, Carbs: 49.1g, Protein: 30.6g, Fat: 13.7g, Sugar: 0.8g, Sodium: 1086mg

Garlic, Chorizo & Black Beans

Serves: 3 , **Prep+ Cook time:** 52 minutes

Ingredients

- Bay leaf, 1.
- Dry chorizo, 2 oz.
- Soaked and rinsed black beans, 1 cup.
- Boiled white rice.
- Yellow onion, ½.
- Cracked pepper, ½ tsp.
- Diced tomatoes, 7.1 oz.
- Sodium-reduced chicken broth, 1 ½ cups.
- Cooking oil, ½ tbsp.
- Garlic cloves, 1 ½.

Directions:

1. Put some oil to the instant pot to cook garlic, chorizo, and onion for 5 minutes on sauté mode.

2. Mix in pepper, beans, and bay leaf to cook for 1 minute, then add the chicken broth and seal the lid.
3. Switch its pressure release handle to the sealing point.
4. Select the manual function to cook for 35 minutes at high pressure.
5. Perform a natural release for 20 minutes immediately after the timer clicks.

6. Mix in the tomatoes to cook for 7 minutes on sauté mode.
7. Enjoy the meal while still hot with tortilla chips of boiled white rice.

Nutritional Information:
Calories: 324, Carbs: 48.8g, Protein: 21.3g, Fat: 5.6g, Sugar: 5.3g, Sodium: 647mg

Brown Rice with Chicken & veggies

Serves: 6 , Prep+ Cook time: 43 minutes

Ingredients
- Worcestershire sauce, 2 tbsps.
- Chicken broth, 2 ¼ cups.
- Garlic cloves, 3.
- Cremini mushrooms, 2 cups.
- Boneless and skinless chicken thigh, 2 lbs.
- Ground black pepper, ⅛ tsp.
- Raw brown rice, 2 cups.
- Baby carrots, 2 cups.
- Canned and condensed chicken, 10 oz.
- Medium onion, 1.
- Olive oil, 1 tbsp.
- Salt, ⅛ tsp.
- Fresh thyme, 1 tbsp.

Directions:

1. Put some oil to the instant pot to cook veggies, onions, and garlic for 2 minutes on sauté mode.
2. Mix in the rest of ingredients with chicken pieces on top and seal the lid.
3. Change its pressure release handle to the sealing spot.
4. Select the manual function key to cook for 31 minutes at high pressure.
5. Perform a natural release for 7 minutes once the timer beeps.
6. Remove the chicken, shred and return back to the rice.
7. Gently stir the meal and serve warm.

Nutritional Information:
Calories: 606, Carbs: 58.8g, Protein: 52.4g, Fat: 16.6g, Sugar: 4.7g, Sodium: 897mg

Parsley Mushroom Risotto

Serves: 2 , Prep+ Cook time: 30 minutes

Ingredients
- Lightly mashed garlic clove, 1.
- Chopped medium onion, ½.
- Arborio rice, ½ cup.
- Chopped celery stalk, ½.
- Olive oil, ½ tbsp.
- Vegetable stock, 2 cups.
- Sliced cremini mushrooms, ½ cup.
- Chopped sprig parsley, 1.

Directions:
1. Put the oil in the instant pot to cook onions for 5 minutes on sauté mode.

2. Put the rest of ingredients to the instant pot then seal the lid.
3. Switch its pressure release handle to the sealing point.
4. Select the manual function to cook for 15 minutes at high pressure.
5. Perform a natural release for 20 minutes once the timer clicks.
6. Give the meal a gentle stir and serve hot.

Nutritional Information:
Calories: 226, Carbs: 42.7g, Protein: 4.4g, Fat: 3.9g, Sugar: 2.3g, Sodium: 59mg

Tasty Mexican Rice

Ingredients

- Smoked paprika, ¼ tsp.
- Long-grain white rice, 1 cup.
- Chicken stock, 2 cups.
- Finely chopped garlic cloves, 2.
- Garlic powder, ¼ tsp.
- Salt, ½ tsp.
- Chopped onion, ¼ cup.
- Sun-dried tomatoes, 2 tbsps.
- Chopped cilantro, 2 tbsps.
- Avocado oil, 1 tbsp.
- Crushed tomatoes, 2 tbsps.
- Cumin, ¼ tsp.

Directions:

1. Put the oil in the instant pot to cook garlic and onion on sauté mode for 3 minutes.
2. Mix in the rice stirring gently.
3. Add all the remaining ingredients and seal the lid.
4. Change its pressure release handle to the sealing point.
5. Select the manual function to cook for 8 minutes at high pressure.
6. Perform a natural release once the timer clicks.
7. Give the meal a gentle stir and serve warm.

Nutritional Information:
Calories: 252, Carbs: 53.1g, Protein: 5.6g, Fat: 1.5g, Sugar: 1.9g, Sodium: 922mg

Flavored Beef Rice

Ingredients

- Cooked corn kernels, ½ cup.
- Diced red onion, ½ cup.
- Water, 1 cup.
- Chili powder, ½ tsp.
- Lean ground beef, ½ lb.
- Chunky salsa, 1 cup.
- Rinsed and drained black beans, 1 cup.
- Salt, ¼ tsp.
- Ground cumin, ¼ tsp.
- Chopped fresh cilantro, 1 tbsp.
- Olive oil, ½ tbsp.
- Rinsed and drained long-grain white rice, ½ cup.

Directions:

1. Put the oil to the instant pot to cook the onion for 3 minutes
2. Mix in cumin, beef, chili powder, and salt to sauté for 5 minutes.
3. Mix in the remaining ingredients then cover the lid.
4. Change its pressure release handle to the sealing position.
5. Select the manual function to cook for 8 minutes at high pressure.
6. Perform a natural release once the timer clicks and remove the lid.
7. Give the meal a gentle stir ad serve warm.

Nutritional Information:
Calories: 378, Carbs: 43.5g, Protein: 31.6g, Fat: 8.8g, Sugar: 5g, Sodium: 868mg

Thyme Cauliflower Risotto

Ingredients

- Vegetable broth, 6 cups.
- Freshly ground black pepper.
- Diced large onions, 2.
- Minced garlic cloves, 4.
- Salt.
- Divided olive oil, 6 tbsps.
- Sprigs thyme, 4.
- Butter, 2 tbsps.
- Olive oil, 2 tbsps.
- Pearl barley, 2 cups.
- Sliced small cauliflower heads, 2.
- Freshly grated parmesan cheese, 1 cup.

- Chopped fresh parsley, 4 tbsps.

Directions:

1. Put the oil in the instant pot to cook the onion and garlic for 3 minutes on sauté mode.
2. Mix in the cauliflower chunks to fry for 5 minutes.
3. Mix in the remaining ingredients with exception of butter and cheese then seal the lid

4. Switch its pressure release handle to the sealing point.
5. Select the manual function to cook for 25 minutes at high pressure.
6. Do a natural release immediately the timer clicks then open the lid.
7. Mix in cheese and butter then serve warm.

Nutritional Information:
Calories: 372, Carbs: 48.2g, Protein: 8.4g, Fat: 18.8g, Sugar: 1g, Sodium: 69mg

Corn & Mixed Veggies Rice

Serves: 3 , Prep+ Cook time: 17 minutes

Ingredients

- Frozen garden peas, ½ cup.
- Turmeric powder, ½ tsp.
- Olive oil, 1 ½ tbsps.
- Frozen sweet corn kernels, ½ cup.
- Diced large onion, ½.
- Chopped green onions, ¼ cup.
- Finely diced large garlic clove, 1.
- Chopped carrots, ½ cup.
- Salt.
- Chopped bell peppers, ¼ cup.
- Butter.
- Rinsed basmati rice, 1 cup.
- Chopped cilantro stalks, 1 ½ tbsps.
- Chicken stock, 1 cup.

Directions:

1. Put the oil to the instant pot to cook all the veggies for 5 minutes on sauté mode.
2. Mix in the remaining ingredients with exception of butter then cover the lid.
3. Change its pressure release handle to the sealing position.
4. Select the manual function to cook for 7 minutes at high pressure.
5. Perform a natural release for 7 minutes once the timer clicks.
6. Mix in the butter to melt into the rice and serve warm.

Nutritional Information:
Calories: 423, Carbs: 66g, Protein: 7.8g, Fat: 14.9g, Sugar: 5.9g, Sodium: 298mg

Turmeric Yellow Potato Rice

Serves: 3 , Prep+ Cook time: 17 minutes

Ingredients

- Turmeric powder, ½ tsp.
- Diced large onion, ½.
- Diced medium-sized potatoes, 3.
- Finely diced large garlic clove, 1.
- Chopped cilantro stalks, 1 ½ tbsps.
- Olive oil, 1 ½ tbsps.
- Butter, 1 tsp.
- Rinsed basmati rice, 1 cup.
- Salt.
- Chicken stock, 1 cup.

Directions:

1. Put the oil to the instant pot to fry all the vegetables for 5 minutes on sauté mode.

2. Add all the remaining ingredients with exception of butter then seal the lid.
3. Switch its pressure release handle to the sealing point.
4. Press the manual function to cook for 7 minutes at high pressure.
5. Do a natural release for 7 minutes once the timer clicks.
6. Mix in the butter to melt into the rice and serve while still warm.

Nutritional Information
Calories: 466, Carbs: 86.1g, Protein: 9g, Fat: 9.2g, Sugar: 3.9g, Sodium: 339mg

Curried Mung Bean

Serves: 4 , **Prep+ Cook time:** 35 minutes

Ingredients

- Chopped baby spinach, 1 cup.
- Vegetable broth, 1 cup.
- Bay leaf, 1.
- Cooking oil, 1 ½ tbsps.
- Grated ginger, ¼ tbsp.
- Turmeric, ¼ tsp.
- Grated garlic, ½ tbsp.
- Salt.
- Coriander powder, ½ tsp.
- Boiled white rice.
- Water, ¾ cup.
- Chili powder, 1 tsp.
- Raw mung beans, ½ cup.
- Chopped onions, ½ cup.

Directions:

1. Put the oil to the instant pot to fry the onions for 5 minutes on sauté mode.
2. Mix in bay leaf, ginger, and garlic paste to cook for 1 minute then add all the spices
3. Stir in broth, water, and mung beans and close the lid.
4. Switch its pressure release handle to the sealing point.
5. Press the manual function key to cook for 15 minutes at high pressure.
6. Perform a natural release for 20 minutes once the timer clicks.
7. Add the spinach to cook for 3 minutes on saute mode.
8. Serve the meal while still hot with white rice.

Nutritional Information:
Calories: 158, Carbs: 19.2g, Protein: 8g, Fat: 5.9g, Sugar: 2.6g, Sodium: 248mg

Spicy Chickpea Tacos

Serves: 6 , **Prep+ Cook time:** 41 minutes

Ingredients

- Shredded carrot, ½.
- Finely chopped green chili, ½.
- Grated garlic, ½ tbsp.
- Coriander powder, ½ tsp.
- Grated ginger, ¼ tbsp.
- Chopped onions, ½ cup.
- Fresh tomato puree, ½ cup.
- Salt.
- Chili powder, 1 tsp.
- Water, ¾ cup.
- Tortillas, 6.
- Turmeric, ¼ tsp.
- Sliced green bell pepper, ½ cup.
- Raw chickpeas, ½ cup.
- Cooking oil, 1 ½ tbsps.
- Fresh cilantro, 1 tbsp.

Directions:

1. Put the oil to the instant pot to fry the onions for 5 minutes on sauté mode.
2. Mix in green chili, ginger, and garlic paste to cook for one minute then add all the spices.
3. Stir in tomato puree, water, and chickpeas then seal the lid.
4. Change its pressure release handle to the sealing point.
5. Allow to cook for 15minutes at high pressure on manual function.
6. Perform a natural release for 20 minutes once the timer clicks.
7. Mix in the bell peppers and shredded carrots to cook for 10 minutes on saute mode.
8. To serve, stuff the tortillas with the prepared fillings.
9. Enjoy.

Nutritional Information:
Calories: 165, Carbs: 25.7g, Protein: 5.3g, Fat: 5.3g, Sugar: 4.3g, Sodium: 58mg

Chapter 4 Beef, Lamb And Pork Delicacies

Apple Flavored Marinated Steak

Serves: 4 , **Prep + Cook time:** 50 minutes

Ingredients:

- Flank steak-2 lbs
- Apple Cider Vinegar-¼ cup
- Dried Onion Soup Mix- 2 tbsp
- Worcestershire sauce -1 tbsp
- Olive oil-½ cup + 1 tbsp
- Salt-¼ tsp
- Pepper-¼ tsp
- ½ cup beef broth or water

Directions:

1. Set Instant Pot on SAUTÉ mode and heat 1 tablespoon of oil
2. Put the flank steak into the pot and season with salt and pepper, Sauté on each side until its start to brown.
3. Put the following ingredients; the broth, vinegar, Worcestershire sauce, Soup mix and a ½ cup of oil, and Stir carefully.
4. At this point, the cooking program should be RESET by pressing the CANCEL button. Close and lock the lid to cook again.
5. Select the MEAT/STEW setting and set the cooking time for 35 minutes.
6. When cooking is done for the stipulated time, use a natural release for 5 minutes then release any remaining pressure manually. Open the lid then Serve.

Healthy Cheese Steak Recipe

Serves: 4-6 , **Prep + Cook time:** 1 hour 15 minutes

Ingredients:

- 2 green bell peppers, sliced
- Sliced mushrooms-8 oz
- Beef stock-1 cup
- Salt-1 tsp
- Ground black pepper-½ tsp
- Mozzarella cheese-1 cup
- Beef chuck roast, cut into chunks (2-3 inch)- 3 lbs
- Oil-1 tbsp
- 2 onions, sliced
- Steak seasoning-2 tbsp

Directions:

1. While the SAUTÉ setting is selected on the Instant Pot, heat the oil.
2. Put the onion and sauté for 3-4 minutes until softened.
3. Also, put the beef chunks and ensure the meat is brown on each side for a few minutes.
4. Put the steak seasoning, bell peppers, mushrooms, and stock and season with salt and pepper. Stir well.
5. At this point, Press the CANCEL key to stop the SAUTÉ function. Close and lock the lid.
6. Ensure to Select MANUAL settings and cook at HIGH pressure for 40 minutes.
7. At the moment timer goes off, use a Quick Release. With utmost care, open the lid. Put the mozzarella cheese on top.
8. Close the lid and let the dish sit for 15 minutes then Serve.

Round Roast with Mushroom-Veggies

Serves: 6 , Prep + Cook time: 40 minutes

Ingredients:

- Round roast (top or bottom)- 2½ lbs
- Ground black pepper-½ tsp
- Thyme-1 tbsp
- Sliced mushrooms-2-3 cups
- 1 large white onion, sliced or diced
- Potatoes (quartered or cubed)- 1 lb
- Olive oil-2 tbsp
- Vegetable or beef broth-2 cups
- Minced garlic-2 tbsp
- Kosher salt-1 tsp

Directions:

1. Combine and mix the olive oil, broth, garlic, salt, pepper, and thyme to the pot.
2. Put the roast, mushrooms, and onion, then stir well.
3. Close and ensure the lid is well locked. Select MANUAL settings and cook at HIGH pressure for 25 minutes.
4. At the moment timer goes off, use a quick release and Carefully open the lid, put the potatoes, stir carefully.
5. Again, Close and ensure the lid is well locked, Select MANUAL settings and cook at HIGH pressure for 10 minutes more.
6. When the timer goes off, use a Quick Release, unlock the lid carefully.

Delicious Roast Beef

Serves: 6-8 , Prep + Cook time: 1 hour 10 minutes

Ingredients:

- Soy sauce_½ cup
- 5 minced cloves garlic
- Granny Smith apple (peeled and chopped)- 1 quantity
- Grated ginger-1 thumb
- Juice of one big orange
- Beef chuck roast, cut into cubes (2 inches)- 4 lbs
- Olive oil-2 tbsp
- Salt1 tsp
- Ground black pepper-1 tsp
- Beef broth -1 cup

Directions:

1. While the SAUTÉ setting is selected on the Instant Pot, add the oil and heat it up. Season the roast with salt and pepper.
2. Put the roast to the pot and cook, ensure the meat has turned light brown on each side. Transfer the meat to a plate.
3. At this point, Press the CANCEL button to stop the SAUTÉ function.
4. Put the beef broth and ensure to deglaze the pot by scraping the bottom to remove all of the brown bits. Pour the soy sauce and stir. Return the roast to the pot.
5. Put the garlic, apple, and ginger on top and also pour over the orange juice.
6. Ensure the lid is Closed and well locked. Select MANUAL mode and cook at HIGH pressure for 45 minutes.
7. At the moment when the timer goes off, use a Quick Release. Unlock the lid carefully then Serve.

Easy Pot Roast

Serves: 6 , Prep + Cook time: 1 hour 10 minutes

Ingredients:

- Olive oil-2 tbsp
- Beef broth-1 cup
- Red wine-1 cup
- Carrots (chopped into large chunks)-4 quantity
- Potatoes (large-sized, quartered)- 4 quantity
- Beef chuck roast-3 lbs
- Chopped celery-2 stalks
- 3 cloves garlic
- 1 onion
- Salt-1 tsp
- Ground black pepper-1 tsp
- steak sauce (optional) -3 tbsp

Directions:

1. While the SAUTÉ setting is selected on the Instant Pot, add the oil and heat it up.
2. Put the roast to the pot and cook until the meat has turned light brown on all sides then transfer the beef to a plate.
3. Put the beef broth and ensure to deglaze the pot by scraping the bottom to remove all of the brown bits. Pour the wine.
4. Put the following ingredients; carrots, potatoes, and celery to the pot and top with the garlic and onion then Season with ½ teaspoon salt.
5. Meanwhile, put the beef on the vegetables. Sprinkle with ½ teaspoon salt and 1 teaspoon pepper, then spread with the steak sauce.
6. At this point, press the CANCEL key to reset the cooking program, then select the MANUAL setting and set at HIGH pressure for 45 minutes.
7. When cooking is done for the stipulated time, use a Natural Release for 15 minutes then release any remaining pressure manually. Carefully open the lid, transfer the roast to a plate and cut it into slices.
8. Serve with the gravy and vegetables

Italian Tasty Bacon-Roast Beef

Serves: 6-8 , Prep + Cook time: 1 hour 25 minutes

Ingredients:

- Parsley (optional)
- Boneless beef chuck roast -2 lbs
- Diced bacon-8 oz
- 2 Chopped onions
- 6 cloves garlic (minced)
- Sliced cremini mushrooms-1 package
- Chicken broth-1 cup
- Tomato paste-1 tsp
- Crushed tomatoes-1 can
- Dried red wine-½ cup
- 2 tsp dried oregano
- Leaves-2 bay
- Italian seasonings-1½ tbsp
- Salt and ground black pepper to taste

Directions:

1. Select SAUTÉ mode to preheat the instant pot.
2. Put the bacon into the pot and cook until lightly crispy and turn to cook the other side.
3. At this point, remove the bacon from the pot. put the onion and garlic and sauté until fragrant.
4. Also put the beef, bacon, mushrooms, broth, tomato paste, tomatoes, red wine, oregano and bay leaves.
5. Sprinkle Italian seasonings all over and season with salt and pepper to taste.
6. At this point, press the CANCEL button to stop the SAUTÉ function, then select the MEAT/STEW mode and set the cooking time for 60 minutes at HIGH pressure.
7. As the timer goes off, allow to Naturally Release for 10 minutes then release any remaining pressure manually. Carefully open the lid.
8. Top with parsley on top then serve.

Simple and Healthy Beef and Broccoli

Serves: 4 , Prep + Cook time: 60 minutes

Ingredients:

- Beef or bone broth-½ cup
- Soy sauce-¼ cup
- Fish sauce-2 tbsp
- (10-12 oz) frozen broccoli -1 bag
- Stew beef meat-1 lb
- 1 onion (quartered)
- 1 clove garlic, large-sized, pressed
- Ground ginger -1 tsp
- Salt-½ tsp

Directions:

1. Combine and mix the beef meat, onion, garlic, ginger and salt in the Instant Pot.
2. Carefully pour the broth, soy sauce, and fish sauce into the pot and stir carefully.
3. Ensure the lid is closed and well locked, then Select MANUAL settings on the pot, at HIGH-pressure cook for 35 minutes.

4. At the point when pressure cooking is complete, use a Quick Release. Unlock and open the lid carefully.

5. Put the broccoli, close the lid and let it sit for 15 minutes then serve.

Buttered-Beef Stroganoff

Serves: 4-6 , Prep + Cook time: 40 minutes

Ingredients:
- Chuck roast, thin slices (½ inch)- 2 lbs
- Butter-4 tbsp
- 1 onion, small-sized
- Kosher salt-1 tsp
- Ground black pepper-1 tsp
- Sliced Mushrooms-1 cup
- 2 cloves garlic, minced
- Beef broth -1¼ cups
- Sour cream-½ cup
- Cooked Egg noodles (optional) -16 oz

Directions:
1. The Instant Pot should be preheated by selecting SAUTÉ mode, then melt the butter.
2. Put the onion and sauté for 3 minutes. Season the meat strips with salt and pepper, and add to the pot.
3. Cook, and stir occasionally, for 2 minutes until it starts to brown, also put the mushrooms and cook for another 2 minutes.
4. Put garlic and sauté for a minute, then press the CANCEL key to stop SAUTE function.
5. Pour the broth and stir well. Close the lid and ensure it is well locked.
6. At this point, Select MANUAL settings on the pot and at HIGH-pressure cook for 15 minutes.
7. The moment the timer goes off, use a Quick Release and carefully open the lid.
8. Put the sour cream and mix properly. Ensure the lid is closed and let it sit for 5 minutes. Serve with cooked egg noodles.

Garlic Herbed Beef and Cabbage

Serves: 4-6 , Prep + Cook time: 1 hour 25 minutes

Ingredients:
- 1 cabbage heat, cut into 6 wedges
- Chopped carrots- 4 quantity
- 3 turnips (cut into quarters)
- 6 potatoes (cut into quarters)
- Horseradish sauce for serving
- Beef brisket -2½ lbs
- Salt-1 tsp
- Ground black pepper -½ tsp
- 3 cloves garlic (chopped)
- Bay leaves- 2 quantity
- Water-4 cups

Directions:
1. While the Instant Pot is ready for use, Put the beef brisket into the pot and season with salt and pepper.
2. Also, put the garlic and bay leaves and pour water into the pot, close the lid and ensure it is well locked.
3. Select the MANUAL setting and set at HIGH pressure and cook for 60 minutes.
4. The moment cooking is complete, use a Quick Release, then carefully open the lid.
5. Put the following ingredients into the pot cabbage, carrots, turnips, and potatoes.
6. Close and ensure the lid is well locked, then select MANUAL settings at HIGH pressure, then cook for 6 minutes.
7. At the point when cooking is complete, select CANCEL and use a Natural Release to put off pressure for 10 minutes.
8. Uncover the pot carefully and serve with horseradish sauce.

Garlic flavor-Beef and Noodles

Serves: 4-6 , Prep + Cook time: 1 hour 10 minutes

Ingredients:

- Boneless beef chuck roast, cut into 2-inch cubes-3 lbs
- Olive oil-2 tbsp
- Salt-1 tsp
- Ground black pepper-½ tsp
- 1 chopped onion
- 2 minced cloves garlic
- Water-2 cups
- 8 oz egg noodles

Directions:

1. Set the instant pot on SAUTÉ mode, then heat the oil in the pot, also put the beef into the pot and sauté until the meat starts to brown on both sides.
2. Season the meat with salt and pepper and add the onion and garlic.
3. Press the CANCEL button to stop the SAUTÉ function then pour a cup of water and lock the lid.
4. At this point, select the MANUAL setting, and at HIGH pressure also set the cooking time for 38 minutes.
5. The moment cooking is done, Release pressure Naturally for 10 minutes and release any remaining steam manually.
6. Take out the meat from the pot, select SAUTÉ on the pot, then put 1 cup of water and boil.
7. Put the noodles and cook for 9-10 minutes return the meat to the pot, stir well.
8. Serve.

Tasty Pork with Apple Sauce

Servings: 4, Prep + Cook time: 35 minutes

Ingredients:

- Chopped apples, 2
- Apple cider, 2 cups
- Dry onion, 1 tbsp.
- Black pepper
- Extra virgin olive oil, 2 tbsps.
- Chopped yellow onion, 1
- Pork loin, 2 lbs.
- Salt

Directions:

1. Melt the oil in the instant pot on sauté mode.
2. Mix in dried onion, pork loin, pepper, and salt.
3. Brown the meat evenly on both sides then put on a plate.
4. Cook the onions in the pot for 2 minutes then return the meat in the pot.
5. Stir in the seasonings, apples, and cider
6. Leave the combination to cook for 20 minutes on high pressure while covered.
7. Release the pressure when the timer clicks and remove the lid.
8. Put the meat on a chopping boars to slice for serving.
9. Enjoy.

Spiced Pork Chops

Servings: 4 , Prep + Cook time: 30 minutes

Ingredients:

- Parsley; ½ bunch.
- Canned cream of mushroom soup, 10 oz.
- Water, 1 cup
- Chicken bouillon powder, 2 tsps.
- Black pepper
- Sour cream, 1 cup.
- Boneless pork chops, 4
- Salt
- Extra virgin olive oil, 2 tbsps.

Directions:

1. Adjust the instant pot to sauté mode to preheat.
2. Put in the pork chops and seasonings to brown evenly and put on a plate

3. Set your instant pot on Sauté mode; add oil and heat it up.
4. Pour the water in the instant pot then add bouillon powder as you stir gently.
5. Stir in the pork chops then cook for 9 minutes at high pressure while covered.
6. Release the pressure naturally when the timer is over and put the pork chops on a platter.
7. Adjust the instant pot to simmer mode to heat the liquid.
8. Stir in mushroom soup to cook for 2 minutes then remove from heat.
9. Mix in the sour cream and parsley then pour over the pork chops.
10. Enjoy.

Beef & Veggies Mix

Servings: 6 , Prep + Cook time: 1 hour and 30 minutes

Ingredients:
- Horseradish sauce
- Beef brisket, 2 ½ lbs.
- Black pepper
- Cabbage head, 1
- Quartered potatoes, 6
- Water, 4 cups.
- Bay leaves, 2
- Chopped carrots, 4
- Quartered turnips, 3
- Salt
- Chopped garlic cloves, 3

Directions:

1. Pour water in the instant pot then add the beef brisket, garlic, pepper, bay leaves and salt.
2. Cook the meat for 1 hour 15 minutes at high pressure with the lid sealed.
3. Quickly release the pressure once the timer click and open the lid.
4. Stir in cabbage, turnips, carrots, and potatoes to cook for 6 minutes at high pressure with the lid sealed.
5. Again release the pressure naturally when the timer beeps and remove the lid.
6. Serve the meal on plates topped with horseradish sauce.
7. Enjoy.

Tasty Pork with Fennel

Servings: 4 , Prep + Cook time: 1 hour 30 minutes

Ingredients:
- White wine, 5 oz.
- Minced garlic cloves, 2
- Chopped yellow onion, 1
- Salt
- Sliced fennel bulbs, 1 lb.
- Boneless pork meat, 2 lbs.
- Chicken stock, 5 oz.
- Black pepper
- Extra virgin olive oil, 2 tbsps.

Directions:
1. Adjust the instant pot to sauté mode to heat the oil.
2. Put in the pork and seasoning then cook until browned evenly and reserve on a plate.
3. In the pot, pour the wine, stock then add garlic to cook for 2 minutes.
4. Return the pork to the pot to cook for 40 minutes at high pressure with the lid sealed.
5. Release the pressure then open the lid.
6. Stir in the fennel and onion to cook for 15 minutes on high pressure.
7. When the time is over, release the pressure and put the pork on a chopping board to slice.
8. Serve the pork slices and fennel as a side topped with cooking sauce.

Cheesy Lamb Meatballs.

Servings: 6, **Prep + Cook time:** 15 minutes

Ingredients:

- Dried oregano, 1 tsp.
- Minced garlic cloves, 4
- Chopped mint, 1 tbsp.
- Crushed tomatoes, 28 oz.
- Chopped onion, 1
- Olive oil, 2 tbsps.
- Black pepper, ¼ tsp.
- Tomato sauce, 6 oz.
- Crumbled feta cheese, ½ cup.
- Breadcrumbs, ½ cup.
- Water, 1 tbsp.
- Ground lamb, 1½ lbs.
- Chopped parsley, 2 tbsps.
- Beaten egg, 1
- Chopped green bell pepper, 1
- Salt, ½ tsp.

Directions:

1. Combine breadcrumbs, lamb, salt, feta, water, parsley, egg, half of the minced garlic, pepper, and mint in a sizable bowl.
2. Shape the combination into medium meatballs.
3. Adjust the instant pot to sauté mode to heat the oil.
4. Add the onion and bell pepper to cook for 2 minutes then add the remaining garlic to cook for 1 minute.
5. Stir in oregano, crushed tomatoes, and tomato sauce then sprinkle in some seasonings.
6. Arrange the meatballs in and ladle over the sauce then seal the cooker lid
7. Press the manual function key to cook on high pressure for 8 minutes.
8. Immediately the timer is over, press the cancel button then perform a quick-release.
9. Enjoy the meatballs with more cheese and parsley.

Instant pot Chili Con Carne

Servings: 4 , **Prep + Cook time:** 40 minutes

Ingredients:

- Black pepper
- Tomato paste, 1 tsp.
- Water, 5 oz.
- Chopped yellow onion, 1.
- Soaked and drained kidney beans, 4 oz.
- Extra virgin olive oil, 4 tbsps.
- Chili powder, 1 tbsp.
- Chopped canned tomatoes, 8 oz.
- Ground beef, 1 lb.
- Ground cumin, ½ tsp.
- Salt
- Minced garlic cloves, 2.
- Bay leaf, 1

Directions:

1. Put the instant pot to sauté mode to heat 1 tablespoon of oil.
2. Put in the meat to brown evenly then place to a bowl.
3. Add the remaining oil to fry the garlic and onion for 3 minutes
4. Put the beef back to the pot then stir in tomato paste, pepper, beans, chili powder, tomatoes, bay leaf, cumin, salt, cumin and water.
5. Cook for 18 minutes at high pressure with the lid sealed
6. Perform a quick release of the pressure then remove the lid
7. Remove the bay leaf and serve chili on bowls right away.

Spicy Braised Pork Recipe

Servings: 6 , Prep + Cook time: 1 hour 30 minutes

Ingredients:

- Paprika, 1 tbsp.
- Chicken stock, 16 oz.
- Extra virgin olive oil, 2 tbsps.
- Pork butt, 4 lbs.
- Chopped onion, ¼ cup.
- Garlic powder, ¼ cup.
- Salt
- Red wine, 16 oz.
- Black pepper
- Lemon juice, 4 oz.

Directions:

1. Combine pork with onion, oil, wine, pepper, stock, garlic powder, lemon juice, salt and paprika in the instant pot.
2. Adjust the cooking time to 45 minute at high pressure with the seal closed.
3. When the time is over, leave the pot for 15 minutes before releasing the pressure quickly.
4. Give the meal a gentle stir then serve immediately.

Mustard Pulled Pork Dish

Servings: 6 , Prep + Cook time: 1 Hour 30 minutes

Ingredients:

- Dried mustard, 2 tsps.
- Salt
- Beer, 11 oz.
- Halved pork shoulder, 3 lbs.
- Smoked paprika, 2 tsps.
- Sugar, 3 oz.
- Water, 8 oz.

For the sauce:

- Cayenne pepper
- Hot water, 4 oz.
- Salt
- Apple cider vinegar, 12 oz.
- Black pepper
- Brown sugar, 2 tbsps.
- Dry mustard, 2 tsps.

Directions:

1. Combine 3 oz. sugar with salt, 2 teaspoons of dry mustard, and Smoked paprika, in a bowl.
2. Brush the meat with the mixture and transfer to the instant pot
3. Stir in 3 oz. water and beer then cook for 1 hour and 15 minutes at high pressure with the lid sealed.
4. Once the timer clicks, release the pressure quickly then remove the lid.
5. Put the meat on a chopping board to shred using 2 forks the reserve.
6. Get rid of half of the cooking oil from the pot.
7. In the meantime, combine brown sugar with vinegar, 4 oz. hot water, pepper, salt, cayenne and 2 tsp. dry mustard in a bowl.
8. Stir the mixture to mix with the remaining cooking sauce in the pot the cook for 3 minutes at high pressure while covered
9. When fully cooked, release the pressure the serve the pork topped with the sauce.

Delightful Pork Chops

Servings: 4 , Prep + Cook time: 25 minutes

Ingredients:

- Minced garlic clove, 1.
- White flour, 1 tbsp.
- Extra virgin olive oil, 2 tbsps.
- Lime juice, 2 tbsps.
- Butter, 2 tbsps.
- Pork chops, 4
- 2 tbsps. cornstarch mixed with 3 tbsp. water
- Salt
- Milk, ½ cup.
- Chopped parsley; 2 tbsps.
- White wine, ½ cup.
- Sliced onions, 1 lb.
- Black pepper

Directions:

1. Adjust the instant pot to sauté mode to heat the oil and butter.
2. Add the pork chops with some seasonings to brown evenly the put in a bowl.
3. Put the onion and garlic in the pot to cook for 2 minutes while stirring gently
4. Mix in milk, parsley, lime juice, and wine then return pork chops to pot.
5. Adjust the cook time to 15 minutes at high pressure while covered.
6. When the timer clicks, release the pressure then open the lid.
7. Stir in flour and cornstarch to cook for 3 minutes on simmer mode.
8. Serve the meal on plates topped with cooking sauce

Marinated Beef and Broccoli

Servings: 4 , Prep + Cook time: 20 minutes

Ingredients:

- Beef stock, ½ cup.
- Peanut oil, 1 tbsp.
- Toasted sesame oil, 2 tsps.
- Stripped chuck roast, 3 lbs.
- Potato starch, 2 tbsps.
- Broccoli florets, 1 lb.
- Chopped yellow onion, 1.

For the marinade:

- Minced garlic cloves, 5.
- Chinese five spice, ½ tsp.
- Sesame oil, 1 tbsp.
- Dried and crushed red peppers, 3.
- Cooked white rice for servings
- Soy sauce, ½ cup.
- Fish sauce, 2 tbsps.
- Black soy sauce, ½ cup.
- Toasted sesame seeds for serving

Directions:

1. Combine black soy sauce fish sauce, with soy sauce, five spice, 1 tablespoon sesame oil, 5 garlic cloves, and crushed red peppers in a mixing bowl.
2. Mix in the beef strips to coat evenly then reserve for 10 minutes
3. Adjust the instant pot o sauté mode to heat the peanut oil to fry the onions for 4 minutes.
4. Stir in the reserved beef strips to cook for 2 minutes
5. Mix in stock the cook for 5minutes on high pressure with the lid sealed.
6. Immediately the timer beeps, release the pressure naturally for 10 minutes then switch the valve to venting to release the remaining pressure and open the lid.
7. Mix ¼ cup of the liquid from the pot with cornstarch then pour the mixture back to the pot.
8. Put the broccoli to the steamer basket to cook for 3 minutes at high pressure with the lid sealed.
9. Again, release the pressure once the timer is over.
10. Serve the beef and rice into bowls with broccoli as a side topped with sesame oil and sesame seed.

Sweet Beef with Mushroom

Servings: 6, Prep + Cook time: 28 minutes

Ingredients:

- beef stew meat: 1½ lbs.
- olive oil: 1½ toss
- garlic: 1½ toss
- diced onions: ¾ cup
- salt: 1½ taps
- chopped mushroom: 2 cups
- water: 1 cup
- black pepper: 1½ taps
- sour cream: ¾ cup

Directions

1. Grease an instant pot and add onions and garlic. Cook under 'sauté' option for 3 minutes.
2. Add all Ingredients except the sour cream. Let it cook at high pressure under 'manual' for 20 minutes.
3. Stir it in the sour cream and serve.

Tasty Lamb Stew

Servings: 7, Prep + Cook time: 1hr 35

Ingredients:

- olive oil: 4 toss
- lamb stew meat: 1 ½ -1¾ lb
- diced onions: 2
- chopped garlic cloves: 8
- salt and pepper: 2 taps
- cumin: 2 taps
- coriander: 2 taps
- turmeric: 2 taps
- cinnamon: 2 taps
- chili flakes: 1 tap
- tomato paste: 4 taps
- apple cider vinegar: ½ cup
- honey or brown sugar: 4 tablespoons
- chicken broth: 2½ cups
- rinsed and drained chickpeas: 2 15 oz. cans
- chopped raisins: ½ cup
- chopped fresh cilantro to garnish: 2 tablespoons

Directions

1. Take a greased instant pot and add all the spices. Cook for 4 minutes under 'sauté' option.
2. Add the remaining ingredients, close the lid and cook till it beeps
3. 'Natural remove' the steam, remove the cover and stir
4. Top with fresh cilantro and serve.

Nutritional value per serving:
Calories: 1010; Carbohydrate: 87.2; Protein: 65.4; Fat: 44.2; Sugar: 27.9; Sodium: 1018

Garlic Beef Sirloin Stew

Servings: 8, Prep + Cook time: 45 minutes

Ingredients:

- beef top sirloin steak : 6 lbs.
- garlic powder: 4 teaspoons
- minced cloves garlic : 8
- butter: 1 cup
- Salt and pepper to taste

Directions

1. Take a greased pot and add the sirloin steaks. Cook for 5 minutes under the 'sauté' option till its brown on both sides.
2. Add all the remaining Ingredients, stir and close the lid. Cook for 30 minutes under the 'meat stew' option till it beeps.
3. 'Natural release' the steam, remove the lid, and serve it hot.

Nutritional Values per Serving: Calories: 865; Carbohydrate: 2; Protein: 103.9; Fat: 44.3; Sugar: 0.4; Sodium: 368

Delicious Lamb Meat Balls

Servings: 3, Prep + Cook time: 45 minutes

Ingredients:

- ground lamb meat: ¾ lbs.
- Freshly ground black pepper and salt
- Roughly chopped tomatoes: 2 small
- Roughly chopped yellow onion: ½ small
- sugar-free tomato sauce: ½ cup
- crushed red pepper flakes: ¼ teaspoon, crushed
- peeled garlic cloves: 2
- mini bell peppers: 5, seeded and halved
- olive oil: ½ tbsp
- adobo seasoning *: 1 tap

Directions

1. Mix the meat and adobo seasoning in a bowl and make meatballs out of it
2. Place it in a greased cooker and cook at 'sauté' mode till they turn golden brown then place it a bowl
3. Add all the remaining Ingredients in the pot close the lid and cook at 'meat stew' mode for 35 minutes till it beeps.
4. 'Natural release' the steam then remove the lid
5. Blend the vegetable mix

6. Stir the meatballs in the vegetable mix, garnish it with herbs and serve it hot.

Nutritional value per serving:
Calories: 445; Carbohydrate: 24.3; Protein: 32; Fat: 25.5; Sugar: 15.7; Sodium: 430

Notes: Adobo Seasoning: * **Directions:** stir Salt, paprika, onion powder, oregano, cumin, garlic powder, black pepper and chili powder in a bowl. Keep it in a sealed jar in a cool, dry place.

Your Traditional Country Steak

Servings: 8, Prep + Cook time: 40 minutes

Ingredients:
- Beef round steak: 4 lbs.
- Vegetable oil: 2 tbsp
- Worcestershire sauce: 4 taps
- Garlic cloves: 6
- All-purpose flour: 1 cup
- Salt: 1 taps
- Black pepper: 1 taps
- Ketchup: 1 cup
- Diced onions: 1 cup

Directions
1. Place the steaks and flour in a bowl and dredge the steaks through such that both sides are covered with flour.
2. Take a greased pot, add steaks in batches and cook at 'sauté' mode till both sides turn brown
3. Add the remaining steaks, secure the lid, and cook at 'manual' mode at high pressure for 30 minute
4. 'Natural release' the steam, remove the cover and serve it hot.

Nutritional value per serving:
Calories: 308; Carbohydrate: 10; Protein: 35.8g; Fat: 12; Sugar: 4.5; Sodium: 365m

Healthy Prime Rib

Servings: 7, Prep + Cooking Time: 51 minutes

Ingredients:
- prime rib roast: ½ 5 lbs.
- olive oil: 1 tbsp
- ground black pepper: 1 tap
- salt: 1 tap
- water: 2 cups
- cloves garlic, minced: 5
- dried thyme: 1 tap

Directions
1. Melt the butter in the instant pot at 'sauté' mode.
2. Gently add the lamb chops, cook for 3 minutes each side then place them in a plate
3. In the pot, carefully place onions and garlic, cook for 3 minutes
4. Add all the remaining ingredient but leave out the arrowroot and water.
5. Secure the lid and let it cook at 'manual' mode under high pressure for 15 minutes till it beeps
6. 'Quick release' the steam then remove the cover.
7. Dissolve the arrowroot flour in water and add it to the pot. Cook for 5 minutes to make a sauce
8. Pour the sauce over the fried chops and serve it hot.

Nutritional value per serving:
Calories: 579; Carbohydrate: 14; Protein: 70.1; Fat: 25.5; Sugar: 5.3; Sodium: 314

Amazing Turmeric Beef Steaks

Servings: 3, Prep + Cook time: 40 minutes

Ingredients:
- beef steak pieces: ½ lb.
- salt: 1tbsp
- oil: 1½ toss
- water: 1 cup
- turmeric powder: 1 tbsp
- red chili powder: 1 tbsp

- coriander powder: 1 tbsp
- lemon juice: 1 tbsp
- cumin powder: 1 tbsp
- vinegar: 1 tbsp
- Boiled white rice to serve

Directions

1. In a bowl, mix red chili powder, cumin powder, salt, coriander powder, vinegar, oil, lemon juice, and turmeric powder.
2. Place the beef in the mixture to marinade it, mix and let pace it in the fridge overnight.
3. Take an instant pot, pour a cup of water inside and place a steamer trivet inside.
4. Arrange the pieces of beef in one layer over the trivet secure the lid and cook at 'meat stew' mode under high pressure for 30 minutes.
5. 'Natural release' the steam, remove the lid and serve hot with boiled rice.

Nutritional value per serving:
Calories: 255; Carbohydrate: 6.8; Protein: 26.6; Fat: 13.1; Sugar: 3.3; Sodium: 1635

Hot 3-peppered Lamb

Servings: 10, **Prep + Cook time:** 40 minutes

Ingredients:

- grass-fed, boneless lamb: 2 lbs. trimmed
- finely chopped tomatoes: 4 cups
- garlic cloves, minced: 6
- water: 2 cups
- olive oil: 2 tbsp
- Salt and black pepper to taste
- dried rosemary, crushed: 2 tbsp
- seeded and sliced large green bell peppers: 2
- seeded and sliced large yellow bell peppers: 2
- seeded and sliced large red bell peppers: 2
- sugar-free tomato sauce: 3 cups

Directions

1. Place the meat, salt and pepper in a greased instant pot and cook for 5 minutes at 'sauté' mode then place it in a plate.
2. While stirring, add water, salt, garlic, tomatoes, rosemary, black pepper, all peppers and tomato sauce
3. Place them all in the pot, secure the lid and cook at 'manual' mode under high pressure for 25 minutes
4. 'Quick release' the steam, remove the cover and serve it hot.

Nutritional value per serving:
Calories: 224; Carbohydrate: 10.1; Protein: 26; Fat: 9.2; Sugar: 6.6; Sodium: 451

Lovely Meal Lamb Shanks

Servings: 3, **Prep + Cook time:** 1 hour

Ingredients:

- grass-fed lamb shanks, trimmed: 1½ lbs.
- olive oil: 1 tbsp
- bone broth: ¾ cup
- dried rosemary, crushed: 1 tap
- melted butter: 1 tbsp
- whole garlic cloves, peeled: 7
- Salt and black pepper to taste
- sugar-free tomato paste: ¾ tbsp
- fresh lemon juice: 1¼ tbsp

Directions

1. Pace the shanks in a greased instant pot, sprinkle salt and pepper over them and cook at 'sauté' mode for 3 minutes each side
2. Add garlic cloves and stir-fry for 2 minutes
3. Add the remaining ingredient except for lemon juice and butter
4. Secure the lid and cook at 'manual' mode under high pressure for 30 minutes
5. 'Natural release' the pressure and remove the cover. Transfer it to a plate
6. Top it with melted butter and lemon juice and serve

Nutritional value per serving:
Calories: 533; Carbohydrate: 1.2; Protein: 69.1; Fat: 23.7; Sugar: 0.6; Sodium: 382

Fragrant Cheesy Beef Meatballs

Servings: 3, Prep + Cook time: 22 minutes

Ingredients:

- ground beef: 1 lb
- Parmesan cheese, grated: 1 tbsp
- dried oregano: ½ taps
- olive oil: ½ taps
- egg: 1
- flaxseed meal: ½ tbsp
- water: 1 cup
- Salt and ground black pepper to taste
- Tomato sauce: ½ 14 oz. Can

Directions

1. Mix parmesan cheese, ground beef, oregano, egg, salt, pepper and flaxseed in a bowl

2. Make meatballs out of the mixture of 1-inch diameter
3. Place the meatballs in an instant pot with oil. Cook at 'sauté' mode until they turn brown
4. Add tomato sauce, secure the lid and cook at 'manual' mode under high pressure for 7 minutes
5. 'Natural release' the steam, remove the cover and serve it warm

Nutritional value per serving:
Calories: 358; Carbohydrate: 3.1; Protein: 50.6; Fat: 15; Sugar: 1.8; Sodium: 411

Coconut Lamb Curry Delicacy

Servings: 4, Prep + Cook time: 45 minutes

Ingredients:

- grass-fed lamb shoulder, cut into bite-sized pieces: 1 lb.
- curry powder, divided: 1 tbsp
- unsweetened coconut milk: ¼ cup
- coconut cream: 2 tbsp
- coconut oil: 1 tbsp
- medium yellow onion, chopped: 1
- garlic cloves, crushed: 2
- chicken broth: ½ cup
- fresh lemon juice: 1 tbsp
- Salt and black pepper to taste
- fresh cilantro to garnish, chopped: 2 tbsp

Directions

1. Mix coconut cream, milk and curry powder in a bowl. Add the lamb and marinate it for 20 minutes

2. Heat a greased instant pot at 'sauté' mode. Gently add onion and garlic. Cook for 4 minutes
3. Add curry powder and cook for 1minuute. Add the lamb without the lamb while keeping the marinade to one side
4. Add chicken broth, pepper, salt and lemon juice, secure the lid and cook at 'manual' mode under high pressure for 20minutes. 'Quick release' the steam and remove the cover
5. Add the cream marinade and cook for 5 minutes at 'sauté' mode
6. Top with fresh cilantro and serve hot.

Nutritional value per serving:
Calories: 340; Carbohydrate: 7.1; Protein: 29.5; Fat: 21.3; Sugar: 4.3; Sodium: 17

Amazing Beef Potato Tots

Servings: 4, Prep + Cook time: 40 minutes

Ingredients:

- lean ground beef: ¾ lbs.
- Frozen potato rounds, tater tots: 16 oz.
- onion, chopped: ¼
- Cream of chicken soup: 8 oz.
- olive oil: 2 tbsps.

Directions

1. Add beef an onion to a greased instant pot. 'Sauté' for 5 minutes

2. Add chicken soup and potato tater tots, secure the lid and cook at 'manual' mode under high pressure for 25 minutes
3. 'Natural release' for 5 minutes remove the cover and serve it warm

Nutritional value per serving:
Calories: 1100; Carbohydrate: 92.7; Protein: 35.2; Fat: 63.4; Sugar: 0.6; Sodium: 1052

Beef Bowl the Japanese Way

Servings: 4, Prep + Cook time: 30 minutes

Ingredients:

- beef ribeye steak, thinly sliced: 1 lb
- large white onions, chopped: 2
- water: 1 cup
- brown sugar: 2 tbsp
- sake: 2 tbsp
- vegetable oil: 2 taps
- soy sauce: 4 tbsp
- mirin: 2 tbsp

Directions

1. Place onions in a greased instant pot and cook till it turns brown
2. Add soy sauce, mirin, sake, water and brown sugar then stir
3. Add beef steaks, secure the lid and cook at 'manual' mode under high pressure for 15 minutes
4. 'Quick release' the steam, remove the cover and serve hot.

Nutritional value per serving:
Calories: 316; Carbohydrate: 16.9; Protein: 22.7; Fat: 16.3; Sugar: 9.8; Sodium: 1174

Healthy Beef & Bacon Casserole

Servings: 4, Prep + Cook time: 45 minutes

Ingredients:

- Ground beef: 1 lb.
- Onion powder: ¼ taps
- Eggs: 4
- Heavy cream: ½ cup
- Ground pepper: ¼ taps
- Garlic cloves, crushed: 1½
- Bacon, cooked and chopped: ½ lb.
- Tomato paste: 3 oz.
- Salt: ¼ taps
- Cheddar cheese, grated: 6 oz.

Directions

1. In a greased instant pot, add beef, bacon, garlic and onion powder. 'Sauté' for 5 minutes
2. In a bowl, mix the cream, eggs, salt, tomato paste and cheddar cheese
3. Pour the bowl mixture on the beef and bacon, secure the lid and cook at 'manual' mode under high pressure for 25 minutes
4. 'Natural release' the steam, remove the cover and serve it hot.

Nutritional value per serving:
Calories: 823; Carbohydrate: 6.7; Protein: 72.9; Fat: 54.9; Sugar: 3.2; Sodium: 1084

Tasty Lamb and Zucchini Curry

Servings: 3, Prep + Cook time: 40 minutes

Ingredients:

- cubed lamb stew meat: 1 lb.
- fresh ginger, grated: 1 tbsp
- lime juice: ½ taps
- black pepper: ¼ taps
- diced tomatoes: ¾ cup
- turmeric powder: ½ taps
- medium carrots, sliced: 1½
- garlic cloves, minced: 2
- coconut milk: ½ cup
- salt: ¼ taps
- olive oil: 1 tbsp
- medium onion, diced: ½
- medium zucchini, diced: ½

Directions

1. In a bowl, mix garlic, ginger, salt, pepper, coconut milk and lime juice
2. Add the meat and let it marinade for 30 minutes
3. Place them in an instant pot, secure the lid and cook at 'manual' mode under high pressure for 20 minutes
4. 'Natural release' the steam for 15 minutes then remove the cover
5. Add zucchini and let it simmer for 5 minutes. Serve it hot

Nutritional value per serving: Calories: 255; Carbohydrate: 12.7; Protein: 9.5; Fat: 19.6; Sugar: 5.6; Sodium: 255

The Juicy Lamb Leg

Servings: 6, Prep + Cook time: 1hour 02 minutes

Ingredients:

- leg of lamb: 2 lbs.
- fine sea salt: 1 tap
- olive oil: 2½ tbsp
- sprigs thyme: 6
- bone broth: 1½ cups
- garlic cloves, minced: 6
- black pepper: 1½ taps
- small onions: 1½
- orange juice: ¾ cup

Directions

1. Marinade the lamb using salt, pepper and garlic

2. Add onions to a greased instant pot and 'sauté' for 4 minutes. Remove them from the pot
3. Place the marinated lamb in the pot, cook for 3 minutes on each side
4. Add the broth, onions, orange juice and thyme, secure the lid, cook at 'meat stew' mode under high pressure for 40 minutes
5. 'Natural release' the steam for 10 minutes remove the lid and serve it hot.

Nutritional value per serving:
Calories: 380; Carbohydrate: 6.3; Protein: 48.1; Fat: 17; Sugar: 3.4; Sodium: 466

Sweet Mexican Beef

Servings: 3, Prep + Cook time: 55 minutes

Ingredients:

- boneless beef: 1 lb.
- salt: ¾ taps
- black pepper: ½ taps
- medium onion, thinly sliced: ½
- garlic cloves, mince 3
- bone broth: ¼ cup
- chili powder: ½ tbsp
- butter: 1 toss
- tomato paste: ½ toss
- red boat fish sauce: ¼ taps

Directions

1. In a bowl, mix beef, chili powder and salt
2. Place onions in an instant pot and 'sauté' for 4 minutes
3. Add tomato paste, garlic, fish sauce, beef and broth, secure the lid and cook at 'meat stew' mode under high pressure for 30 minutes
4. 'Natural release' the steam for 15 minutes and remove the lid
5. Top it with salt and pepper. Serve it hot.

Nutritional value per serving:
Calories: 649; Carbohydrate: 4.1; Protein: 23.9; Fat: 59; Sugar: 1.2; Sodium: 723

Tasty Lamb

Servings: 2, Prep + Cook time: 40 minutes

Ingredients:

- Lamb meat, ground: 1 lb.
- Garlic cloves: 4
- Rosemary: 1 taps
- Salt: ¾ taps
- Black pepper: ¼ taps
- Small onion, chopped: ½
- Dried oregano: 1 taps
- Ground marjoram: 1 taps
- Water: ¾ cup

Directions

1. Using a food processor, chop garlic, onions, rosemary and marjoram
2. Add ground lamb meat and salt and pepper

3. Compress the mixture to make a compact 'loaf.'
4. Cover it with a tin foil then make holes on it
5. In an instant pot, pour water and place trivet inside
6. Place the 'loaf' over the trivet, secure the lid and cook at 'manual' mode under high pressure for 15 minutes
7. 'Quick release' the pressure, remove the lid and serve warm

Nutritional value per serving:
Calories: 664; Carbohydrate: 4.8; Protein: 56.9; Fat: 44.8; Sugar: 0.8; Sodium: 1061

Broccoli Beef Stew

Servings: 3, Prep + Cook time: 1 hour

Ingredients:

- Beef stew chunks: 1¼ lbs.
- Zucchini, chopped: 1
- Curry powder: 1 tbsp
- Salt: ½ taps
- Broccoli florets: ½ lb.
- Chicken broth: ¼ cup
- Garlic powder: ½ tbsp
- Coconut milk: ½ cup

Directions

1. Place all the ingredient except the coconut milk in an instant pot, secure the lid and cook at 'manual' mode under high pressure for 45 minutes
2. 'Natural release' the steam, remove the lid and add coconut milk
3. Let it simmer for 2 minutes then serve it hot

Nutritional value per serving:
Calories: 227; Carbohydrate: 24.4; Protein: 12; Fat: 16.2; Sugar: 5.9; Sodium: 1097

Cool Beef-Pork Stew

Servings: 3, **Prep + Cook time:** 4 hours 40 minutes

Ingredients:

- olive oil: ¼ tbsp
- Grass-fed ground beef: ¼ lbs.
- Ground pork: ¼ lbs.
- medium tomatillo, chopped: 1
- small yellow onion, chopped: ⅛
- jalapeño pepper, chopped: ½
- garlic clove, minced: ½
- sugar-free tomato sauce: ¼ 6oz can
- chili powder: ¼ tbsp
- ground cumin: ¼ tbsp
- Freshly ground black pepper and Salt
- water: 1 tbsp
- cheddar cheese, shredded: 2 tbsp

Directions

1. Place all the ingredient in a greased instant pot and cook at 'slow cook' mode under high pressure for 4 hours
2. 'Natural release' the steam, remove the lid and serve it hot

Nutritional value per serving:
Calories: 181; Carbohydrate: 4.8; Protein: 20.4; Fat: 8.5; Sugar: 1;Sodium: 122

Lovely Wine-Glazed Short Ribs

Servings: 2, Prep + Cook time: 1hour 15 minutes

Ingredients:

- Boneless beef short ribs: 1 lb.
- Curry powder: 1 tbsp
- Water: 1 cup
- White wine: 1 tbsp
- Large onion, diced: ½
- Tamari sauce: 1½ tablespoons
- Salt: ½ tbsp

Directions

1. Place all the ingredient in a greased instant pot, secure the lid and cook at 'slow cook' mode under high pressure for 1 hour
2. 'Natural release' the steam, remove the lid and serve it hot.

Nutritional value per serving:
Calories: 482; Carbohydrate: 8.3; Protein: 74.8; Fat: 14.7; Sugar: 2.6; Sodium: 570

Chapter 5 Poultry and Chicken Delicacies

Spiced Whole Chicken

Servings 8 , Prep + Cook time 45 minutes;
Ingredients:

- Whole chicken – 3 lbs
- Sugar – 2 tbsps
- Salt – 2 tsps
- Onion powder – 1 tbsp
- Garlic powder – 1 tbsp
- Paprika – 1 tbsp
- Ground black pepper – 2 tsps
- Cayenne pepper – ½ tsp
- Water – 1 cup
- Cooking wine – 1 tbsp
- Soy sauce – 2 tsps
- Minced green onion – 1

Directions:

1. Plug in and switch on the instant pot, pour in water, then insert steam or trivet stand, and pour in soy sauce and wine.
2. Place remaining ingredients except for chicken and onions in a bowl, stir until mixed and rub the mixture all over the chicken until evenly coated.
3. Place the seasoned chicken on the rack in the instant pot, then shut with lid, press the Manual button and press timer pad to cook for 18 minutes at high pressure.
4. When timer beeps, let the pressure naturally for 15 minutes and then carefully open the lid.
5. Garnish chicken with green onions and serve.

Scrumptious Chicken Thighs

Servings 8 , Prep + Cook time 35 minutes;
Ingredients:

- Chicken thighs – 5 lbs
- Minced garlic – 2 tsps
- Soy sauce – ½ cup
- White vinegar – ½ cup
- Black peppercorns – 1 tsp
- Bay leaves – 3
- Salt – ½ tsp
- Ground black pepper – ½ tsp

Directions:

1. Plug in and switch on the instant pot, add all the ingredients except for chicken thighs and stir until mixed.
2. Then add chicken thighs, stir until evenly coated and shut with lid.
3. Press the Poultry button and press timer pad to cook for 15 minutes at high pressure.
4. When timer beeps, let the pressure naturally for 10 minutes and then carefully open the lid.
5. Remove and discard bay leaves from the chicken, stir well and serve immediately.

Italian Chicken with Cremini Mushrooms and Carrots

Servings 6 , Prep + Cook time 25 minutes;
Ingredients:

- Chicken thighs, boneless, skinless – 8
- Salt – 1 tsp
- Ground black pepper – ½ tsp
- Olive oil – 1 tbsp
- Medium carrots, chopped – 2
- Cremini mushrooms, stemmed and quartered – 1 cup
- White onion, peeled and chopped – 1
- Minced garlic – 1 ½ teaspoon
- Tomato paste – 1 tbsp
- Cherry tomatoes – 2 cups
- Green olives, pitted – ½ cup
- Fresh basil, sliced – ½ cup
- Fresh Italian parsley, chopped – ¼ cup

Directions:

1. Plug in and switch on the instant pot, press the sauté button, add oil and wait until the instant pot is hot.
2. In the meantime, season chicken pieces with ½ teaspoon salt and black pepper.
3. Add onion, mushrooms, and carrots into the heated instant pot, season with remaining salt, stir well and cook for 5 minutes or until vegetables are softened.
4. Add garlic and tomato paste and continue cooking for 30 seconds.
5. Then add seasoned chicken thighs, tomatoes, and olives, stir well and press the cancel button.
6. Shut with lid, press the Manual button and press timer pad to cook for 10 minutes at high pressure.
7. When timer beeps, do quick pressure release and then carefully open the lid.
8. Garnish chicken with parsley and basil and serve.

Fantastic Thai Chicken

Servings 4 , Prep + Cook time 25 minutes;
Ingredients:

- Chicken thighs, boneless and skinless – 2 lbs
- Lime juice – 1 cup
- Fish sauce – ½ cup
- Olive oil – ¼ cup
- Coconut nectar – 2 tbsps
- Grated ginger – 1 tsp
- Chopped mint – 1 tsp
- Cilantro, chopped – 2 tsps

Directions:

1. Place all the ingredients except for chicken in a bowl and whisk until mixed.
2. Plug in and switch on the instant pot, add chicken thighs, then pour prepared marinade all over the chicken and toss until evenly coated.
3. Shut with lid, press the Manual button and press timer pad to cook for 10 minutes at high pressure.
4. When timer beeps, do quick pressure release and then carefully open the lid.
5. Serve straightaway.

Simple and Spiced Chicken Wings

Servings 4 , Prep + Cook time 20 minutes;
Ingredients:

- Chicken wings – 3 lbs
- Olive oil – 2 tbsps
- Brown sugar – ¼ cup
- Garlic powder – ½ tsp
- Cayenne pepper – ½ tsp
- Ground black pepper – ½ tsp
- Paprika – ½ tsp
- Salt – ½ tsp
- Chicken broth – 1½ cups

Directions:

1. Place all the ingredients except for chicken wings and broth in a bowl and stir until mixed.

2. Rub this mixture all over the chicken wings until evenly coated.
3. Plug in and switch on the instant pot, pour in the broth, then add chicken wings and shut with lid.
4. Press the Manual button and press timer pad to cook for 10 minutes at high pressure.

5. When timer beeps, do quick pressure release and then carefully open the lid.
6. Transfer chicken wings onto a sheet pan and place it under the broiler to cook chicken for 5 to 6 minutes or until crispy.
7. Serve straightaway.

Chicken Wings with Hot Buffalo Sauce

Servings 6 , Prep + Cook time 25 minutes;
Ingredients:
- Chicken wings, sectioned, fresh – 4 lbs
- Cayenne pepper hot sauce – ½ cup
- Salt – ½ tsp
- Brown sugar – 2 tbsps
- Worcestershire sauce – 1 tbsp
- Butter – ½ cup
- Water – 1½ cups

Directions:
1. Prepare sauce and for this, take a heatproof container and whisk together hot sauce, salt, sugar, Worcestershire sauce until mixed.
2. Add more butter into the sauce to make it milder in taste or add more hot sauce to make it hotter.

3. Place the bowl into the microwave and cook for 20 seconds at high heat setting or until butter melts, set aside.
4. Plug in and switch on the instant pot, pour in water, then insert steam or trivet stand, and place chicken wings on it.
5. Shut with lid, press the Manual button and press timer pad to cook for 10 minutes at high pressure.
6. When timer beeps, do quick pressure release and then carefully open the lid.
7. Transfer chicken wings onto a sheet pan, brush the top with prepared sauce and then place the pan under the broiler for 5 minutes or until crispy.
8. Serve straightaway.

Honey and Lime Chicken Wings

Servings 4 , Prep + Cook time 35 minutes;
Ingredients:
- Chicken wings – 2 lbs
- Honey – 3 tbsps
- Soy sauce – 2 tbsps
- Small lime, juiced – 1
- Sea salt – ½ tsp
- Water – ½ cup

Directions:
1. Whisk together honey, soy sauce, lime juice, and salt until combined and then pour the mixture into a large plastic bag.
2. Add chicken wings, seal the bag, turn it upside down to coat chicken wings and let marinate for 60 minutes in the refrigerator.

3. Then plug in and switch on the instant pot, pour in water and chicken wings along with the marinade and shut with lid.
4. Press the Manual button and press timer pad to cook for 15 minutes at high pressure.
5. When timer beeps, release pressure naturally for 10 minutes and then carefully open the lid.
6. Press the sauté button and cook for 3 to 5 minutes or until sauce is thickened to desired consistency.
7. Serve straightaway.

Sweet Chili Chicken with Sesame Seeds

Servings 6 , Prep + Cook time 35 minutes;
Ingredients:

- Chicken thigh fillets, boneless – 6
- Sweet chili sauce – 5 tbsps
- Hoisin sauce – 5 tbsps
- Grated ginger – 1 tsp
- Minced garlic – 2 tsps
- Rice vinegar – 1 tbsp
- Sesame seeds – 1½ tbsp
- Soy sauce – 1 tbsp
- Chicken stock – ½ cup

Directions:

1. Place all the ingredients except for chicken in a bowl and whisk until combined.
2. Plug in and switch on the instant pot, add chicken thighs and then pour prepared sauce over chicken.
3. Shut with lid, press the Manual button and press timer pad to cook for 15 minutes at high pressure.
4. When timer beeps, release pressure naturally for 10 minutes and then carefully open the lid.
5. Serve chicken with mashed potatoes or boiled rice.

Awesome Chicken with Salsa Verde

Servings 6 , Prep + Cook time 25 minutes;
Ingredients:

- Chicken breasts, boneless – 2½ lbs
- Smoked paprika – 1 tsp
- Cumin – 1 tsp
- Salt – 1 tsp
- Salsa verde – 2 cups

Directions:

1. Plug in and switch on the instant pot, add chicken, then season with salt, cumin, and paprika and pour salsa on top.
2. Shut with lid, press the Manual button and press timer pad to cook for 20 minutes at high pressure.
3. When timer beeps, do quick pressure release and then carefully open the lid.
4. Shred chicken with two forks and serve straightaway.

Honey-Sriracha Chicken

Servings 4 , Prep + Cook time 20 minutes;
Ingredients:

- Chicken breasts, diced – 4
- Soy sauce – 5 tbsps
- Honey – 3 tbsps
- Sugar – ¼ cup
- Cold water – 4 tbsps
- Minced garlic – 1 tbsp
- Sriracha – 3 tbsps
- Cornstarch – 2 tbsps

Directions:

1. Plug in and switch on the instant pot, add all the ingredients except for chicken, cornstarch and 2 tablespoons water and whisk until combined.
2. Add chicken, toss until evenly coated and shut with lid.
3. Press the Manual button and press timer pad to cook for 9 minutes at high pressure.
4. In the meantime, stir together cornstarch and remaining water until smooth.
5. When timer beeps, do quick pressure release and then carefully open the lid.
6. Stir cornstarch mixture into the chicken, press the sauté button and simmer for 3 minutes or until sauce is reduced to desired thickness.
7. Serve straightaway.

Sweet and Sour Chicken Dish

Servings 4 , Prep + Cook time 45 minutes;
Ingredients:

- Chicken thighs, boneless – 2 lbs
- Soy sauce – ¼ cup
- Organic ketchup – 3 tbsps
- Coconut oil – ¼ cup
- Honey – ¼ cup
- Garlic powder – 2 tsps
- Ground black pepper – ½ tsp
- Sea salt – 1½ tsp

Directions:

1. Plug in and switch on the instant pot, add all the ingredients except for chicken and whisk until mixed.
2. Add chicken, toss until well coated and shut with lid.
3. Press the Manual button and press timer pad to cook for 18 minutes at high pressure.
4. When timer beeps, do quick pressure release and then carefully open the lid.
5. Press the sauté button and simmer chicken for 5 minutes or until sauce is reduced to desired thickness.
6. Serve straightaway.

Coconut Chicken Curry

Servings 4 , Prep + Cook time 40 minutes;
Ingredients:

- Chicken breast – 2 lbs
- Coconut milk – 16 oz
- Tomato sauce – 16 oz
- Tomato paste – 6 oz
- Minced garlic – 1 teaspoon
- Medium white onion, peeled and chopped – 1 cup
- Curry powder – 2 tbsps
- Honey – 3 tbsps
- Salt – 1 tsp

Directions:

1. Plug in and switch on the instant pot, add all the ingredients except for chicken and stir until well combined.
2. Then add chicken, stir until mixed and shut with lid.
3. Press the Manual button and press timer pad to cook for 15 minutes at high pressure.
4. When timer beeps, release pressure naturally for 15 minutes and then carefully open the lid.
5. Stir the chicken curry and serve with boiled rice.

Delicious Chicken Curry

Servings 4 , Prep + Cook time 35 minutes;
Ingredients:

- Chicken breast, chopped – 1 lb
- Olive oil – 1 tbsp
- Medium white onion, peeled and sliced – 1
- Chicken curry base – 1 tbsp
- Coconut cream – 5 oz
- Medium potatoes, cut into halves – 6
- Coriander, chopped – ½ bunch

Directions:

1. Plug in and switch on the instant pot, press the sauté button, add oil and when hot, add chicken and cook for 2 minutes or until it begins to brown.
2. Then add onion and continue cooking for 1 minute.
3. In the meantime, whisk together chicken curry base coconut cream until combined.
4. Add this mixture into the instant pot, then add potatoes, stir well until evenly coated and press the cancel button.
5. Shut with lid, press the Manual button and press timer pad to cook for 15 minutes at high pressure.
6. When timer beeps, do quick pressure release and then carefully open the lid.
7. Garnish the curry with coriander and serve.

Easy Chicken Cacciatore

Servings 4 , Prep + Cook time 45 minutes;
Ingredients:

- Chicken thighs, with the bone, skinless – 4
- Olive oil – 2 tbsps
- Salt – 1 tsp
- Ground black pepper – 1 tsp
- Diced green bell pepper – ½ cup
- Diced red bell pepper – ¼ cup
- Diced white onion – ½ cup
- Crushed tomatoes – 7 ounce
- Chopped parsley – 2 tbsps
- Dried oregano – ½ tsp
- Bay leaf – 1

Directions:

1. Plug in and switch on the instant pot, press the sauté button, add 1 tablespoon oil and heat until hot.
2. In the meantime, season chicken with salt and black pepper.
3. Then add seasoned chicken into the instant pot and cook for 2 minutes per side or until nicely browned.
4. Transfer chicken to a plate, set aside, and then add remaining oil into the instant pot.
5. Add onion and peppers and cook for 5 minutes or until nicely golden brown.
6. Add chicken thighs along with tomatoes, oregano and bay leaves, stir until mixed and press the cancel button.
7. Shut with lid, press the Manual button and press timer pad to cook for 25 minutes at high pressure.
8. When timer beeps, release pressure naturally for 5 minutes then do quick pressure release and carefully open the lid.
9. Serve straightaway.

Tasty Chicken Nachos

Servings 6 , Prep + Cook time 45 minutes;
Ingredients:

- Chicken thighs, boneless and skinless – 2 lbs
- Olive oil – 1 tbsp
- Taco seasoning mix – 1 teaspoon
- Mild red salsa – 2/3 cup
- Salsa verde – 1/3 cup

Directions:

1. Plug in and switch on the instant pot, press the sauté button, add oil and heat until hot.
2. Then add chicken and cook for 2 to 3 minutes per side or until nicely brown.
3. Stir together red salsa, salsa verde, and taco seasoning, pour this mixture over chicken, stir well and press the cancel button.
4. Shut with lid, press the Manual button and press timer pad to cook for 15 minutes at high pressure.
5. When timer beeps, release pressure naturally for 10 minutes then do quick pressure release and carefully open the lid.
6. Shred chicken with two forks, stir until mixed and serve with tortilla chips.

Mouthwatering Chicken Piccata

Servings 4 , Prep + Cook time 30 minutes;
Ingredients:

- Chicken breasts skinless and boneless – 1½ lbs
- Olive oil – 1 tbsp
- Ground black pepper – ¼ tsp
- Salt – ½ tsp
- Chicken broth – 1 cup
- Lemon juice – ¼ cup
- Butter – 2 tbsps
- Brined capers, drained – 2 tbsps
- Parsley, chopped – 2 tbsps
- Cooked rice or pasta – 2 cups

Directions:

1. Plug in and switch on the instant pot, press the sauté button, add oil and heat until hot.
2. In the meantime, season chicken with salt and black pepper.

3. Add seasoned chicken into the instant pot and cook for 3 minutes per side or until nicely golden brown.
4. Pour in broth, stir and shut with lid.
5. Press the Manual button and press timer pad to cook for 5 minutes at high pressure.
6. When timer beeps, do quick pressure release and carefully open the lid.
7. Transfer chicken into a serving bowl, then press the saute button and simmer the sauce for 5 minutes or until reduced to desired thickness.
8. Stir in lemon juice and butter until smooth, then add capers and parsley and press the cancel button.
9. Drizzle this sauce over the chicken and serve immediately with cooked rice.

Yummy Chicken Adobo

Servings 4 , Prep + Cook time 40 minutes;
Ingredients:
- Chicken drumsticks – 4
- Salt – ½ tsp
- Ground black pepper – 1 tsp
- Olive oil – 2 tbsps
- White vinegar – ¼ cup
- Soy sauce – 1/3 cup
- Sugar – ¼ cup
- Medium white onion, peeled and chopped – 1
- Minced garlic – 2 ½ tsps
- Bay leaves – 2

Directions:
1. Plug in and switch on the instant pot, press the saute button, add oil and wait until hot.
2. In the meantime, season chicken with salt and ½ teaspoon black pepper.
3. Add seasoned chicken into the instant pot and cook for 4 minutes per side or until brown.
4. Whisk together remaining black peppers and ingredients until smooth, then add to instant pot and shut with lid.
5. Press the Manual button and press timer pad to cook for 10 minutes at high pressure.
6. When timer beeps, do quick pressure release and carefully open the lid.
7. Press the sauté button and simmer for 10 minutes or until sauce reduce to desired thickness.
8. Remove bay leaves and serve chicken immediately.

Appetizing Chicken Congee

Servings 6 , Prep + Cook time 65 minutes;
Ingredients:
- Chicken drumsticks – 6
- Water – 7 cups
- Jasmine rice, rinsed – 1 cup
- Grated ginger – 1 tbsp
- Salt – 1 tsp
- Scallions, chopped – ½ cup
- Sesame oil, optional – 2 tbsp

Directions:
1. Plug in and switch on the instant pot, add ginger, chicken, and rice, then pour in water and stir until mixed.
2. Shut with lid, press the Manual button and press timer pad to cook for 25 minutes at high pressure.
3. When timer beeps, release pressure naturally for 10 minutes and carefully open the lid.
4. Transfer chicken to a plate, shred with two forks, discard the bones and return chicken into the instant pot.
5. Press the sauté button and cook for 10 minutes or until sauce reduce to desired thickness.
6. Top chicken with scallion, drizzle with sesame oil and serve.

Fantastic Chicken Puttanesca

Servings 6 , Prep + Cook time 45 minutes;

Ingredients:

- Chicken thighs, skin on – 6
- Olive oil – 2 tbsps
- Water – 1 cup
- Chopped tomatoes – 14 oz
- Minced garlic – 1 tsp
- Red chili flakes – ½ tsp
- Pitted black olives – 6 oz
- Capers, rinsed and drained – 1 tbsp
- Fresh basil, chopped – 1 tbsp
- Salt – 1 tsp
- Ground black pepper – 1 tsp

Directions:

1. Plug in and switch on the instant pot, press the saute button, add oil and when hot, add chicken thighs, skin-side down.
2. Cook chicken for 4 to 6 minutes or until nicely brown and then transfer to a plate.
3. Add tomatoes, olives, capers, and garlic into the instant pot, season with salt, black pepper and basil, pour in water and stir until just mixed.
4. Return chicken into the instant pot, press the cancel button and shut with lid.
5. Press the Manual button and press timer pad to cook for 16 minutes at high pressure.
6. When timer beeps, release pressure naturally for 10 minutes and carefully open the lid.
7. Serve straightaway.

Italian Flavored Chicken and Potatoes

Servings 4 , Prep + Cook time 35 minutes;

Ingredients:

- Chicken thighs, skinless and boneless – 2 lbs
- Olive oil – 2 tbsp
- Chicken stock – ¾ cup
- Dijon mustard – 3 tbsps
- Lemon juice – ¼ cup
- Italian seasoning – 2 tbsps
- Red potatoes, peeled and cut into quarters – 2 lbs
- Salt – 1 tsp
- Ground black pepper – 1 tsp

Directions:

1. Plug in and switch on the instant pot, press the sauté button, add oil and wait until hot.
2. Meanwhile, season chicken thighs with ½ teaspoon salt and black pepper.
3. Add chicken into the instant pot and cook for 3 minutes per side or until nicely brown.
4. Whisk together mustard, Italian seasoning, lemon juice, and mustard until combined and then pour this mixture all over the chicken.
5. Add potatoes, season with remaining salt and black pepper, stir until mixed and press the cancel button.
6. Shut with lid, press the Manual button and press timer pad to cook for 15 minutes at high pressure.
7. When timer beeps, release pressure naturally for 5 minutes then do quick pressure release and carefully open the lid.
8. Serve straightaway.

Barbeque Chicken Wings

Servings: 4 , Prep + Cook time: 35 minutes

Ingredients:

- Chicken wings -2 lbs.
- Water -1/2 cup
- Basil; dried -1/2 tsp.
- Honey BBQ sauce -3/4 cup
- Apple juice -1/2 cup
- Red pepper; crushed -1 tsp.
- Paprika -2 tsp.
- Brown sugar -1/2 cup
- Salt and black pepper - to the taste
- Cayenne pepper - a pinch

Directions:

1. Place the wings in the insert of your Instant Pot.
2. Add apple juice, BBQ sauce, pepper, salt, red pepper, basil, sugar, water, and paprika.
3. Mix well and seal the lid. Cook for 10 minutes on manual mode at High.
4. Once done, release the pressure quickly, then remove the lid.
5. Spread the wings in a baking sheet and pour the remaining sauce over them.
6. Broil the wings for 7 minutes then flip them to broil again for 7 minutes.
7. Serve fresh.

Saucy Duck with Potatoes

Servings: 4 , **Prep + Cook time:** 30 minutes

Ingredients:
- Duck, cut into small chunks -1
- Garlic cloves; minced -4
- Sugar -4 tbsp.
- Green onions; roughly chopped -2
- Soy sauce -4 tbsp.
- Sherry wine -4 tbsp.
- Water -1/4 cup
- Potato; cut into cubes -1
- Ginger root; sliced -1-inch
- Salt -a pinch
- Black pepper - to the taste

Directions:
1. Choose Sauté mode on your Instant Pot.
2. Add duck pieces and sauté until brown.
3. Stir in ginger, garlic, soy sauce, green onions, wine, sugar, black pepper, a pinch of salt, and water.
4. Seal the lid and cook on Poultry mode for 18 minutes.
5. Allow the pressure to release quickly, then remove the lid.
6. Add potatoes and seal the lid again.
7. Cook for 5 minutes at High on manual mode.
8. Again, quick release the pressure to remove the lid.
9. Serve fresh.

Dijon Chicken with Potatoes

Servings: 4 , **Prep + Cook time:** 30 minutes

Ingredients:
- Chicken thighs; skinless and boneless -2 lbs.
- Chicken stock -3/4 cup
- Lemon juice -1/4 cup
- Red potatoes; peeled and cut into quarters -2 lbs.
- Extra virgin olive oil -2 tbsp.
- Dijon mustard -3 tbsp.
- Italian seasoning -2 tbsp.
- Salt and black pepper - to the taste

Directions:
1. Choose Sauté mode on your Instant Pot and add oil to its insert.
2. Add chicken thighs along with salt and pepper.
3. Sauté for 2 minutes from all the sides.
4. Whisk mustard with lemon juice and Italian seasoning.
5. Pour this mixture over the chicken and add potatoes.
6. Seal the lid and cook for 15 minutes on manual mode at High.
7. Once done, release the pressure quickly, then remove the lid.
8. Serve fresh.

Chicken Roux Gumbo

Servings: 4 , **Prep + Cook time:** 55 minutes

Ingredients:
- Chicken thighs; cut into halves -1 lb.
- Vegetable oil -1 tbsp.
- Smoky sausage; sliced -1 lb.
- Salt and black pepper - to the taste

For the roux:
- Flour -1/2 cup

- Vegetable oil -1/4 cup
- Cajun spice -1 tsp.

Aromatics:
- Bell pepper; chopped -1
- Quarts' chicken stock -2
- Canned tomatoes; chopped -15 oz.
- Celery stalk; chopped -1
- Salt - to the taste
- Garlic cloves; minced -4
- Okra -1/2 lbs.
- Yellow onion; chopped -1
- Tabasco sauce - a dash

For serving:
- White rice; already cooked
- Parsley; chopped -1/2 cup

Directions:
1. Select the Sauté mode on your Instant Pot.
2. Add a tbsp of oil to its insert and add sausage.
3. Sauté for 4 minutes then transfer the sausages to a plate.
4. Add chicken pieces to the instant pot and sauté for 6 minutes.
5. Transfer them to a plate then add a ¼ cup of oil to the Instant Pot.
6. Stir in Cajun spices, onion, garlic, celery, salt, pepper, onion and bell pepper.
7. Sauté for 5 minutes then return the sausage and chicken.
8. Add tomatoes and stock, mix well.
9. Seal the lid and cook on manual mode for 10 minutes at High.
10. Once done, release the pressure naturally in 15 minutes then remove the lid.
11. Add okra and switch the pot to Sauté mode.
12. Cook for 10 minutes then add salt, pepper and Tabasco sauce.
13. Serve fresh with rice and garnish with parsley.

Coca cola Braised Chicken

Servings: 4 , Prep + Cook time: 20 minutes

Ingredients:
- Chicken drumsticks -4
- Extra virgin olive oil -2 tbsp.
- Coca-cola -15 oz.
- Balsamic vinegar -1 tbsp.
- Chili pepper; chopped -1
- Yellow onion; minced -1
- Salt and black pepper - to the taste

Directions:
1. Choose Sauté mode on your Instant pot and add oil its insert.
2. Add chicken and sear each until golden brown from all the sides.
3. Transfer it to a plate then add vinegar and coca cola to the Instant Pot.
4. Cook for 2 minutes on Sauté mode then return the chicken.
5. Add salt and pepper, seal the lid.
6. Cook for 10 minutes on manual mode at High.
7. Once done, release the pressure quickly, then remove the lid.
8. Serve fresh.

Chunky Chicken Salsa

Servings: 5 , Prep + Cook time: 35 minutes

Ingredients:
- Chicken breast, skinless and boneless -1 lb.
- Chunky salsa -1 cup
- Cumin -3/4 tsp.
- Oregano - a pinch
- Salt and black pepper - to the taste

Directions:
1. Pat dry the chicken and rub it with salt and pepper.
2. Place this chicken in the insert of the Instant Pot.
3. Add cumin, oregano and chunky salsa.
4. Mix well then seal the lid of the Instant Pot.
5. Cook on poultry mode for 25 minutes.
6. Once done, release the pressure quickly then shred meat with a fork.
7. Serve the meat with its salsa.
8. Enjoy.

Chicken Thighs with Vegetables

Servings: 4 , Prep + Cook time: 50 minutes

Ingredients:

- Chicken thighs -6
- Vegetable oil -1 tsp.
- Canned tomatoes; chopped -15 oz.
- Yellow onion; chopped -1
- Tomato paste -2 tbsp.
- White wine -1/2 cup
- Chicken stock -2 cups
- Potatoes; chopped -1 ½ lb.
- Celery stalk; chopped -1
- Baby carrots; cut into halves -1/4 lb.
- Thyme; dried -1/2 tsp.
- Salt and black pepper - to the taste

Directions:

1. Choose Sauté mode on your Instant Pot and add oil to its insert.
2. Add the chicken along with salt and pepper.
3. Sear them for 4 minutes per side then transfer the chicken to a plate.
4. Add carrots, celery, onion, tomato paste and thyme to the Instant Pot.
5. Mix well and cook for 5 minutes on Sauté mode.
6. Stir in white wine and salt, cook for another 3 minutes.
7. Add seared chicken, stock and tomatoes.
8. Place the steamer basket over the chicken and place the potatoes in it.
9. Seal the lid and cook for 30 minutes on manual mode at High.
10. Once done, release the pressure quickly, then remove the lid.
11. Remove the potatoes and the chicken. Shred the meat using a fork.
12. Return both the chicken and potatoes to the Instant Pot.
13. Mix well and serve fresh.

Chicken Dipped in Tomatillo Sauce

Servings: 6 , Prep + Cook time: 35 minutes

Ingredients:

- Chicken thighs; skinless and boneless -1 lb.
- Extra virgin olive oil -2 tbsp.
- Canned garbanzo beans; drained -5 oz.
- Yellow onion; thinly sliced -1
- Garlic clove; crushed -1
- Canned green chilies; chopped -4 oz.
- Handful cilantro; finely chopped -1
- Rice; already cooked -15 oz.
- Tomatoes; chopped -5 oz.
- Cheddar cheese; grated -15 oz.
- Black olives; pitted and chopped -4 oz.
- Salt and black pepper - to the taste
- Canned tomatillos; chopped -15 oz.

Directions:

1. Choose Sauté mode on your Instant Pot and add oil to its insert.
2. Add onions, stir cook for 5 minutes then add garlic.
3. Sauté for 15 seconds then add chilies, chicken, pepper, salt, cilantro, and tomatillos.
4. Mix well then seal the lid and cook for 8 minutes on Poultry mode.
5. Once done, allow the pressure to release quickly then remove the lid.
6. Shred the chicken using a fork then return it to the Instant Pot.
7. Add beans, and rice then switch the Instant pot to sauté mode.
8. Cook for 1 minute then add tomatoes, cheese, and olive.
9. Stir cook for 2 minutes then serve fresh.
10. Enjoy.

Crispy Italian Chicken

Servings: 4 , **Prep + Cook time:** 50 minutes

Ingredients:

- Chicken thighs -6
- Garlic cloves; chopped -4
- Rosemary; dried - a pinch
- Cold water -1 cup
- Soy sauce -1 tbsp.
- Extra virgin olive oil -2 tbsp.
- Butter -2 tbsp.
- White flour -1 cup
- Eggs; whisked -2
- Yellow onion; thinly sliced -1
- Cornstarch mixed -2 tbsp.
- Water -2 ½ tbsp.
- Panko breadcrumbs -1 ½ cups
- Salt and black pepper - to the taste

Directions:

1. Add garlic, onion 1 cup water, and rosemary to the insert of the Instant Pot.
2. Place a steamer basket over the water and set the chicken thighs in the basket.
3. Seal the lid and cook for 9 minutes on manual mode at High.
4. Once done, release the pressure naturally in 10 minutes then remove the lid.
5. Take a suitable pan and melt butter in it over medium-high heat.
6. Add 1.5 cups breadcrumbs and cook until slightly golden.
7. Remove the chicken from the pot and pat them dry.
8. Rub the chicken with salt and pepper then dredge them through the flour.
9. Whisk egg in a bowl and dip the chicken in the gg.
10. Coat the pieces with the breadcrumbs.
11. Place the chicken thighs in a baking sheet lined with parchment paper.
12. Place the chicken in the oven and bake for 10 minutes at 300 degrees F.
13. Meanwhile, switch the Instant pot to Sauté mode and warm up the cooking liquid.
14. Stir in 1 tbsp soy sauce, cornstarch, salt, and pepper.
15. Mix well and cook for 2 minutes then transfer it to a serving bowl.
16. Serve the sauce with baked chicken thighs.
17. Enjoy fresh.

Cacciatore Olive Chicken

Servings: 4 , **Prep + Cook time:** 25 minutes

Ingredients:

- Canned tomatoes and juice; crushed -28 oz.
- Chicken drumsticks; bone-in -8
- Black olives; pitted and sliced -1/2 cup
- Chicken stock -1 cup
- Bay leaf -1
- Garlic powder -1 tsp.
- Yellow onion; chopped. -1
- Oregano; dried -1 tsp.
- Salt - to the taste

Directions:

1. Choose Sauté mode on your Instant Pot.
2. Add bay leaf, salt, and stock to the insert of the Instant Pot.
3. Stir in onion, oregano, chicken, tomatoes, and garlic powder.
4. Mix well and seal the lid. Cook for 15 minutes at High on Manual mode.
5. Once done, release the pressure quickly, then remove the lid.
6. Remove the bay leaf and transfer the chicken to the serving plates.
7. Pour the cooking liquid over the chicken and garnish with olives.
8. Enjoy fresh.

Chili Adobo Chicken Stew

Servings: 6, Prep + Cook time: 31 minutes

Ingredients:
- boneless, skinless chicken breasts: 6
- water: ½ cup
- turmeric: 1 tbsp
- GOYA Adobo all-purpose seasoning with pepper: 1 tbsp
- diced tomatoes: 2 cups
- diced green chilies: 1 cup
- White rice or fill tacos to serve

Directions
1. Put the chicken breast in the inner pot
2. Sprinkle adobo seasoning on both sides
3. Add diced tomatoes and a half cup of water, secure the lid and cook at 'manual' mode for 25 minutes till it beeps
4. 'Natural release, for 15 minutes then 'quick release,' remove the lid and shred the chicken using 2 forks
5. Serve it with the rice
6. Alternatively, fill the tacos with the shredded chicken and serve

Nutritional value per serving:
Calories: 204; Carbohydrate: 7.6; Protein: 32.9; Fat: 4.2; Sugar: 2.2; Sodium: 735

Honeyed Chicken Curry

Servings: 4, Prep + Cook time: 31 minutes

Ingredients:
- yellow mustard: ¼ cup
- unsalted butter, melted: ¼ cup
- cayenne pepper: ¼ taps
- boneless, skinless chicken thighs or breasts: 1½ lbs.
- hot curry powder: 1½ taps
- salt: 1 tap
- honey: ½ cup
- Boiled rice to serve

Directions
1. Place mustard, curry powder, honey, cayenne pepper, salt, and melted butter in the inner pot and mix them well
2. Place the pot in the cooker with trivet
3. Place the chicken on the trivet and cook at 'manual' mode under high pressure for 18 minutes
4. 'Natural release' the steam for 10 minutes and remove the lid
5. Shred the chicken and place them aside\let the remaining ingredients 'sauté' for 5 minutes
6. Boil the sauce until it is thick
7. Pour it over the shredded chicken, stir
8. Serve it hot with boiled rice

Nutritional value per serving:
Calories: 1895; Carbohydrate: 41.3; Protein: 132.8; Fat: 133.6; Sugar: 34.9; Sodium: 894

Smoked Paprika Chicken Stew

Servings: 6, Prep + Cook time: 20 minutes

Ingredients:
- olive oil: 1 tap
- strips bacon, chopped: 3
- small onion, chopped: 1
- garlic cloves, minced: 2
- small red bell pepper, chopped: 1
- smoked paprika: 2 taps
- salt: 1 tap
- beer: 1 12 oz. can
- chicken breasts which are cut into small pieces: 1½ lbs.
- white rice: 1 cup
- 2 strips bacon, cooked topping

Directions
1. 'Sauté' oil and bacon in the pot for 3 minutes without covering
2. Add bell pepper and 'sauté' for 3 more minutes
3. Add chopped onion and garlic and let it sauté for a further 2 minutes and turn off the heat
4. Add all the seasoning and beer. Mix well

5. Add chicken and rice then cook at 'manual' mode under high pressure for 10 minutes.
6. 'Quick release' the steam
7. Remove the lid

8. Top with bacon strips and serve.
Nutritional value per serving:
Calories: 524; Carbohydrate: 29.3; Protein: 68.5; Fat: 10.3; Sugar: 1.2; Sodium: 310

Spiced Chicken Breasts

Servings: 4, Prep + Cook time: 20 minutes

Ingredients:
- water: 1 cup
- chicken broth: 2 cups
- chicken breast, cubed: 1½ lbs
- chopped carrots: 1 cup
- olive oil: 1 taps
- frozen peas: 1 cup
- oregano: 2 taps
- onion powder: 1 taps
- Refrigerated biscuits: 1 tube 16 oz.
- basil: 1 taps
- salt: ½ taps
- cloves minced garlic : 2
- pepper: ½ taps

Directions

1. Press the biscuits to make them flat and cut them to 2-inch strips
2. In a pot, mix olive oil, onion powder, oregano, chicken, garlic, salt, pepper and basil then 'sauté' them till the chicken turns brown
3. While stirring, add water, peas, the biscuits strips carrots and chicken broth, cover with a lid and cook at 'manual' mode for 5 minutes till it beeps
4. 'Natural release' the steam for 10 minutes remove the lid and serve.

Nutritional value per serving:
Calories: 610; Carbohydrate: 13.6; Protein: 100.5; Fat: 12.1; Sugar: 4.4; Sodium: 717

Honeyed Chicken Teriyaki

Servings: 4, Prep + Cook time: 20 minutes

Ingredients:
- boneless, skinless chicken breasts: 1 lb.
- soy sauce: ½ cup
- honey: 1/3 cup
- apple cider vinegar: 2 tbsp
- sesame oil: 1 tap
- garlic cloves, minced: 2
- minced ginger: 2 taps
- corn starch: 2 tbsp
- water: 3 tbsp
- Garnish: sliced green onions, sesame seeds

Directions
1. Take a pressure cooker pot and place the chicken in it
2. Mix soy sauce, sesame oil, ginger, garlic, vinegar and honey in a bowl
3. Pour the mixture over the chicken, secure the lid and cook at 'manual' mode under high pressure for 5 minutes till it beeps
4. 'Natural release' the steam for 15 minutes. Shred the chicken with 2 forks. Put it aside
5. In the remaining mixture in the pot, add water and corn-starch, 'sauté' it while stirring till it thickens
6. Place the chicken in and mix well
7. On top, add sesame seeds and green onions then serve.

Nutritional value per serving:
Calories: 645; Carbohydrate: 30.9; Protein: 97.2; Fat: 12.4; Sugar: 23.8; Sodium: 1427

Flavorsome Chicken

Servings: 4, Prep + Cook time: 20 minutes

Ingredients:
- olive oil: 1 tbsp
- clove garlic, minced: 1
- medium onion, chopped: 1
- chicken broth: 2 cups
- Sliced mushrooms: 7 oz.
- Large lettuce leaves

- buffalo wing sauce: ½ cup
- low sodium soy sauce: 1/3 cup
- boneless, skinless chicken breast: 2 lbs.
- shredded carrots: ½ cup

Directions
1. 'Sauté' onions and oil in an instant pot
2. Add chicken and let it sit for 5 minutes till its brown
3. While stirring, add mushrooms, garlic, chicken broth, wing sauce, and soy sauce,

secure the lid and cook at 'manual' mode for 4 minutes.
4. Let it sit for 10 minutes. After which you remove the valve to venting and the lid
5. Stir the mixture
6. Pour the chicken and the sauce over the lettuce
7. Garnish with shredded carrots and serve

Nutritional value per serving:
Calories: 564; Carbohydrate: 6.2; Protein: 99.2; Fat: 11.9; Sugar: 4.3; Sodium: 823

Cheesy Chicken

Servings: 4, Prep + Cook time: 16 minutes

Ingredients:
- small onion chopped: 1
- diced tomatoes with juice: 4 cups
- boneless, skinless chicken breasts: 2 lbs.
- chipotle peppers: 1 tbsp
- water: ½ cup
- Jasmine rice uncooked: 1 cup
- lime, juiced: ½ tbsp
- Sea salt: 2 taps.
- ground black pepper: ½ teaspoon
- Butter: 2 tablespoons.
- drained and rinsed organic black beans: 1 can

- cheddar cheeses for serving, shredded: 2 cups

Directions
1. in your instant pot, place chicken, tomatoes, peppers, water, rice, salt, lemon juice, butter and onion then cook at 'manual' mode under high pressure for 6 minutes till it beeps
2. 'Quick pressure release' the steam
3. Add black beans, salt and pepper and stir
4. Top with shredded cheese and serve.

Nutritional value per serving:
Calories: 447; Carbohydrate: 15.2; Protein: 66.2; Fat: 11.7; Sugar: 3.9; Sodium: 188

Garlicky Chicken Breasts

Servings: 3, Prep + Cook time: 14 minutes

Ingredients:
- garlic powder: ¼ taps
- Boneless chicken breasts: 2 lbs.
- black pepper: 1 tbsp
- dried oregano: ⅛ taps
- dried basil: ⅛ taps
- olive oil: 1 toss
- water: 1 cup
- Salt to taste
- For serving: lime wedges, sprinkled oregano, and basil

Directions
1. 'Sauté' oil in the pot without the lid on
2. Season the chicken and gently place it in the pot. Cook each side for 4 minutes till its

brown
3. Place water in the pot and set the trivet
4. On the trivet, place chicken pieces and cook at 'manual' mode under high pressure for 5 minutes.
5. 'Natural release' to release the steam then 'quick release' to ensure al steam is vented remove the lid and place the chicken on a platter
6. Top it with lime wedges, sprinkled oregano, and basil then serve.

Nutritional value per serving:
Calories: 155; Carbohydrate: 0.3; Protein: 21.3; Fat: 7.2; Sugar: 4.3; Sodium: 62

Buttered Chicken

Servings: 5, Prep + Cook time: 12 minutes

Ingredients:

- chicken breasts: 2 lbs.
- rice vinegar: ¼ cup
- smooth cashew butter: ½ cup
- Jasmine rice uncooked: 1 cup
- Soy Sauce: ¼ cup
- chili sauce: 1 toss
- chicken broth: ½ cup
- honey: ¼ cup
- cloves garlic minced:3
- fresh cilantro for topping chopped : 3 toss
- cashews for topping chopped : 3 toss

Directions

1. Cut the chicken breasts into 1-inch chunks. place the pieces into each
2. Mix cashew butter, honey, rice, soy sauce, chili sauce, vinegar, chicken broth and garlic in a bowl and pour it over the chicken pieces
3. Secure the lid with a pot and cook at 'manual' mode under high pressure for 7 minutes till it beeps
4. 'Quick release' the steam
5. Top it with chopped cashews and fresh cilantro then serve

Nutritional value per serving:

Calories: 640: Carbohydrate: 26.3: Protein: 69.9: Fat: 27.6: Sugar: 13.7: Sodium: 754

Chili Chicken

Servings: 5, Prep + Cook time: 20 minutes

Ingredients:

- Boneless skinless chicken breasts: 2 lbs.
- sea salt: 1 tap
- black pepper: ¼ taps
- onion, chopped: 1
- Olive oil: 2 tbsps.
- garlic cloves, minced: 4
- organic chicken broth: ½ cup
- dried parsley: 1 tap
- chili powder: 1½ taps
- medium or large sized limes, juiced: 2
- arrowroot flour – optional: 4 taps

Directions

1. Place oil and onions in an instant pot then 'sauté' for 5 minutes
2. Add all the remaining ingredients
3. stir well
4. Secure the lid
5. cook under high pressure for 10 minutes
6. 'Natural release' the steam and check if the sauce is thick enough
7. If it's not thick enough, add dissolved arrowroot flour
8. Place the chicken on a platter
9. serve hot

Nutritional value per serving:

Calories: 697: Carbohydrate: 2.9: Protein: 127.3: Fat: 46.1: Sugar: 0.7: Sodium: 501

Herbaceous Turkey

Servings: 4, Prep + Cook time: 25 minutes

Ingredients:

- turkey thighs with skin and bones: 4
- Salt and pepper to taste
- olive oil: 2 toss
- cloves garlic, minced: 8
- fresh thyme, chopped: 2 taps
- fresh oregano, chopped: 2 taps
- Sherry, or dry red wine: ½ cup
- chicken broth: ½ cup
- Fresh herbs for topping

Directions

1. Season the turkey thighs using salt and pepper
2. 'Sauté' oil in instant pot
3. Gently add turkey thighs and cook for 5 minutes till they turn golden brown on both sides
4. . Remove it from the pot
5. On the pot, place oil, garlic, thyme and oregano then 'sauté' for 2 minutes

6. Add sherry or wine, chicken broth and fried turkey thighs
7. Secure the lid and cook t 'manual' mode under high pressure for 20 minutes till it beeps
8. 'Natural release' the steam
9. Top with fresh herbs and serve

Nutritional value per serving:
Calories: 545; Carbohydrate: 3.2; Protein: 66.7; Fat: 24.1; Sugar: 0.7;Sodium: 229

Healthy Tso's Chicken

Servings: 6, Prep + Cook time: 13 minutes

Ingredients:
- white wine vinegar: 1/3 cup
- tomato paste: 2 toss
- arrowroot powder: 3 toss
- chicken breast cut into small pieces: 1½ lbs.
- honey: 1 toss
- soy sauce: ½ cup
- olive oil: 2 tablespoons
- coconut sugar: ¼ cup
- cloves garlic crushed: 2
- minced ginger: 2 toss
- red hot chili pepper: 3 toss
- water: ½ cup
- sesame seeds for topping: 2 toss
- chopped green onion for topping: ¼ cup

Directions

1. Cover the chicken with arrowroot flour by rolling it in the flour
2. 'Sauté' the chicken, oil and garlic in the port while occasionally stirring till the chicken turns golden brown
3. Max the remaining ingredient in a bowl to make a paste and add it to the pot
4. Secure the lid and cook at 'manual' mode under high pressure for 8 minutes
5. Carefully release the steam and remove the lid
6. Top it with sesame seeds together with green onions then serve

Nutritional value per serving:
Calories: 617; Carbohydrate: 15: Protein: 96.6: Fat: 16.1: Sugar: 9.4: Sodium: 1432

Mustard Chicken

Servings: 5, Prep + Cook time: 35 minutes

Ingredients:
- olive oil: 2 toss
- lemon juice: ¼ cup
- chicken broth: ¾ cup
- chicken thighs, boneless: 2 lbs.
- Italian seasoning: 2 toss
- red potatoes, quartered: 3 lbs.
- Dijon mustard: 3 toss
- Salt and pepper as needed

Directions
1. Ina pot, place oil and chicken

2. Sprinkle salt and pepper to taste
3. Mix lemon juice, the chicken broth and the Dijon mustard in a bowl
4. Add potatoes with the remaining seasonings
5. Secure the lid and cook at 'manual' mode under high pressure for 15 minutes till it beeps
6. 'Natural release' the steam and serve

Nutritional value per serving:
Calories: 748; Carbohydrate: 4.3; Protein: 127.5; Fat: 19.9; Sugar: 4.4; Sodium: 656

Honeyed Chicken

Servings: 2, Prep + Cook time: 27 minutes

Ingredients:
- cold water: 3 cups
- salt: ½ tsp
- boneless, skinless chicken breast: 1 lb.
- Dijon mustard: 1 toss
- honey: 1 toss
- balsamic vinegar: 1 toss
- cloves garlic, finely minced: 3
- olive oil: 3 toss

- Field greens.
- Grape tomatoes, cut in half

Directions

1. Take a large bowl, into it add 2 cups of water and chicken pieces and place it in the fridge for 45 minutes
2. In an instant pot, place 1 cup of water and a trivet on top
3. Place the chicken on the trivet and cook at 'manual' mode under high pressure for 7 minutes till it beeps
4. 'Natural release' the steam and let the chicken sit aside for 5 minutes
5. Mix Dijon mustard, olive oil, garlic, balsamic vinegar and honey in a bowl
6. Slice the chicken, add field greens and tomatoes and pour honey mixture over it then serve.

Nutritional value per serving:
Calories: 407; Carbohydrate: 11; Protein: 32; Fat: 25; Sugar: 9; Sodium: 262

Delicious Turkey

Servings: 2, Prep + Cook time: 1 hour 05 minutes

Ingredients:

- chicken broth: 1¼ cup
- turkey breast boneless : 1 lb
- butter, melted: 4 toss
- turkey herb rub: 2 toss
- large onion, quartered: 1
- celery, cut into large pieces: 4 stalks
- cloves garlic, crushed: 5
- A few sprigs of fresh herbs - rosemary, sage and thyme
- turkey gravy mix: 2 0.87 oz. packets

Directions

1. Pour chicken broth in the instant pot and set the trivet
2. Place turkey roast on the trivet
3. Pour melted butter over it
4. Sprinkle the seasonings and herbs over it
5. Add garlic, onion and celery, secure the lid and cook at 'manual' mode under high pressure for 55 minutes
6. 'Natural release' the steam, remove the lid and slice turkey road
7. Slice the turkey
8. Place gravy packets in the pot and 'sauté.' Let it boil for 5 minutes to form a thick paste
9. Pour the paste over the turkey then serve

Nutritional value per serving:
Calories: 220; Carbohydrate: 12.9; Protein: 12.3; Fat: 13.4; Sugar: 6.1; Sodium: 1104

Tasty Turkey Breasts

Servings: 8, Prep + Cook time: 50 minutes

Ingredients:

- bone-in, skin-on turkey breast: 6½ lbs
- pepper, powdered onion, garlic powder, salt and paprika spices
- turkey or chicken broth: 1 14 oz. can
- large onion, quartered: 1
- butter, melted: 4 toss
- celery, cut into large pieces: 1 stock
- thyme: 1 sprig
- cloves of garlic : 3
- Salt and pepper as needed
- corn-starch: 3 tablespoons
- cold water: 3 toss

Directions

1. Add all the spices to the turkey and cover with a thin layer of seasoning
2. Stuff garlic, thyme, celery and onion in the turkey breast
3. 'Sauté' butter and the turkey, cook it till its golden brown then turn the heat off
4. Add chicken broth, secure the lid and cook at 'manual' mode under high pressure for 30 minutes till it beeps
5. 'Natural release' the steam for 10 minutes then 'quick release' and Remove the lid
6. Add corn-starch dissolved in water and let it 'sauté' till the broth thickens
7. Add pepper and salt, Slice the turkey and serve with the steaming broth

Nutritional value per serving:
Calories: 360; Carbohydrate: 3; Protein: 49; Fat: 16; Sugar: 0.9; Sodium: 869

Awesome Turkey Thighs

Servings: 4, Prep + Cook time: 50 minutes

Ingredients:

- melted butter, unsalted: ½ cup
- fresh rosemary, chopped: 1 tap
- fresh thyme, chopped: 1 tap
- smoked paprika: 1 toss
- Dijon mustard: 2 toss
- maple syrup: ½ cup
- turkey thighs bone-in skin-on, washed and dried: 2 3 lbs.
- salt: 1 tap
- pepper: ½ taps
- water: 1 cup
- large onion, chopped: 1
- celery, chopped: 5 stalks
- carrots, chopped: 5
- Rosemary: 4 sprigs
- thyme: 2 sprigs

Directions

1. Place melted butter, thyme, rosemary, maple syrup, smoked paprika and Dijon mustard in an instant pot and 'sauté' while stirring occasionally
2. Add water, celery, onion, sprig rosemary, thyme, and carrots
3. Set the trivet and place turkey on it
4. Pour the remaining maple syrup over the turkey and cook at 'manual 'mode under high pressure for 30 minutes till it beeps
5. 'Natural release' the steam for 10 minutes then 'quick release.'
6. Remove the lid and let the turkey sit aside for 10 minutes
7. Cut eh turkey into slices and pour maple mustard mixture over it
8. Serve

Nutritional value per serving:
Calories: 633; Carbohydrate: 41; Protein: 44; Fat: 34; Sugar: 30;Sodium: 1410

Saucy Turkey

Servings: 7, Prep + Cook time: 50 minutes

Ingredients:

- cranberries, fresh or frozen: 3 cups
- orange juice: 1 cup
- apple jelly: 1 cup
- five-spice: ½ taps
- corn-starch: 3 toss
- Turkey breast with skin: 4 lbs.
- fresh rosemary, chopped: 1 toss
- dried thyme: ½ taps
- chicken broth: ½ cup
- Salt and pepper as needed
- unsalted butter, melted: 4 toss
- medium onions, chopped: 2

Directions

1. Blend 2 cups of cranberries, apple jelly, five Spice, orange juice and corn-starch
2. Sprinkle salt, pepper, thyme, and rosemary over turkey breast
3. Add 2 tablespoons of butter and 'sauté' till the turkey is golden brown. Let it sit aside
4. Add 2 tablespoons of butter, onion, salt, and pepper to the pot then 'sauté' for 5 minutes
5. Add cranberry and bring it to boil while stirring occasionally
6. Add the remaining cranberries and mix
7. Add chicken broth and turkey, secure the lid and cook at 'manual' mode under high pressure for 25 minutes till it beeps
8. Release the steam, remove the lid and serve it hot with cranberry sauce

Nutritional value per serving:
Calories: 600; Carbohydrate: 51.8; Protein: 70.8; Fat: 9.6; Sugar: 32.2; Sodium: 195

Creamy Turkey Breasts

Servings: 3, Prep + Cook time: 35 minutes

Ingredients:

- olive oil: 3 toss
- turkey breast cut into long strips: ½ lb.
- Salt and pepper to taste
- cloves garlic, minced: 5
- dried basil: 2 tbsp
- Fire-roasted tomatoes: 15 oz.
- heavy cream, 125 ml: ½ cup
- basil leaves to garnish, chopped: 8

Directions

1. Blend the roasted tomatoes
2. Season the chicken breasts using salt and pepper
3. Place oil in an instant pot and 'sauté.'
4. Gently add turkey breasts and cook till golden brown. Then put them aside.
5. Place oil, garlic and basil to the pot and 'sauté' for 1 minute
6. Add tomato paste and heavy cream and cook for 3 minutes
7. Add turkey breasts, secure the lid and cook at 'manual' mode under high pressure for 15 minutes till it beeps
8. Release the steam and remove the lid
9. Garnish with basil leaves and serve

Nutritional value per serving:
Calories: 355; Carbohydrate: 11.5; Protein: 36.5; Fat: 18.3; Sugar: 5.6; Sodium: 624

Hot Turkey

Servings: 4, Prep + Cook time: 20 minutes

Ingredients:

- ground turkey: 2 lbs.
- Salt and pepper to taste
- cayenne pepper: ¼ teaspoon
- Herbs de Provence: 1 teaspoon
- olive oil: 1 tablespoon
- Swiss cheese: 4 slices
- water: 1 cup
- eggs, fried: 4
- tomato cut into four slices: 1
- turkey bacon: 4 slices
- lettuce leaves: 4

Directions

1. Mix ground turkey, cayenne pepper, salt, herbs de Provence and pepper in a bowl
2. Make four burger patties out of the mixture
3. Place olive oil in the pot and 'sauté.'
4. Carefully add the turkey patties in the pot and cook until both sides turn golden brown. Put them aside
5. Add 1 cup of water in the pot, set the trivet and place the fried patties on it
6. Cover each patty with a cheese slice
7. Place bacon strips on the trivets, secure the lid and cook at 'manual' function under high pressure for 5 minutes till it beeps
8. Release the steam and remove the lid
9. Top it with lettuce leaves, a tomato slice, turkey patty, bacon and fried egg and serve

Nutritional value per serving:
Calories: 720; Carbohydrate: 1.7; Protein: 122.3; Fat: 18.9; Sugar: 0.7;Sodium: 534

Apricot Glazed Whole Turkey with Veggies

Servings: 8 to 10 , Prep + Cooking Time: 60 minutes

Ingredients:

- Carrot, diced – 1
- Cumin – ½ tsp.
- Turmeric – ½ tsp.
- Chicken Stock – 2 cups
- Salt – 1 tsp.
- Apricot Jam – 6 oz.
- Black Pepper, grounded – 1 tsp.
- Coriander – ½ tsp.
- Turkey, washed & patted dry – 9lb.
- Onion, peeled & diced – 1

Directions

1. Mix the apricot jam with coriander, cumin, pepper, turmeric, and salt in a bowl.
2. Apply this spice mix generously over the turkey.

3. Pour the broth to the instant pot along with carrot and onions. Stir well.
4. Add the turkey. Mix and close the lid.
5. Select the 'poultry' setting of the instant pot and set the cooking time to 40 minutes.
6. When the time is over, allow the steam to release naturally for 10 min and release the remaining manually.

7. Open the lid and serve it hot.

Notes: If you prefer a crispy and browned meat, you can broil it for 3 to 4 minutes.

Nutritional Information per Serving:
Calories: 745, Total Fat: 20.6g, Saturated Fat: 6.7g, Carbs: 13g, Protein: 120g

Instant Pot Salsa Verde Turkey

Servings: 4 to 6, **Prep + Cooking Time:** 40 minutes

Ingredients:
- Cumin – ¼ tsp.
- Turkey Breast, 1 ½-inch cubed – 2 lb.
- Black Pepper, grounded – ¼ tsp.
- Smoked Paprika – ¼ tsp.
- Cumin – ¼ tsp.
- Salsa Verde – 16 oz.
- Turmeric – ¼ tsp.
- Garlic Salt – ¼ tsp.

Directions
1. Mix all the ingredients excluding the turkey in the instant pot until well combined.

2. Stir in the turkey cubes and give everything a good stir.
3. Close and lock the lid. Press the 'manual' setting of the instant pot and set the cooking time to 20 minutes at high pressure.
4. Once the cooking duration is over, allow the pressure to be released quickly. Open the lid carefully.

Notes: If you want to make it a nutritious fare, you can add beans to it.

Nutritional Information per Serving:
Calories: 745, Total Fat: 20.6g, Saturated Fat: 6.7g, Carbs: 13g, Protein: 120g

Turkey Wings with Cranberries & Walnuts

Servings: 4 , **Prep + Cooking Time:** 55 minutes

Ingredients:
- Yellow Onion, sliced – 1
- Turkey Wings – 4
- Butter – 2 tbsp.
- Vegetable Oil – 2 tbsp.
- Orange Juice – 1 cup
- Kosher Salt – 1 tsp.
- Cranberries – 1 ½ cup
- Thyme, chopped roughly – Bunch
- Walnuts – 1 cup

Directions
1. Pre-heat the instant pot with the 'sauté' setting and to this, spoon in the oil.
2. Once the oil becomes hot, stir in butter.
3. In the meantime, marinate the turkey with salt and pepper. Set it aside.
4. When the butter has melted, add the seasoned turkey and sear them for 4 minutes or until lightly browned. Transfer them to a plate.
5. Stir in the cranberries, thyme, walnuts, and onion to the instant pot and mix well.

6. Then, pour the orange juice and return the turkey to the pot. Combine.
7. Close and lock the lid. Press the 'manual' setting of the instant pot and set the cooking time to 20 minutes at high heat.
8. When the time is up, allow the pressure to be released naturally for 10 minutes and the remaining manually.
9. Carefully open the lid and remove the turkey to a serving bowl.
10. Press the 'sauté' setting and simmer the cranberry juice for 5 to 10 minutes or until thickened.
11. Serve the cranberry sauce over the turkey and enjoy.

Notes: For more crunchy veggies, you can add celery to it.

Nutritional Information per Serving:
Calories: 608, Total Fat: 41.2g, Saturated Fat: 6.1g, Carbs: 26g, Protein: 31.3g

One Pot Turkey Casserole

Servings: 6 , **Prep + Cooking Time:** 50 minutes

Ingredients:

- Creamy Mushroom Soup Can – 2
- Onion, medium & sliced – 1
- Salt – ½ tsp.
- Turkey Breast, boneless – 2 lb.
- Black Pepper, grounded – ½ tsp.
- Celery Stalk, sliced – 1
- Chicken Stock – 1 cup
- Mixed Vegetables, frozen – 10 oz.
- Pepperidge Farm Herb Stuffing Mix – 14 oz.

Directions

1. Stir in the frozen vegetables, celery and onion to the instant pot.
2. Marinate the turkey with salt and pepper. Set it aside.
3. Add the seasoned turkey to the pot along with the broth and mix well.
4. Close and lock the lid. Press the 'poultry' setting and set the timer to 25 minutes.
5. Once the time is over, allow the pressure to release quickly.
6. Open the lid and pour the mushroom soup and stuffing mix.
7. Select the 'sauté' button of the instant pot and sauté them for 5 to 8 minute or until thickened while stirring it frequently.
8. Serve the turkey in a bowl and top it with the sauce.

Notes: For more crunchy veggies, you can add celery to it.

Nutritional Information per Serving:
Calories: 253, Total Fat: 3.2g, Saturated Fat: 1.2g, Carbs: 16.7g, Protein: 41.7g

Simple Turkey Chilli

Servings: 4, **Prep + Cooking Time:** 45 minutes

Ingredients:

- Cayenne – 1/8 tsp.
- Vegetable Stock – 1 ½ cup
- Turkey, grounded (85% lean)– 1lb.
- Onion, diced – 1
- Tomato Juice, canned – 10 oz.
- Water – ½ cup
- Chili Powder – 2 ½ tbsp.
- Chickpeas, cooked – 2 cups
- Cumin – 1 ½ cup
- Garlic, peeled – 2
- Tomato Juice – 5 ½ oz.
- Yellow Bell Pepper, diced – 1

Directions

1. Place the turkey and water in the instant pot and stir well.
2. Close and lock the lid. Press the 'manual' button of the instant pot and set the timer to 5 minutes at high pressure.
3. Once the cooking time is up, allow it to rest for 5 to 10 minutes and then release the pressure quickly.
4. Open the lid. Break down the turkey with a wooden spoon.
5. Stir in all the remaining ingredients to the instant pot and give everything a good stir.
6. Close the lid and select the 'manual' button again and cook them for 5 minutes at high pressure.
7. Allow it to rest for 8 to 10 minutes and then release the pressure quickly.
8. Serve it hot.

Notes: For more crunchy veggies, you can add celery to it.

Nutritional Information per Serving:
Calories: 731, Total Fat: 20.4g, Saturated Fat: 5.7g, Carbs: 96.8g, Protein: 61.1g

Juicy Turkey Breast Roast

Servings: 4, Prep + Cooking Time: 60 minutes

Ingredients:

- Salt – 2 tsp.
- Turkey Breast Roast, boneless – 3 lb.
- Chicken Broth – 1 ½ cup
- 4 tbsp. Garlic Infused Oil divided

Directions

1. Apply half the garlic infused oil and salt all over the turkey. Set it aside.
2. Preheat the pot by pressing the 'sauté' button.
3. Stir in the remaining oil into the instant pot and then place the marinated turkey into it.
4. Sear the turkey for a few minutes or until they are browned.
5. Select the 'cancel' button. Transfer the turkey to a bowl.
6. Once transferred, pour the broth into the instant pot and deglaze it by scraping the browned bits.
7. Place the steam rack in the instant pot and keep the turkey on top of it.
8. Close and lock the lid. Press the 'manual' button and set the timer to 30 minutes at high pressure.
9. When the time is up, allow the pressure to release for 10 minutes. Release the remaining pressure manually.
10. Serve it hot.

Notes: You can add white wine for more flavour.

Nutritional Information per Serving:
Calories: 515, Total Fat: 36.4g, Saturated Fat: 5.4g, Carbs: 4.4g, Protein: 66.9g

Thanksgiving Herb Turkey Roast

Servings: 6, Prep + Cooking Time: 50 minutes

Ingredients:

- Celery Stalks, chopped roughly – 3
- Turkey Breast – 3lb.
- Oregano, dried – 1 tsp.
- Chicken Broth – 2 cup
- Salt – 1 tsp.
- Rosemary Sprigs, fresh – 2
- Red Onion, quartered – 1
- Thyme, fresh – 1 sprig
- Black Pepper, grounded – 1 tsp.
- Basil, dried – 1 tsp.

Directions

1. Prepare the instant pot by pouring water to the pot and then place a steamer rack inside.
2. Stir in the rosemary and thyme to it.
3. Marinate the turkey with salt, basil, pepper, and oregano. Set it aside.
4. Place the seasoned turkey on the steamer rack with the breast side up.
5. Keep onion and celery into it.
6. Close and lock the lid. Select the 'manual' button and set the cooking duration to 35 minutes at high pressure.
7. Once the cooking time is over, allow the pressure to release for 10 minutes and release the remaining manually.
8. Open the lid carefully and serve it by slicing it. Spoon the gravy over it.

Notes: Serve it on a bed of your favourite vegetables.

Nutritional Information per Serving:
Calories: 263, Total Fat: 4.5g, Saturated Fat: 1g, Carbs: 12.9g, Protein: 40.7g

Chapter 6 Fish and Seafood

Orange Flavored Fish with

Servings: 4 , Prep + Cook time: 17 minutes

Ingredients:

- Chopped small ginger piece, 1.
- Orange juice and zest, 1.
- Black pepper.
- Extra virgin olive oil
- White fish fillets, 4
- Fish stock, 1 cup
- Chopped spring onions, 4.
- Salt.

Directions:

1. Dry the fillets with paper towel then rub them with olive oil and some seasonings.
2. In the instant pot, pour the stock, onions, orange juice, orange zest and ginger in your instant pot.
3. Set the fillets in the steamer basket.
4. Cook for 7 minutes at high pressure with the lid sealed
5. Release the pressure quickly and serve the fish sprinkled with orange sauce.

Simple Salmon

Servings: 2 , Prep + Cook time: 15 minutes

Ingredients:

- Extra virgin olive oil, 2 tbsps.
- Salt.
- Water, 1 cup.
- Frozen salmon fillets, 2.
- Black pepper.

Directions:

1. In the instant pot, add the water
2. Set the salmon fillet in the steamer basket

3. Cook for 3 hours on low pressure with the lid covered
4. Perform a quick release of pressure when the timer is over.
5. Put the salmon to paper towels and pat dry.
6. Set a pan with on fire to heat the oil.
7. Add the fillets with the skin facing down, sprinkle with some pepper and salt then cook for 2 minutes.
8. Serve the salmon with a salad of your choice.

Thyme Salmon

Servings: 4 , Prep + Cook time: 25 minutes

Ingredients:

- Parsley springs, 4.
- Sliced tomatoes, 3.
- Extra virgin olive oil, 3 tbsps.
- Sliced lemon, 1.
- Water, 2 cups.
- Chopped white onion, 1.
- Salt.
- Salmon fillets, 4.
- Thyme springs, 4.
- Black pepper.

Directions:

1. Sprinkle the oil on a parchment paper

2. Arrange the tomatoes then some seasonings and oil, followed by the fish with some seasonings, add some oil, then thyme, parsley sprigs, onions, lemon slices, and then finish with the seasonings.
3. Pour 2 cups of water to the instant pot
4. Fold and wrap packet then transfer to the steamer basket of the instant pot
5. Cook for 15 minutes on low with the lid closed
6. Release the pressure quickly then remove the lid
7. Serve the fish while still warm and enjoy.

Buttered Almond Cod.

Ingredients:
- Almond milk, ½ cup.
- Minced garlic, 1 tsp.
- Fish sauce, ¼ cup.
- Soy sauce, 3 tbsps.
- Lime zest, 1 tbsp.
- Cod, 8 oz.
- Almond flakes, 3 tbsps.
- Butter, 1 tbsp.

Directions:
1. Combine soy sauce and fish sauce in a bowl well.
2. Rub the fish with minced garlic and lime.
3. Pour on the almond milk and leave the fish to marinate for 10 minutes.
4. Melt the butter in the instant pot.
5. Turn the instant pot on sauté mode and cook for 10 minutes with the lid covered.
6. When the timer is over, open the lid then add the almond flakes to cook for 3 minutes as you stir gently.
7. Enjoy the meal while still hot.

Instant Pot Fish and Potatoes

Ingredients:
- Half and half, 14 oz.
- Peeled and sliced potatoes, 13 oz.
- Salt.
- Milk, 13 oz.
- Chopped yellow onion, 1.
- Water, 14 oz.
- Sliced white fish, 17 oz.
- Chicken stock, 14 oz.
- Black pepper.

Directions:
1. In your instant pot Combine fish with water, stock, potatoes, onions, and milk.
2. Cook for 10 minutes at high pressure with the lid covered
3. Release the pressure quickly when the timer is over then open the lid and put the pot to simmer mode.
4. Taste and adjust the seasonings then add half and half to cook for 10 minutes.
5. Serve and enjoy the meal.

Macaroni and Tuna Casserole.

Ingredients:
- Tuna, 2 cans.
- Salt, ½ tsp.
- Shredded cheddar cheese, 1 cup.
- Macaroni pasta, 2 ½ cups.
- Water, 3 cups.
- Mushroom cream soup, 1 can.
- Pepper, ½ tsp.
- Frozen peas, 1 cup.

Directions:
1. Combine water and the soup to the instant pot.
2. Mix in the remaining ingredients with exception of cheese.
3. Turn the steam valve to sealing and select manual.
4. Cook for 4 minutes at high pressure with the lid locked.
5. Release the pressure quickly and remove the lid.
6. Add the cheese on top then cook for 5 minutes with the lid sealed to melt the cheese.
7. Serve and enjoy.

Easy Mustard Halibut

Servings: 2, **Prep + Cook time:** 10 minutes

Ingredients:

- Dijon mustard, 2 tsp.
- Water, 1 cup.
- Firm fish fillets or steaks, 2.
- Steamer basket.

Directions:

1. Rub 1 teaspoon of Dijon mustard on the fish fillets.
2. Put cup of water to the instant pot and set the steamer basket to the pot.
3. Add the fish in the steamer basket with the skin facing down.
4. Select manual function key with default settings.
5. Cook the fish with the lid covered.
6. Switch the steam valve to release the pressure quickly when the timer beeps.
7. Serve immediately.

Instant Garlic Shrimp

Servings: 4, **Prep + Cook time:** 15 minutes

Ingredients:

- Beer, 16 oz.
- Old bay seasoning, 1 tbsp.
- Sliced sweet onions, 2.
- Black pepper.
- Cooked and chopped Andouille sausage, 12 oz.
- Crushed red pepper flakes, 1 tsp.
- Crushed garlic cloves, 8.
- Sliced corn ears, 4.
- French baguettes.
- Shrimp, 1 ½ lbs.
- Sliced potatoes, 1 lb.
- Salt.

Directions:

1. Combine beer with red pepper flakes, old bay seasoning, onions, shrimp, black pepper, sausage pieces, garlic, potatoes, corn, and salt in the instant pot.
2. With the pot covered, cook for 5 minutes at high pressure.
3. Release the pressure quickly then remove the lid.
4. Serve the shrimp with French baguettes as a side.

Cheesy Tuna with Noodle

Servings: 4, **Prep + Cook time:** 30 minutes

Ingredients:

- Drained canned tuna, 14 oz.
- Chopped parsley, 1 tbsp.
- Chopped red onion, ½ cup.
- Basil.
- Drained and chopped artichoke hearts, 8 oz.
- Black pepper.
- Extra-virgin olive oil, 1 tbsp.
- Crumbled feta cheese
- Water, 1 ¼ cups.
- Garlic.
- Egg noodles, 8 oz.
- Chopped canned tomatoes, 14 oz.
- Oregano.
- Salt.

Directions:

1. Switch the instant pot to sauté mode to heat the oil to fry the onions for 2 minutes.
2. Mix in the salt, noodles, water, pepper and tomatoes.
3. Turn the pot to simmer mode to cook for 10 minutes
4. Stir in artichokes and tuna.
5. With the lid sealed, cook for 5 minutes at high pressure.
6. Release the pressure quickly when the timer clicks.
7. Serve the meal topped with parsley and cheese.

Delight Salmon Fillets with Rice.

Servings: 2 , **Prep + Cook time:** 20 minutes

Ingredients:
- Olive oil, 2 tbsps.
- Salt.
- Cold tap water, 1 cup.
- Frozen salmon fillets, 2.
- Pepper.

Directions:
1. In the instant pot, add 1 cup of water.
2. Put the steamer rack in its place then put the fillets in the rack.
3. Lock and seal the steamer valve.
4. Select manual function and cook for 1 minute on low pressure.
5. Quickly release the pressure when the timer beeps and remove the lid.
6. Remove the fish and dry with a paper towel
7. Set the skillet on fire over medium-high heat
8. Rub the fish fillet skins with 1 tablespoon olive oil then season with black pepper and salt.
9. Cook the salmon fillets on the skillet with the skin facing down for 2 minutes.
10. Serve the salmon with rice.

Lemony Clams

Servings: 4 , **Prep + Cook time:** 25 minutes

Ingredients:
- Baby red potatoes, 1 lb.
- Chopped parsley, 2 tbsps.
- Sliced chorizo links, 2.
- Scrubbed and de-bearded mussels, 30.
- Lemon wedges.
- Extra virgin olive oil, 1 tsp.
- Small clams, 15.
- Chopped yellow onion, 1.
- Beer, 10 oz.

Directions:
1. Heat the oil in the instant pot on sauté mode
2. Stir in onions and chorizo to cook for 4 minutes.
3. Mix in potatoes, beer, mussels, and clams; then stir well.
4. Cook for 10 minutes at high pressure with the lid sealed.
5. Quickly release the pressure when the timer clicks then open the lid.
6. Stir in parsley and sever immediately with lemon wedges.

Salmon in White wine

Servings: 4, **Prep + Cook time:** 15 minutes

Ingredients:
- Black peppercorns, 3.
- White wine vinegar, 1 tsp.
- Dry white wine, ½ cup.
- Chopped dill, ¼ cup.
- Chicken stock, 2 cups.
- Bay leaf, 1.
- Black pepper.
- Fennel seeds, ½ tsp.
- Salmon fillet, 16 oz.
- Lemon zest, 1.
- Chopped scallions, 4.
- Salt.

Directions:
1. Rub the salmon fillets with seasonings then transfer them to the steamer basket of the instant pot.
2. Mix in lemon zest, dill, scallions, vinegar, peppercorns, stock, bay leaf, wine, and fennel.
3. With the lid closed, cook for 5 minutes at high pressure.
4. Release the pressure quickly when the timer clicks then open the lid.
5. Serve the salmon on plates.
6. Switch the pot to steamer mode to cook the liquid for 3 minutes.
7. Sprinkle the liquid over the salmon and enjoy.

One Pot Salmon and Raspberry Sauce

Servings: 6 , Prep + Cook time: 2 hours 5 minutes

Ingredients:

- Clam juice, 1 cup.
- Sherry, 1 tsp.
- Lemon juice, 2 tbsps.
- Finely chopped dill, 1/3 cup.
- Extra virgin olive oil, 2 tbsps.
- Chopped parsley, 2 tbsps.
- White pepper.
- Minced garlic cloves, 2.
- Raspberries.
- Salmon steaks, 6.
- Sliced leeks, 4.
- Salt.

For the raspberry vinegar:

- Red raspberries, 2 pints.
- Cider vinegar, 1-pint.

Directions:

1. In a bowl, combine vinegar with raspberries
2. Mix in the salmon fillets then refrigerate for 2 hours.
3. Switch the instant pot to sauté mode to heat the oil
4. Stir in garlic, leeks, and parsley to cook for 2 minutes
5. Mix in sherry, clam, pepper dill, salt, lemon juice, and the salmon steaks.
6. Cook for 3 minutes at high pressure with the lid sealed.
7. Perform a quick release of pressure then open the lid.
8. Serve the meal with fresh raspberries and leeks.

Capers and Cod Fillets

Servings: 4, Prep + Cook time: 20 minutes

Ingredients:

- Chopped parsley, 1 tbsp.
- Pitted and chopped olives, 1 cup.
- Cod fillets, 4.
- Crushed garlic clove, 1.
- Black pepper.
- Extra-virgin olive oil, 1 tbsp.
- Halved tomatoes, 17 oz.
- Drained and chopped capers, 2 tbsps.
- Salt.

Directions:

1. Set the tomatoes on the bottom of a heat proof bowl.
2. Mix in the seasonings and parsley then fish on top
3. Add olive oil, capers, garlic, pepper, olives and salt
4. Transfer the bowl in the steamer basket of the pot
5. With the lid closed, cook for 5 minutes at high pressure.
6. Release the pressure naturally and serve immediately.

Mustard Salmon Burger

Servings: 4, Prep + Cook time: 20 minutes

Ingredients:

- Mustard.
- Panko, ½ cup.
- Black pepper.
- Lemon zest, 2 tbsps.
- Extra virgin olive oil, 1 tsp.
- Arugula.
- Minced salmon meat, 1 lb.
- Tomatoes slices.
- Salt.

Directions:

1. Process the salmon in the blender then put in a bowl
2. Stir in lemon zest, salt, panko and pepper.
3. Mould 4 patties out of the mixture.
4. Switch the instant pot to sauté mode to heat the oil
5. Fry the parties for 3 minutes each side then place on the buns.
6. Serve the burger with arugula, tomatoes, and mustard.

Shrimp & Potato Curry

Servings: 4 , Prep + Cook time: 25 minutes

Ingredients:

- Ground coriander, 1 tsp.
- Chopped onions, 4.
- Salt.
- Peeled and chopped tomatoes, 1 lb.
- Quartered potatoes, 8.
- Curry powder, 1 tsp.
- Extra virgin olive oil, 4 tbsps.
- Lemon juice, 1.
- Peeled and deveined shrimp, 2 lbs.
- Watercress, 1 tbsp.

Directions:

1. Pour some water to the instant pot then put the potatoes in the steamer basket.
2. Cook for 10 minutes at high pressure with the lid sealed
3. Release the pressure quickly when the timer clicks then transfer the potatoes to a bowl and clean the pot.
4. Switch the instant pot to sauté mode to heat the oil for frying the onions for 5 minutes
5. Stir in the curry, coriander and salt to cook for 5 minutes
6. Mix in the shrimp, tomatoes, lemon juice and add the reserved potatoes.
7. Cook for 3 minutes t high pressure with the lid sealed.
8. Again, release the pressure then serve the shrimp with watercress

Flounder & Shrimp mix

Servings: 4, Prep + Cook time: 20 minutes

Ingredients:

- Water, ½ cup.
- Flounder, 2 lbs.
- Black pepper.
- Butter, 2 tbsps.
- Lemon wedges, 4.
- Cooked and deveined shrimp, 1/2 lb.
- Salt.

Directions:

1. Rub the fish with some seasonings then put in the steamer basket then add water to the pot.
2. Cook for 10 minutes at high pressure with the lid sealed
3. Immediately the timer beeps, release the pressure then open the lid and put the fish on plates.
4. Clean up the pot and turn it to sauté mode to melt the butter
5. Stir in the shrimp and seasonings.
6. Top the shrimp on the fish with lemon wedges on the side.

Herbed Shrimp and Risotto

Servings: 4, Prep + Cook time: 30 minutes

Ingredients:

- Grated parmesan, ¾ cup
- Minced garlic cloves, 2.
- Chopped tarragon and parsley, ¼ cup.
- Arborio rice, 1 ½ cups.
- Butter, 4 tbsps.
- Salt.
- Chicken stock, 4 ½ cups.
- Chopped yellow onion, 1.
- Peeled and deveined shrimp, 1 lb.
- Dry white wine, 2 tbsps.
- Black pepper.

Directions:

1. Switch the instant pot to sauté mode to melt 2 tablespoons of butter
2. Stir in the onion and garlic to cook for 4 minutes then add the rice and cook for another minute followed by the wine.
3. Mix in pepper, salt, and 3 cups of stock

4. Cook for 9 minutes at high pressure with the lid sealed
5. Release the pressure quickly then remove the lid
6. Mix in the remaining stock and shrimp.

7. Turn the instant pot to sauté mode and cook for 5 minutes as you stir.
8. Mix in the remaining butter, cheese, parsley, and tarragon
9. Serve immediately and enjoy.

Buttered Shrimp Paella

Servings: 4, **Prep + Cook time:** 15 minutes

Ingredients:
- Melted butter
- Jasmine rice, 1 cup.
- Black pepper.
- Minced garlic cloves, 4.
- Lemon juice, 1.
- Water, 1½ cups.
- Saffron, ¼ tsp.
- Grated hard cheese
- Chopped parsley, ¼ cup.
- Deveined shrimps, 20.
- Butter, ¼ cup.
- Crushed red pepper, ¼ tsp.
- Salt.
- Parsley.

Directions:
1. In the instant pot, add the shrimp
2. Mix in pepper, saffron, butter, salt, rice, red pepper, garlic, lemon juice, water and parsley.
3. With the lid closed, cook for 5 minutes at high pressure
4. Quickly release the pressure when the timer is over then open the lid.
5. Remove the shrimps and peel them
6. Put the shrimp back to pot then give them a gentle stir.
7. Serve into bowls topped with parsley and cheese.

Cherry tomatoes and Alaskan Cod.

Servings: 3 , **Prep + Cook time:** 15 minutes

Ingredients:
- Pepper.
- Olive oil
- Any seasoning
- Butter, 2 tbsps.
- Large filet wild Alaskan cod, 1.
- Cherry tomatoes, 1 cup.
- Salt.

Directions:
1. Select a heatproof dish that fits in the air fryer well then add the tomatoes
2. Divide the fish fillets into 3 pieces and top them on the tomatoes
3. Sprinkle the seasonings on the fish then add 1tablespoon of butter on each fillet and some oil.
4. Pour water to the instant pot then put in the trivet and transfer the dish to the trivet.
5. Press the manual function to cook for 9 minutes in the case of a frozen fish and 5 minutes for a thawed fish.
6. Release the pressure naturally when the timer clicks and serve immediately.

Japanese Style Mackerel

Servings: 4 , **Prep + Cook time:** 60 minutes

Ingredients:
- Sliced shallot, 1.
- Rice vinegar, 1 tbsp.
- Water, 1 cup.
- Miso, ¼ cup.
- Crushed garlic clove, 1.
- Japanese hot mustard, 1 tsp.
- Sake, 1/3 cup.
- Sliced celery stalks, 2.
- Chopped ginger piece, 1-inch.
- Thinly sliced sweet onion, 1.
- Salt
- Sliced mackerel, 2 lbs.
- Mirin, 1/3 cup.
- Sugar, 1 tsp.

Directions:

1. Switch the instant pot to sauté mode to cook ginger, sake, shallot, garlic and mirin, for 2 minutes.
2. Stir in water and miso then add the mackerel.
3. Cook for 45 minutes at high pressure with the lid sealed.
4. In the meantime, combine ice water with onion and celery in a bowl and cover.
5. Combine vinegar with mustard, sugar and salt in another bowl
6. Release the pressure from the pot naturally for 10 minutes and serve the mackerel on plates.
7. Strain the celery and onions the combine with mustard dressing and top on the mackerel

Lemony Mackerel

Servings: 4 , **Prep + Cook time:** 20 minutes

Ingredients:
- Lemon wedges, 3.
- Vegetable oil, 1 tbsp.
- Breadcrumbs, 3 oz.
- Lemon juice and rind, 1.
- Finely chopped chives, 1 tbsp.
- Salt.
- Butter, 1 tbsp.
- Margarine, 2 tbsps.
- Black pepper.
- Mackerels, 4.
- Whisked egg, 1.
- Water, 10 oz.

Directions:

1. Combine breadcrumbs with lemon rind, egg, pepper, lemon juice, salt, and chives in a sizable bowl.
2. Coat the fish with the mixture.
3. Turn the instant pot to sauté mode to melt the butter and oil to brown the fish evenly then reserve on a plate.
4. Wash the pot then pour some water in it.
5. Take a heatproof dish the grease with the margarine, add fish and put it in the pot.
6. With the lid closed, cook for 6 minutes at high pressure.
7. Release the pressure once the timer clicks.
8. Serve the mackerel with lemon wedges

Coconut Squid Masala

Servings: 4, **Prep + Cook time:** 25 minutes

Ingredients:
- Cumin seeds, ½ tsp.
- Mustard seeds, ¼ tsp.
- Red chili powder, 1 ½ tbsp.
- Extra virgin olive oil, 3 tbsps.
- Salt.
- Minced garlic cloves, 4.
- Coconut pieces, 5
- Squids, 17 oz.
- Turmeric powder, ¼ tsp.
- Black pepper.
- Water, 2 cups.
- Chopped ginger pieces, 1-inch

Directions:

1. In the instant pot, add the squids

2. Stir in turmeric, chili powder, water, pepper and salt.
3. With the lid sealed, cook for 15 minutes at high pressure.
4. In the meantime, process the ginger, coconut, cumin, and garlic in the blender

5. Set the pan on fire to melt the oil then cook the mustard seeds for 3 minutes over medium-high heat.
6. Quickly release the pressure when the timer clicks and transfer squid and water to the pan
7. Stir in the coconut blend to cook until well thicken then serve immediately.

Buttered Crab Legs

Servings: 4 , Prep + Cook time: 8 minutes

Ingredients:
- Water, 1 cup.
- Butter, ¼ cup.
- Lemon wedges, 3.
- Halved king crab legs, 4 lbs.

Directions:
1. Set the crab legs in the steamer basket of the pot.

2. Pour water to the pot.
3. Cook for 3 minutes at high pressure with the lid sealed.
4. Quickly release the pressure when the timer clicks and remove the lid.
5. Serve the crab legs to a bowl with butter and lemon wedges on the side.

Easy Tuna and Mushrooms.

Servings: 6, Prep + Cook time: 15 minutes

Ingredients:
- Egg noodles, 16 oz.
- Water, 3 cups.
- Bread crumbs, ¼ cup.
- Drained tuna, 5 oz.
- Cheddar cheese, 4 oz.
- Canned cream mushroom soup, 28 oz.
- Frozen peas, 1 cup.

Directions:
1. In the instant pot, put the noodles then pour water to cover them

2. Mix in the tuna, soup, and the frozen peas the seal the lid
3. Select the manual function key to cook for 4 minutes at high pressure
4. Press the cancel button when the timer clicks then unplug the pot.
5. Switch the steam valve to release the pressure.
6. Open the lid and stir in the cheese and serve.

Chili Salmon

Servings: 4, Prep + Cook time: 15 minutes

Ingredients:
- Lemon juice, 1.
- Assorted chili pepper, 2 tbsps.
- Salt.
- Sliced lemon, 1.
- Salmon fillets, 4.
- Water, 1 cup.
- Black pepper.

Directions:
1. Set the salmon fillets in the steamer basket of the pot

2. Sprinkle with some seasonings and lemon juice.
3. Top with lemon slices, the chili peppers, then pour 1 cup of water to the pot.
4. With the lid sealed, cook for 5 minutes at high pressure.
5. Quickly release the pressure when the timer goes off.
6. Serve the salmon with lemon slices.

Sea Food Mix

Servings: 4 , Prep + Cook time: 25 minutes

Ingredients:

- Mussels, 12.
- Bay leaves, 2.
- Clam juice, 8 oz.
- Chopped yellow onions, 2.
- Dried marjoram, ½ tsp.
- White wine, 1 ½ cups.
- Salt.
- Peeled and deveined big shrimp, 1 ½ lb.
- Dried basil, 1 tbsp.
- Sliced fish fillets, 1 ½ lb.
- Chopped canned tomatoes, 20 oz.
- Shell clams, 12.
- Minced garlic cloves, 3.
- Butter, 1 cup.
- Chopped parsley, ½ cup.
- Black pepper.

Directions:

1. Switch the instant pot to sauté mode to melt the butter
2. Stir in the garlic and onion to cook for 2 minutes.
3. Mix in parsley, pepper, tomatoes, clam juice, salt, bay leaves, marjoram, wine and basil.
4. Cook for 10 minutes at high pressure with the lid closed.
5. Release the pressure and turn pot to Sauté mode
6. Stir in the mussels and clams to cook for 8 minutes
7. Get rid of the unopened clams and mussels
8. Mix in the shrimp and fish to cook for 4 minutes.
9. Serve the meal right away.

Olives Steamed Fish

Servings: 4 , Prep + Cook time: 20 minutes

Ingredients:

- Pitted and chopped olives, 1 cup.
- Halved cherry tomatoes, 1 lb.
- Water, 1 cup.
- Black pepper.
- Dried thyme, ¼ tsp.
- Olive oil
- White fish fillets, 4.
- Minced garlic clove, 1.
- Salt.

Directions:

1. Add the water in the instant pot.
2. Set the fish fillets in the steamer basket of the pot.
3. Top with olives, tomatoes, thyme, pepper, garlic, oil, and salt.
4. Cook for 10 minutes on low pressure with the lid sealed.
5. Release the pressure quickly then open the lid.
6. Serve the fish mix immediately.

Spiced Mussels with Sauce

Servings: 4, Prep + Cook time: 15 minutes

Ingredients:

- Chicken stock, ½ cup.
- Dried oregano, 2 tsps.
- Red pepper flakes, ½ tsp.
- Chopped yellow onion, 1.
- Extra virgin olive oil, 2 tbsps.
- Minced garlic, 2 tsps.
- Scrubbed and de-bearded mussels, 2 lbs.
- Chopped tomatoes, 14 oz.

Directions:

1. Turn the instant pot to sauté mode to heat the oil and fry the onions for 3 minutes
2. Stir in the garlic and pepper flakes to cook for 1 minute
3. Mix in oregano, mussels, tomatoes, and stock.
4. Cook for 2 minutes on low with the lid sealed
5. Release the pressure quickly, remove the unopened mussels and serve.

Easy Parmesan Shrimp

Servings: 4, **Prep + Cook time:** 15 minutes

Ingredients:
- Chopped canned tomatoes, 10 oz.
- Grated parmesan, 1 cup.
- Water, 1/3 cup.
- Finely chopped parsley, 1 tbsp.
- Already cooked spaghetti.
- Extra virgin olive oil, 2 tbsps.
- Dried oregano, ¼ tsp.
- Peeled and deveined shrimp, 1 lb.
- Tomato paste, 1/3 cup.
- Minced garlic clove, 1.

Directions:
1. Switch the instant pot to sauté mode to heat the oil for 2 minutes for frying the garlic
2. Stir in water, parsley, tomato paste, tomatoes, shrimp, oregano, and tomato paste.
3. Cook for 3 minutes at high pressure with the lid sealed.
4. Release the pressure quickly the serve with spaghetti topped with parmesan.

Creamed Tilapia.

Servings: 4 , **Prep + Cook time:** 35 minutes

Ingredients:
- Onion, 1.
- Tilapia, 12 oz.
- Cream, ½ cup.
- Ground ginger, 1 tsp.
- Butter, 1 tbsp.
- Cheddar cheese, 5 oz.
- Ground black pepper, 1/3 tsp.

Directions:
1. Divide the tilapia into medium fillets
2. Mix ground black pepper and ground ginger.
3. Coat the tilapia fillets with the mixture then allow to rest for 5 minutes
4. In the meantime, grate the Cheddar cheese, then peel and slice the onion.
5. Select the manual function to melt the butter in the instant pot.
6. Mix in the tilapia fillets to cook for 2 minutes each side.
7. Top the tilapia with sliced onions then cover.
8. Spread the grated cheese on top then pour the cream on top.
9. Cook for 10 minutes on stew mode with the lid closed
10. Remove the lid once the timer clicks and serve the fillets right away.

Steamed Mussels and Spinach

Servings: 4 , **Prep + Cook time:** 15 minutes

Ingredients:
- Chopped white onion, 1.
- Dry white wine, ½ cup.
- Crushed garlic clove, 1.
- Sliced radicchio, 1.
- Water, ½ cup.
- Extra virgin olive oil.
- Cleaned and scrubbed mussels, 2 lbs.
- Baby spinach, 1 lb.

Directions:
1. Put the radicchio and baby spinach on appetizer plates
2. Switch the instant pot to sauté mode to heat the oil
3. Stir in the onion and garlic to cook for 4 minutes then stir in wine to cook for 1 more minute.
4. Set the mussels in the steamer basket of the pot.
5. Cook for 1 minute on low pressure with the lid sealed.
6. Immediately the timer goes off, release the pressure.
7. Serve the spinach and radicchio topped with mussels and cooking liquid.

Herbed Catfish.

Servings: 6, Prep + Cook time: 20 minutes

Ingredients:
- Garlic cloves, 3.
- Dill, 1 tsp.
- Fresh thyme, ¼ cup.
- Fresh parsley, 1 tsp.
- Salt, 1 tbsp.
- Olive oil, 1 tbsp.
- Catfish, 14 oz.
- Soy sauce, 2 tbsps.
- Water, ¼ cup.

Directions:
1. Clean the fresh thyme and fresh parsley and chop the greens
2. Mix the chopped greens with salt and dill.
3. Peel and slice the garlic cloves,
4. Heat the oil in the instant pot to sauté the garlic for 1 minute.
5. Mix the catfish and with green beans, water and soy sauce and put everything to the instant pot.
6. Cook for 4 minutes on sauté mode to a golden brown color then serve immediately.

Easy Jalapeno Mussels

Servings: 3, Prep + Cook time: 15 minutes

Ingredients:
- Minced garlic cloves, 2.
- Cleaned and scrubbed mussels, 2 lbs.
- Dry white wine, ¼ cup.
- Balsamic vinegar, ¼ cup.
- Chopped white onion, ½ cup.
- Lemon wedges
- Chopped jalapeno peppers, 2.
- Red pepper flakes, 2 tbsps.
- Salt.
- Crushed canned tomatoes, 28 oz.
- Extra virgin olive oil, ¼ cup.
- Chopped basil, ½ cup.

Directions:
1. Turn the instant pot to sauté mode then add wine, vinegar, onion, jalapenos, oil, tomatoes, garlic and pepper flakes to boil.
2. Stir in the mussels.
3. Cook for 4 minutes on low pressure with the lid sealed.
4. Release the pressure quickly and remove the lid
5. Remove the unopened mussels.
6. Stir in the basil and some salt then serve with lemon wedges.

Lime Salmon with Veggies mix

Servings: 2, Prep + Cook time: 20 minutes

Ingredients:
- Canola oil, 1 tbsp.
- Broccoli florets, 2 cups.
- Bay leaf, 1.
- Water, 1 cup.
- Baby carrots, 1 cup.
- Salmon fillets, 2.
- Black pepper
- Cinnamon stick, 1.
- Cloves, 3.
- Salt.
- Lime wedges

Directions:
1. In the instant pot, add the cinnamon stick, bay leaf, and cloves.
2. Brush the steamer basket with canola oil then put the salmon fillets on the basket.
3. Add some seasonings, carrots, and broccoli.
4. With the lid covered, cook for 6 minutes at high pressure.
5. Release the pressure naturally for 4 minutes.
6. Shift the valve to venting to release the remaining pressure then open the lid.
7. Remove the cinnamon, bay leaves, and cloves
8. Serve the salmon and veggies topped with cooking sauce and lime wedges on the side.

Simple Raisins Shrimp

Servings: 4, Prep + Cook time: 16 minutes

Ingredients:

- Raisins, ½ cup.
- Bouillon, 1 cup.
- Sliced mushrooms, ¼ cup.
- Flour, 3 tbsps.
- Chopped yellow onion, ¼ cup.
- Salt.
- Curry powder, ½ tsp.
- Milk, 1 cup.
- Shortening, 2 tbsps.
- Peeled and deveined shrimp, 1 lb.
- Lemon slices, 4.
- Black pepper.

Directions:

1. Turn the pot to sauté mode to heat the shortenings.
2. Stir in the mushroom and onion to cook for 2 minutes
3. Mix in the seasonings, bouillon, curry powder, lemon, shrimp, and raisins
4. With the lid covered, cook for 2 minutes at high pressure.
5. In the meantime, whisk together milk and flour
6. Release the pressure quickly and remove the lid
7. Stir in the flour and milk then cook until curry thickens on Simmer mode
8. Enjoy.

Shrimp Delight

Servings: 4, Prep + Cook time: 15 minutes

Ingredients:

- Chopped parsley, 2 tbsps.
- Minced garlic cloves, 4.
- Hot paprika, 2 tsps.
- Extra virgin olive oil, 2 tbsps.
- Tomato sauce, 1 cup.
- Dry white wine, ¼ cup.
- Black pepper.
- Bay leaf, 1.
- Chopped yellow onion, 1 cup.
- Sugar, ¼ tsp.
- Dried thyme, ¼ tsp.
- Saffron, ¼ tsp.
- Crushed hot pepper, 1 tsp.
- Peeled and deveined shrimp, 1 ½ lbs.
- Fish stock, ½ cup.
- Salt.

Directions:

1. Switch the instant pot to sauté mode to heat the oil.
2. Stir in the shrimp to cook for 1 minute then reserve on a platter
3. Fry the onion for 2 minutes
4. Stir in wine, parsley, paprika, and garlic to cook for 2 minutes.
5. Mix in red pepper, salt, tomato sauce, bay leaf, sugar, pepper, thyme, stock, and saffron.
6. Cook for 4 minutes at high pressure with the lid closed
7. Quickly release the pressure when the timer clicks then remove the lid then mix in the shrimp.
8. Cook for 2 minutes at high pressure with the lid sealed.
9. Release the pressure quickly then open the lid.
10. Serve the shrimp immediately.

Instant Pot Cod and Peas

Servings: 4 , Prep + Cook time: 20 minutes

Ingredients:

- Chopped garlic cloves, 2.
- Wine, 9 oz.
- Salt.
- Cod fillets, 16 oz.
- Paprika, ½ tsp.
- Dried oregano, ½ tsp.
- Peas, 10 oz.
- Chopped parsley, 1 tbsp.
- Pepper.

Directions:

1. Combine parsley, paprika, garlic, and oregano in the food processor to blend.
2. Mix in the wine, process again and reserve.
3. Rub the fish with pepper and salt then put it in the steamer basket of your instant pot.
4. Cook for 2 minutes at high pressure with the lid covered.
5. Release the pressure and set the fish on plates
6. Put the peas to the steamer basket.
7. Cook for 2 minutes at high pressure with the lid covered,
8. Release the pressure again and arrange peas next to fish fillets.
9. Enjoy the meal topped with herbs dressing

Dilly Shrimp,

Servings: 4,Prep + Cook time: 20 minutes

Ingredients:

- Cornstarch, 2 tbsps.
- Milk, ¾ cup.
- Dill weed, 1 tsp.
- Chopped yellow onion, 1 tbsp.
- Shortening, 2 tbsps.
- Peeled and deveined shrimp, 1 lb.
- White wine, 1 cup.

Directions:

1. Set the instant pot on sauté mode to heat the shortening.
2. Stir in onions to cook for 2 minutes.
3. Mix in wine and shrimp and cover the lid to cook for 2 minutes on High pressure.
4. When the timer goes off, quick release the pressure and remove the lid.
5. Switch the instant pot to simmer mode.
6. Stir milk and cornstarch in a mixing bowl.
7. Add the cornstarch mx to the shrimp until it becomes thick.
8. Mix in dill weed then cook for 5 minutes on simmer mode.
9. Serve and enjoy.

Stewed Seafood

Servings: 10 , Prep + Cook time: 35 minutes

Ingredients:

- Celery seeds, 1 tsp.
- Vegetable oil, ¾ cup.
- Flour, 1 ¼ cups.
- Oysters, 24.
- Onion powder, ½ tsp.
- Crawfish tails, 24.
- Chicken stock, 2 quarts.
- Chopped plum tomatoes, 6.
- Peanut oil, 2 tbsps.
- Dried thyme, 1 tsp.
- Cayenne pepper, ¼ tsp.
- Chopped garlic cloves, 4.
- Chopped white onions, 1 cup.
- Sliced sausage, 1 lb.
- Peeled and deveined shrimps, 24.
- Chopped green bell pepper, 1 cup.
- Sweet paprika, 1 tsp.
- Salt.
- Garlic powder, ½ tsp.
- Bay leaves, 3.
- Crab meat, ½ lb.
- Chopped celery, ½ cup.
- Black pepper.

Directions:

1. Set a pan on fire to heat the vegetable oil over medium heat then stir in flour to cook for 4 minutes.
2. Switch the pot to sauté mode to heat the peanut oil
3. Stir in garlic, peppers, celery and onions to cook for 10 minutes.
4. Stir in stock, tomatoes, sausage, cayenne, bay leaves, celery seeds, thyme, paprika, garlic powder and onion for 3 minutes.
5. Mix in flour mix to combine.
6. Add oysters, crab, shrimp, crawfish and seasonings and cover the lid to cook for 15 minutes on High.
7. Immediately the timer click, quick release the pressure and open the lid
8. Serve and enjoy.

Turmeric Shrimp with Rice

Servings: 4, Prep + Cook time: 30 minutes

Ingredients:
- Halved green chilies, 2.
- Mustard oil, 3 oz.
- Beaten curd, 4 oz.
- Turmeric powder, 1 tsp.
- Salt
- Chopped ginger, 1-inch.
- Mustard seeds, ½ tbsp.
- Already cooked rice
- Peeled and deveined shrimp, 18 oz.
- Finely chopped onions, 2.

Directions:
1. Soak the mustard seeds in water then reserve for 10 minutes then strain the water and grind well.
2. Combine the shrimp, turmeric, chilies, mustard oil, curd, mustard paste, ginger and onions in a bowl to coat then reserve for 10 minutes.
3. Put everything in the instant pot.
4. Cook for 5 minutes on low pressure with the lid closed
5. Release the pressure quickly and serve the shrimp with boiled rice.

Curried Coconut Fish

Servings: 6, Prep + Cook time: 25 minutes

Ingredients:
- Finely grated ginger, 1 tbsp.
- Chopped tomato, 1.
- Ground turmeric, ½ tsp.
- Sliced capsicums, 2.
- Sliced fish fillets, 6.
- Coconut milk, 14 oz.
- Hot pepper flakes, 1 tsp.
- Salt.
- Curry leaves, 6.
- Lemon juice, 2 tbsps.
- Ground coriander, 1 tbsp.
- Minced garlic cloves, 2.
- Ground fenugreek, ½ tsp.
- Sliced onions, 2.
- Ground cumin, 2 tsps.
- Black pepper.

Directions:
1. Turn the instant pot to sauté mode to heat the oil for frying curry leaves for 1 minute.
2. Stir in garlic, onion and ginger to cook for 2 minutes.
3. Mix in fenugreek, hot pepper, coriander, cumin and turmeric to cook for 2 minutes.
4. Stir in the tomatoes, capsicum, fish and coconut milk to cook for 5 minutes on Low pressure with the lid closed.
5. Naturally release the pressure and adjust the seasonings.
6. Divide into bowls to serve with a lemon juice topping.
7. Enjoy.

One Pot Assorted Clams

Servings: 4 , **Prep + Cook time:** 15 minutes

Ingredients:

- Water, 2 cups.
- Chopped parsley, ¼ cup.
- Butter, 4 tbsps.
- Dried oregano, 1 tsp.
- Grated parmesan cheese, ¼ cup.
- Lemon wedges
- Shucked clams, 24.
- Breadcrumbs, 1 cup.
- Minced garlic cloves, 3.

Directions:

1. Set up a mixing bowl in place to combine garlic, oregano, parmesan, butter and parsley.
2. Add a tablespoon of this mix in the exposed clams.
3. Transfer the clams in the steamer basket and add 2 cups of water to cook for 4 minutes at High pressure.
4. Release the pressure quickly before opening the lid.
5. Serve on plates with lemon wedges.
6. Enjoy.

Easy Squid in White wine

Servings: 4 , **Prep + Cook time:** 30 minutes

Ingredients:

- Fresh peas, 1 lb.
- Crushed canned tomatoes, ½ lb.
- Salt.
- White wine.
- Chopped yellow onion, 1.
- Cleaned and sliced squid, 1 lb.
- Olive oil
- Black pepper.

Directions:

1. Add some oil to the instant pot to heat up on Sauté mode.
2. Stir in onion to cook for 3 minutes.
3. Mix in squid and allow to cook for another 3 minutes.
4. Add peas, wine and tomatoes then cover the lid to cook for 20 minutes.
5. When the timer beeps, quick release the pressure and open the lid.
6. Add the seasonings then serve right away.

Cardamom Shrimp

Servings: 4 , **Prep + Cook time:** 40 minutes

Ingredients:

- Dried fenugreek leaves, 1 tsp.
- Bay leaves, 2.
- Cardamom pods, 3.
- Butter, 1/3 cup.
- Cream, ½ cup.
- Cashews, ½ cup.
- Cinnamon stick, 1.
- Cloves, 10.
- Chopped green chilies, 3.
- Sugar, 1 tsp.
- Chopped tomatoes, 4.
- Chopped red onions, 2.
- Garlic paste, 1 tbsp.
- Salt.
- Peeled and deveined big shrimp, 1 lb.
- Dried red chilies, 14.
- Ginger paste, 1 tbsp.

Directions:

1. Set the instant pot on sauté mode to melt butter.
2. Stir in cinnamon stick, bay leaves, onion and cardamom to cook for 3 minutes.
3. Mix in cashews, red chilies, ginger paste, green chilies, garlic paste and tomatoes.
4. Stir in salt and cover the lid to cook for 15 minutes on High.
5. Do a quick release of pressure and set everything in the blender to pulse well.

6. Sieve into a pan to heat up over medium High heat.
7. Stir in shrimp and cover the pot to cook for 12 minutes.

8. Add sugar, cream and fenugreek to cook for 2 minutes and remove from heat.
9. Serve on plates and enjoy.

Creamy Tuna and Crushed Crackers.

Servings: 8 , Prep + Cook time: 25 minutes

Ingredients:
- Heavy cream, ¼ cup.
- Butter, 3 tbsps.
- Chicken stock, 3 ½ cups.
- All-purpose flour, 3 tbsps.
- Crushed buttery crackers, 1 cup.
- Frozen peas, 1 cup.
- Salt, 2 tsps.
- Shredded cheddar, 1 cup.
- Fresh ground black pepper
- Pasta, 2 cups.
- Fresh tuna, 8 oz.
- Celery, 1 cup.
- Onion, 1 cup.

Directions:
1. Preheat the instant pot until hot on Sauté and add onion and celery.
2. Cook until the onion is transparent and pour in pasta, chicken stock and seasonings.
3. Stir gently then add the fresh tuna on top of the pasta mix.
4. Select the cancel function then seal the lid
5. Press the manual function on sauté mode for 5 minutes.
6. In the meantime, heat the sauté pan over medium high heat.
7. Melt the butter on the pan then stir in flour to cook for 2 minutes and remove from heat.
8. Switch the steam valve to venting once the timer beeps then transfer tuna onto a plate and reserve.
9. Put the butter mix to the instant pot to cook until it thickens on sauté mode.
10. Switch off the pot then stir in peas, tuna, and heavy cream.
11. Cover the mix with grated cheese and crackers.
12. Cover it to settle for 5 minutes and serve.
13. Enjoy.

Simple Teriyaki Shrimp

Servings: 4 , Prep + Cook time: 15 minutes

Ingredients:
- Chicken stock, 1 cup.
- Sugar, 3 tbsps.
- Pea pods, ½ lb.
- Soy sauce, 2 tbsps.
- Pineapple juice, ¾ cup.
- Peeled and deveined shrimp, 1 lb.
- Vinegar, 3 tbsps.

Directions:
1. Add the pea pods and shrimp to the instant pot
2. Set up a mixing bowl to combine pineapple juice, soy sauce, stock, vinegar and sugar.
3. Transfer the mixture into the pot and cover the lid to cook for 3 minutes on High.
4. Immediately the timer clicks, quick release the pressure and open the lid.
5. Serve the mean and enjoy.

Spiced Mussels with Sausage

Servings: 4 , **Prep + Cook time:** 10 minutes

Ingredients:
- Paprika, 1 tbsp.
- Spicy sausage, 8 oz.
- Chopped yellow onion, 1.
- Amber beer, 12 oz.
- Scrubbed and de-bearded mussels, 2 lbs.
- Extra-virgin olive oil, 1 tbsp.

Directions:
1. Add oil to the instant pot to heat on Sauté mode.
2. Stir in onion to cook for 2 minutes.
3. Add sausages and let them cook for 4 minutes.
4. Stir in mussels, paprika and beer and cover the pot to cook for 2 minutes on Low.
5. Quick release the pressure before opening the lid and discarding unopened mussels.
6. Put into bowls and serve.
7. Enjoy.

Garlic Butter Crab Legs

Servings: 2 , **Prep + Cook time:** 15 minutes

Ingredients:
- Salted butter, 4 tbsps.
- Olive oil, 1 tsp.
- Water, 1 cup.
- Halved lemon, 1.
- Frozen crab legs, 2 lbs.
- Minced garlic clove, 1.

Directions:
1. Add water to the Instant Pot before lowering the steamer basket and add crab legs.
2. Select the steam option with a cook time of 3minutes in the case of fresh and 4 minutes for frozen.
3. Meanwhile, heat the oil in a skillet.
4. Stir in the garlic for 1 minute
5. Mix in the butter to melt then squeeze the halved lemon in the butter.
6. Select the cancel option then quick release the pressure
7. Enjoy the crabs with the garlic butter on the side

Chicken Stew With Carrots And Tomatoes

Servings: 6, **Prep + Cooking Time:** 1 hour 35 minutes

Ingredients:
- Chicken thighs- 6
- White wine- ½ cup
- Tomato paste-2 tbsp.
- Dried thyme- ½ tsp.
- New potatoes- ½ Ib.
- Baby carrots- ¾ Ib.
- Chopped celery stalk- 1
- Sliced baby carrots- ¼ Ib.
- Chicken stock- 2 cups
- Chopped yellow onion- 1
- Chopped canned tomatoes- 15 oz.
- Vegetable oil- 1 tsp.
- Salt and black pepper

Directions:
1. Press 'Sauté' on the Instant Pot and pour in the vegetable oil.
2. Season the chicken with salt and pepper and put it in the Instant Pot to brown for 4 minutes on both sides and then set aside.
3. Mix in the tomato paste, onion, celery, salt, thyme, and pepper and let it cook for 5 minutes.
4. Pour the wine into the pot then let it simmer for 3 minutes and add the tomatoes, the chicken stock, and the chicken.
5. Put the potatoes on a steaming rack and put it in the pot then seal the pot and set to cook at high pressure for 30 minutes.
6. Natural release the pressure for 15 minutes then quick release the pressure by moving the valve to venting position.

7. Remove the potatoes from the basket and set aside.
8. Remove the chicken from the pot and set on a chopping board to cool then shred the meat and remove the bones then put the chicken inside the stew.
9. Season with salt and pepper and serve into bowls.

Seafood Jambalaya with White Rice

Servings: 3, **Prep time + Cook time:** 5 hours 5 minutes

Ingredients
- Dried oregano, ½ tsp.
- Chopped onion, ½ cup.
- Peeled and deveined shrimp, 4 oz.
- Sliced celery stalk, ¾ cup.
- Chopped bacon slices, 2.
- Dried thyme, ¼ tsp.
- Cajun seasoning, ½ tbsp.
- Vegetable broth, 1 1/5 cups.
- Canned diced tomatoes, 1 cup.
- Freshly ground black pepper.
- Uncooked long-grain white rice, 1 cup.
- Sliced catfish, 4 oz.
- Olive oil, 1 tbsp.
- Minced garlic, ¼ tsp.
- Cayenne pepper, ¼ tsp.
- Salt.

Directions
7. On the instant pot, tap the "Sauté" function and add oil.
8. Add garlic, bacon, celery and onion to cook for 10 minutes.
9. Mix in the remaining ingredients and reserve the seafood.
10. Stir well before covering with the cooker lid.
11. Set the cooker to cook on a medium mode.
12. Set the pressure release handle to cook for 4 hours on "venting" position.
13. Open the cooker lid and add seafood to the gravy.
14. Cover the lid again keeping the pressure in the venting position.
15. Let it cook for 45 more minutes before serving.
16. Enjoy.

Nutritional Information:
Calories: 505, Carbs: 58.6g, Protein: 27.4g, Fat: 16.8g, Sugar: 3.1g, Sodium: 818mg

Shrimp Creole and Seasoned Sauce

Servings: 4 , **Prep + Cook time:** 7 hrs. 30 minutes

Ingredients
- Worcestershire sauce, 1 tbsp.
- Chopped white onion, ¾ cup.
- Crushed whole tomatoes, 28 oz.
- Minced garlic, ½ tsp.
- Chopped green bell pepper, ½ cup.
- Sliced celery stalk, 1 cup.
- White rice.
- Tomato sauce, 8 oz.
- Salt.
- Ground black pepper, ¼ tsp.
- Peeled and deveined shrimp, 1 lb.
- Olive oil, 1 tbsp.
- Hot pepper sauce, 4 drops.

Directions
1. Add oil and other ingredients except shrimp into the pot.
2. Cover the cooker lid and maintain the pressure handle valve in venting position.
3. Tap the "slow cook" function on the cooker to cook over medium heat.
4. Cook the mixture for 6 hours.
5. Uncover the lid to add shrimp.
6. Stir to cook the shrimp for 1 more hour on "Slow cook" function
7. Ensure the lid is covered with the pressure release in venting position.
8. Pour juice over white rice to serve.
9. Enjoy.

Nutritional Information:
Calories: 146, Carbs: 13.5g, Protein: 19.5g, Fat: 1.7g, Sugar: 0.9g, Sodium: 894mg

Salmon Casserole with Mushroom Soup

Servings: 4, Prep + Cook time: 8 hours 20 minutes

Ingredients
- Ground nutmeg, ¼ tsp.
- Peeled and sliced medium potatoes, 3.
- Water, ¼ cup.
- Salt.
- Drained and flaked salmon, 16 oz.
- Flour, 3 tbsps.
- Freshly ground black pepper.
- Olive oil, ½ tbsp.
- Mushroom soup cream, 8 oz.
- Chopped scallion, ½ cup.

Directions
1. Mix water and mushroom soup in a mixing bowl.
2. Add olive oil and grease the pot lightly.
3. Add half of the potatoes in the pot to season with pepper, salt and half of the flour over it.
4. Add half of the salmon and half of the scallion layers.
5. Add more layers and top up with mushroom soup mix.
6. Evenly add a nutmeg topping. Cover the lid before setting pressure release handle to the venting position.
7. Let the instant pot cook for 8 hours over medium heat.
8. Serve and enjoy.

Nutritional Information:
Calories: 235, Carbs: 27.5g, Protein: 18g, Fat: 6.3g, Sugar: 1.2g, Sodium: 310mg

Tuna Chowder with Chicken Flavor

Servings: 3 , Prep + Cook time: 7 hours 20 minutes

Ingredients
- Chicken broth, 7 oz.
- Chopped celery, ½ cup.
- Cayenne pepper, ½ tsp.
- Chopped medium red potato, 1.
- Crushed dried thyme, ½ tsp.
- Diced tomatoes with juice, 8 oz.
- Peeled and roughly shredded carrot, ½ cup.
- Drained water-packed tuna chunks, 6 oz.
- Chopped onion, ½ cup.
- Freshly ground black pepper, ½ tsp.
- Salt.

Directions
1. In an instant pot, combine all the ingredients with exception of tuna.
2. Close the lid and maintain the pressure release handle on venting position.
3. Tap the "Slow Cook" function to cook for 7 hours over medium heat.
4. Uncover the pot after 7 hours and add tuna.
5. Secure the lid then steam tuna for 5 minutes in the hot gravy.
6. Serve the chowder while hot.

Nutritional Information:
Calories: 158, Carbs: 18.7g, Protein: 18.3g, Fat: 1.2g, Sugar: 4.4g, Sodium: 772mg

Salmon Soup with Carrots and Parsley

Servings: 3, Prep + Cook time: 37 minutes

Ingredients
- Homemade chicken broth, 2 cups.
- Peeled and chopped carrots, 1 cup.
- Coconut oil, 1 tbsp.
- Chopped yellow onion, ½ cup.
- Freshly ground black pepper.
- Chopped fresh parsley, 2 tbsps.
- Salmon fillets, 1 lb.
- Chopped celery stalk, ½ cup.
- Salt.
- Chopped cauliflower, 1 cup.

Directions
1. Add a cup of water to the instant pot and put trivet inside.
2. Put a single salmon fillet layer over the trivet.
3. Cover the lid and adjust the pressure release handle to "Sealed" position.
4. Choose the "Manual" function and cook at a high pressure for 9 minutes.

5. Release the steam after the beep.
6. Remove trivet, salmon and water from the pot.
7. Cut the salmon into small edible chunks.
8. Add coconut oil to the instant pot, then choose the "Sauté" function to cook.
9. Stir in onions, celery and carrots to cook for 5 minutes.
10. Mix in cauliflower and chicken broth then cover the cooker lid.
11. Set to "Manual" and allow to cook at high pressure for 8 minutes.
12. Naturally release the steam once it beeps.
13. Uncover the pot then add salmon chunks along with seasonings.
14. Add a parsley topping and serve.

Nutritional Information:
Calories: 284, Carbs: 41.3g, Protein: 132.8g, Fat: 16.4g, Sugar: 23.8g, Sodium: 508mg

Salmon Curry with Cumin Flavor

Servings: 8 , Prep + Cook time: 22 minutes

Ingredients
- Unsweetened coconut milk, 4 cups.
- Curry leaves, 4.
- Ground turmeric, 1 tsp.
- Red chili powder, 2 tsps.
- Curry powder, 4 tbsps.
- Ground coriander, 4 tsps.
- Minced garlic cloves, 4.
- Fresh cilantro leaves.
- Chopped small yellow onions, 2.
- Chopped Serrano peppers, 2.
- Chopped tomatoes, 2 ½ cups.
- Sliced salmon fillets, 3 lbs.
- Olive oil, 2 tbsps.
- Ground cumin, 4 tsps.
- Fresh lemon juice, 2 tbsps.

Directions
1. Add curry leaves and oil into the instant pot then choose the "Sauté" function to cook for 30 seconds.
2. Transfer onions and garlic to the pot to cook for 5 minutes.
3. Mix in all the spices to cook for 1 more minute.
4. Add Serrano pepper, tomatoes, fish and coconut milk while cooking.
5. Cover and tighten the lid then close the pressure release valve.
6. Allow to cook at low pressure for 5 minutes.
7. Naturally release all the steam after the beep.
8. Uncover the lid to squeeze in the lemon juice.
9. Serve and garnish with cilantro leaves.

Nutritional Information:
Calories: 559, Carbs: 12.2g, Protein: 36.9g, Fat: 43.2g, Sugar: 6.5g, Sodium: 106mg

Salmon Fillets with Lemon

Servings: 3, Prep + Cook time: 13 minutes

Ingredients
- Fresh lemon juice, 1 tsp.
- Ground black pepper.
- Salmon fillet, 5 oz.
- Lemon slices, 3.
- Water, 1 cup.
- Salt.
- Fresh cilantro

Directions
1. Add water into the pot before placing trivet inside.
2. Put salmon in a medium bowl and rub it with seasonings.
3. Top the salmon with lemon juice and put a lemon slice over it.
4. Cover the lid and tighten it before setting the pressure release handle to "Sealing" position.
5. Allow the cooker to cook for 3 minutes under the "Steam" function.
6. Release the steam after the beep.
7. Uncover the cooker to serve. Top up with fresh cilantro and lemon slice.

Nutritional Information:
Calories: 63, Carbs: 0.2g, Protein: 9.2g, Fat: 2.9g, Sugar: 0.1g, Sodium: 48mg

Spicy Salmon with Stevia Taste

Servings: 8 , Prep + Cook time: 12 minutes

Ingredients

- Ground cumin, 2 tsps.
- Powdered stevia, 2 tsps.
- Freshly grated black pepper.
- Minced garlic cloves, 2.
- Red chili powder, 2 tbsps.
- Sliced salmon fillet, 2 lbs.
- Water, 2 cups.
- Lemon slices, 8.
- Salt.

Directions

1. Add two cups of water into the pot before setting trivet into it.

2. Combine all the ingredients in a mixing bowl with exception of lemon slices.
3. Rub the mixture all over salmon fillets.
4. Put a single layer of salmon fillets over the trivet.
5. Add a lemon slice topping. Secure the lid and tap the "Steam" function to cook for 2 minutes.
6. Do a quick release and remove the lid after the beep.
7. Serve while hot and enjoy.

Nutritional Information:
Calories: 159, Carbs: 1.5g, Protein: 22.4g, Fat: 7.4g, Sugar: 0.2g, Sodium: 109mg

Garlicky Salmon

Servings: 6 , Prep + Cook time: 8 minutes

Ingredients

- Freshly ground black pepper
- Dried oregano, ½ tsp.
- Olive oil, ¼ cup.
- Minced feta cheese, 1 ½ tbsps.
- Fresh lemon juice, 3 tbsps.
- Water, 1 ½ cup.
- Salmon fillets, 1 ½ lbs.
- Minced garlic clove, 1 ½.
- Salt.
- Fresh rosemary sprigs, 3.
- Lemon slices, 3.

Directions

1. Whisk feta cheese, oregano, lemon juice, garlic and seasonings in a large mixing bowl.

2. Add water into the pot before setting the steamer trivet in it.
3. Put a single layer of salmon fillets over the trivet.
4. Rub the fillets with cheese mixture.
5. Put a rosemary sprig and a lemon slice over every fillet.
6. Tighten the lid and tap the "Steam" function to cook for 3 minutes.
7. Do a Quick release after the cooking. Uncover to serve while hot.
8. Enjoy.

Nutritional Information:
Calories: 270, Carbs: 1.1g, Protein: 22.5g, Fat: 20.3g, Sugar: 0.3g, Sodium: 117mg

Spicy Mahi-Mahi with the Lime Taste

Servings: 4 , Prep + Cook time: 22 minutes

Ingredients

- Minced garlic cloves, 4.
- Freshly ground black pepper.
- Mahi-mahi fillets, 16 oz.
- Erythritol, 4 tbsps.
- Crushed red pepper flakes, 2 tsps.
- Water, 1 ½ cup.
- Salt.

- Fresh lime juice, 4 tbsps.

Directions

1. Season the Mahi-Mahi fillets with pepper and salt.
2. Set up a separate mixing bowl to combine all the remaining ingredients.
3. Place a single layer of seasoned fillets over the trivet.

4. Top the prepared sauce on each fillet.
5. Cover and tighten the lid.
6. On the cooker, set the "Steam" function to cook for 5 minutes.
7. Do a quick release and uncover the lid once it beeps.

8. Serve the Mahi-Mahi while steaming hot.
9. Enjoy.

Nutritional Information:
Calories: 108, Carbs: 18.6g, Protein: 21.4g, Fat: 1.2g, Sugar: 15.1g, Sodium: 189mg

Mahi-Mahi with Spices and Tomatoes

Servings: 3 , Prep + Cook time: 19 minutes

Ingredients

- Fresh lemon juice, 1 tbsp.
- Sliced yellow onion, ½.
- Freshly ground black pepper.
- Dried oregano, ½ tsp.
- Mahi-mahi fillets, 12 oz.
- Sugar-free diced tomatoes, 14 oz.
- Butter, 1 ½ tbsps.
- Salt.

Directions

1. Add butter into the pot before selecting the "Sauté" function.
2. Mix all the ingredients in the pot except the fillets to cook for 10 minutes.

3. Tap the "Cancel" key before adding Mahi-Mahi to the sauce.
4. Use a spoon to cover the sauce and fillets.
5. Cover and tighten the lid then set the "Manual" function at a high pressure for 4 minutes.
6. Do a quick release and uncover the lid after the beep.
7. Serve the fillets topped with the sauce.
8. Enjoy.

Nutritional Information:
Calories: 184, Carbs: 8.2g, Protein: 22.6g, Fat: 7.1g, Sugar: 4.4g, Sodium: 187mg

Cod with Cherry Tomatoes

Servings: 6, Prep + Cook time: 25 minutes

Ingredients

- Minced garlic cloves, 3.
- Freshly ground black pepper.
- Olive oil, 2 tbsps.
- Chopped fresh rosemary, 2 ½ tbsps.
- Halved cherry tomatoes, 1 ½ lbs.
- Cod fillets, 24 oz.
- Salt.

Directions

1. Add rosemary, half of the tomatoes and olive oil to the pot.
2. Put cod fillets over the tomatoes and add more tomatoes to the pot.

3. Add garlic and cover with the lid. Tap the "Manual" function and allow to cook for 5 minutes under high pressure.
4. Using quick release, release all the steam after the beep.
5. Serve the cold fillets with tomatoes the season with pepper and salt.
6. Enjoy.

Nutritional Information:
Calories: 149, Carbs: 6g, Protein: 21.4g, Fat: 5g, Sugar: 3g, Sodium: 116mg

Dinner Mussels with Rosemary Flavor

Servings: 8, **Prep + Cook time:** 17 minutes

Ingredients

- Fresh lemon juice, ¼ cup.
- Crushed dried rosemary, 1 tsp.
- Cleaned and de-bearded mussels, 4 lbs.
- Ground black pepper.
- Minced garlic cloves, 2.
- Chicken broth, 2 cups.
- Olive oil, 2 tbsps.
- Chopped medium yellow onions, 2.
- Salt.

Directions

1. Add oil to the pot then select the "Sauté" function to cook.
2. Stir in onions to cook for 5 minutes.
3. Stir in garlic and rosemary then cook for 1 minute.
4. Transfer the chicken broth and lemon juice into the cooker to season with black pepper and salt.
5. Put the trivet in the cooker before arranging mussels over it.
6. Set the "Manual" function for 1 minute at low pressure.
7. Cover and tighten the lid to cook the mussels.
8. Do a quick release and remove the lid after the beep.
9. Serve into a bowl with steaming hot soup.
10. Enjoy.

Nutritional Information:
Calories: 249, Carbs: 11.7g, Protein: 28.6g, Fat: 9g, Sugar: 1.5g, Sodium: 881mg

Seasoned Lobsters

Servings: 4 , **Prep + Cook time:** 23 minutes

Ingredients

- Sliced lobster tails, 4 lbs.
- Black pepper.
- Melted unsalted butter, 4 tbsps.
- Water, 1 cup.
- Salt.

Directions

1. In an instant pot, pour a cup of water and put trivet in it.
2. Put the lobster tails over the trivet with the shell side facing down.
3. Cover the lid and tighten it then choose the "Manual" function at low pressure for 3 minutes.
4. Tap cancel and do a quick release after the beep.
5. Uncover the pot and remove the trivet.
6. Put the lobster on a serving plate.
7. Add melted butter over the lobster tails.
8. Season with pepper and salt before serving.
9. Enjoy.

Nutritional Information:
Calories: 507, Carbs: 0g, Protein: 86.3g, Fat: 15.3g, Sugar: 0g, Sodium: 1240mg

Coconut Curry Cod

Servings: 8 , **Prep + Cook time:** 17 minutes

Ingredients

- Ground coriander, 4 tsps.
- Finely grated fresh ginger, 2 tbsps.
- Unsweetened coconut milk, 4 cups.
- Chopped medium onions, 4.
- Chopped tomatoes, 2 ½ cups.
- Fresh lemon juice, 2 tbsps.
- Minced garlic cloves, 4.
- Red chili powder, 2 tsps.
- Ground turmeric, 1 tsp.
- Curry leaves, 4.
- Seeded and chopped Serrano peppers, 2.
- Sliced cod fillets, 3 lbs.
- Olive oil, 2 tbsps.
- Curry powder, 4 tbsps.
- Ground cumin, 4 tsps.

Directions

1. Add oil and choose the "Sauté" function to cook.
2. Add curry leaves to cook for 30 seconds.
3. Stir in ginger, garlic and onion to cook for 5 minutes.
4. Add all the spices to the mixture to cook for 1 ½ more minutes.
5. Tap "cancel" and add tomatoes, coconut milk, Serrano pepper and fish.
6. Secure the lid before choosing "Manual" settings to cook at low pressure for 5 minutes.
7. Do a quick release and remove the lid after the beep.
8. Add lemon juice to the curry and stir.
9. Serve immediately and enjoy.

Nutritional Information:

Calories: 758, Carbs: 47.3g, Protein: 29.8g, Fat: 54.1g, Sugar: 8.2g, Sodium: 940mg

Shrimp, Beans and Delicious Spices

Servings: 3, **Prep + Cook time:** 35 minutes

Ingredients

- Cayenne pepper, ½ tsp.
- Chopped celery stalk, ½.
- Bay leaf, 1.
- Seeded and chopped small green bell pepper, ½.
- Peeled and deveined medium shrimp, ½ lb.
- Chopped fresh parsley, 1 tbsps.
- Chopped medium onion, 1.
- Rinsed, soaked and drained great northern beans
- Chopped red pepper flakes, ½ tsp.
- Olive oil, 1 ½ tbsps.
- Minced garlic clove, 1.
- Chicken broth, 1 cup.

Directions

1. Tap the "Sauté" function on the instant pot then add bell pepper, onion, oil and celery to cook for 5 minutes.
2. Add spices, bay leaf, parsley and garlic to cook for 2 more minutes.
3. Put the beans and chicken broth in the pot before covering with the lid.
4. Tap the "Manual" function to cook for 15 minutes at medium pressure.
5. Do a natural release for 10 minutes and uncover the lid after the beep.
6. To the beans, add shrimp to cook on "Manual" function for 2 minutes at a high pressure.
7. Perform a "Quick release" and reserve for 10 minutes.
8. Remove the lid to serve while hot.
9. Enjoy.

Nutritional Information:

Calories: 320, Carbs: 39.9g, Protein: 26.3g, Fat: 7g, Sugar: 3.4g, Sodium: 331mg

Chapter 7 Vegetable and Vegetarian

Eggplant Ratatouille Delicacy

Servings: 6 , Prep + Cook time: 22 minutes

Ingredients:

- Big eggplant, peeled and thinly sliced: 1
- Red bell pepper; chopped: 1
- Water: 1/2 cup
- Garlic cloves; minced: 2
- Extra virgin olive oil: 3 tbsp.
- Onion; chopped: 1 cup
- Green bell pepper; chopped: 1
- Thyme: 1 Tsps
- Canned tomatoes; chopped: 14 oz
- Sugar: 1 pinch
- Basil, chopped: 1 cup
- Salt and black pepper to the taste

Directions:

1. 'Sauté' oil in an instant pot
2. Gently add green and red bell pepper, onion and garlic then stir. Let it cook for 3 minutes
3. Carefully add eggplant, water, salt, pepper, thyme, sugar and tomatoes then secure the lid. Cook it for 4 minutes on high
4. 'Quick release' the steam. Remove the lid
5. Top it with basil and serve

Cheesy Endives Risotto

Servings: 2 , Prep + Cook time: 30 minutes

Ingredients:

- Belgian endives, trimmed and cut into halves lengthwise and roughly chopped: 2
- Rice: 3/4 cup
- Yellow onion; chopped: ½
- Heavy cream: 3 tbsp.
- Extra virgin olive oil: 2 tbsp.
- White wine: 1/2 cup
- Veggie stock: 2 cups
- Parmesan, grated: 2 oz
- Salt and black pepper to the taste

Directions:

1. 'Sauté' oil in an instant pot
2. Add onions and stir. Let it cook for 4 minutes
3. While stirring, add endives and let it cook for 4 minutes
4. Add rice, wine, salt, pepper and stock, stir, secure the lid and cook for 10 minutes on high
5. 'Quick release' the pressure, remove the lid and let it 'sauté.'
6. Add cheese and heavy cream, stir and let it cook for 1 minute then serve.

Saucy Artichokes

Servings: 2 , Prep + Cook time: 30 minutes

Ingredients:

- Artichokes; washed, stems and petal tips cut off: 2
- Bay leaf: 1
- Water: 1 cup
- Garlic cloves; chopped: 2
- Lemon cut into halves: 1
- For the sauce:
- Coconut oil: 1/4 cup
- Extra virgin olive oil: 1/4 cup
- Anchovy fillets: 3
- Garlic cloves: 3

Directions:

1. In the steamer basket of the instant pot, put artichokes
2. Add water, lemon halves, 2 garlic cloves and bay leaf, secure the lid and cook for 20 minutes on high
3. 'Natural release' the pressure for 10 minutes and remove the lid
4. Blend coconut oil, anchovy, 3 garlic cloves and olive oil in your food processor
5. Dip the artichokes into the blend and serve.

Garlicky Zucchinis

Servings: 4 , **Prep + Cook time:** 22 minutes

Ingredients:
- Zucchinis, roughly chopped: 6
- Tomato puree: 1 cup
- Cherry tomatoes cut into halves: 1 lb.
- Olive oil: 1 drizzle
- Yellow onions; chopped: 2
- Vegetable oil: 1 tbsp.
- Garlic cloves; minced: 2
- Bunch basil; chopped: 1
- Salt and black pepper to the taste

Directions:
1. 'Sauté' vegetable oil in an instant pot
2. Add onion then stir and let it cook for 5 minutes
3. While stirring, add tomatoes, tomato puree, zucchinis, salt and pepper, secure the lid and cook it for 5 minutes on high
4. 'Quick release' the steam. Remove the lid
5. Add garlic and basil then stir
6. Top it with olive oil and serve

Cauliflower-sauced Pasta

Servings: 4 , **Prep + Cook time:** 20 minutes

Ingredients:
- Cauliflower florets: 8 cups
- Spinach; chopped: 2 cups
- Fettuccine paste: 1 lb.
- Garlic cloves; minced: 2
- Chicken stock: 1 cup
- Butter: 2 tbsp.
- Green onions; chopped: 2
- Gorgonzola cheese, grated: 1 tbsp.
- Sun-dried tomatoes; chopped: 3
- Salt to the taste
- Balsamic vinegar: 1 splash

Directions:
1. 'Sauté' butter in the instant pot for it to melt
2. Add garlic and stir then let it cook for 2 minutes
3. While stirring, add the stock, salt and cauliflower, secure the lid and cook for 6 minutes on high
4. 'Natural release' the steam for 10minutes then turn the valve to venting to remove the remaining pressure
5. Blend the cauliflower
6. Add spinach and green onions then stir
7. Take a pot, add water and salt then bring it to boil over medium-high heat
8. Add pasta to the boiling water. Cook as per the instructions. Drain it when it's cooked
9. Top the pasta with cauliflower sauce, gorgonzola, sun-dried tomatoes and a splash of vinegar, toss it and serve

Creamy Savoy Cabbage

Servings: 4 , **Prep + Cook time:** 20 minutes

Ingredients:
- Bacon; chopped: 1 cup
- Bay leaf: 1
- Yellow onion; chopped: 1
- Bone stock: 2 cups
- Nutmeg: 1/4 Tsps.
- Coconut milk: 1 cup
- Parsley flakes: 2 tbsp.
- Medium Savoy cabbage head; chopped: 1
- Salt and black pepper to the taste

Directions:
1. 'Sauté' bacon and onion in an instant pot while stirring. Cook it until it becomes crispy
2. Add stock, cabbage, bay leaf, salt, pepper and nutmeg, stir, secure the lid and let it cook for 5 minutes on high
3. 'Quick release' the steam and remove the lid. Let it remain in 'sauté' mode
4. Add milk, more salt and pepper and parsley then stir and let it cook for 4 minutes.
5. Serve

Quick Maple-Glazed Carrots

Servings: 4 , Prep + Cook time: 15 minutes

Ingredients:

- Carrots; peeled and sliced diagonally: 2 lb.
- Maple syrup: 1 tbsp.
- Raisins: 1/4 cup
- Butter: 1 tbsp.
- Water: 1 cup
- Black pepper to the taste

Directions:

1. In an instant pot, place carrots, water and raisins, secure the lid and cook on high for 4 minutes
2. 'Quick release' the steam. Remove the lid
3. Add butter, stir and top it with pepper then serve.

Cheesed Beets

Servings: 6 , Prep + Cook time: 30 minutes

Ingredients:

- Beets: 6
- Water: 1 cup
- Blue cheese, crumbled: 1/4 cup
- Salt and black pepper to the taste

Directions:

1. In the steamer basket of the instant pot, place the beets and add 1 cup of water, secure the lid and cook for 20minutes on high
2. 'Natural release' the steam and remove the lid then let the beets cook
3. Peel the beets and cut them to quarters
4. Top it with blue cheese, salt and pepper then serve

Spicy Sausages

Servings: 4 , Prep + Cook time: 15 minutes

Ingredients:

- Canned tomatoes; chopped: 15 oz
- Yellow onion; chopped: 1/2 cup
- Butter: 3 tbsp.
- Sausage links, sliced: 1 lb.
- Turmeric: 2 Tsps.
- Green cabbage head; chopped: 1
- Salt and black pepper to the taste

Directions:

1. 'Sauté' sausage slices in a greased instant pot and stir them occasionally till they become brown. Drain the excess grease afterward
2. Add butter, cabbage, tomatoes salt, pepper, onion and turmeric, stir, secure the lid and cook for 2 minutes on high
3. 'Quick release' the steam and remove the lid then serve.

Buttered Leeks

Servings: 4 , Prep + Cook time: 20 minutes

Ingredients:

- Leeks; washed, roots and ends cut off: 4
- Butter: 1 tbsp.
- Water: 1/3 cup
- Salt and black pepper to the taste

Directions:

1. In an instant pot, place the leeks, water and butter, salt and pepper, stir and secure the lid. cook for 5 minutes on high
2. 'Quick release' the steam. Remove the lid
3. Let it sit for 5 minutes at 'sauté' then serve

Potatoes with Mixed Vegetable Stew

Servings: 4, Prep + Cook time: 28 minutes

Ingredients

- Peas, ¾ cups.
- Olive oil, 1 tbsp.
- Peeled and diced white potatoes, 1 lb.
- Paprika, ½ tbsp.
- Chopped celery ribs, 1½.
- Tomato paste, ¼ cup.
- Chopped garlic, ¾ tbsp.
- Diced medium carrots, 1½.
- Chopped fresh parsley, ¼ cup.
- Italian herbs, ½ tbsp.
- Chopped large yellow onions, ¾.
- Water, 2½ cups.
- Fresh rosemary, 1 tsp.

Directions

1. Set the instant pot to sauté all the vegetables and oil for 5 minutes.
2. Mix in the rest of ingredients and cover with the lid.
3. Cook at high pressure for 13 minutes under the "Manual" function.
4. Naturally release the steam and uncover the lid after the beep.
5. Add a fresh parsley garnishing to serve while hot.
6. Enjoy.

Nutritional Information:
Calories: 230, Carbs: 38.8g, Protein: 6.9g, Fat: 6.3g, Sugar: 9.6g, Sodium: 115mg

Garlicky Potato and Tomatoes

Servings: 2, Prep + Cook time: 40 minutes

Ingredients

- Thyme, 1½ tbsps.
- Fresh tomatoes, 8 oz.
- Peeled and diced small onion, 1.
- Rosemary, ½ tbsp.
- Olive oil, 1 tbsp.
- Pepper.
- Grated garlic cloves, 2 tbsps.
- Peeled and diced large potatoes, 2.
- Water, 1 cup.
- Cayenne pepper, ½ tbsp.
- Salt.

Directions

1. Add a cup of water to the pot then put the trivet in it.
2. Put half the garlic and potatoes over the trivet and season with pepper and salt.
3. Cover the lid to cook for 20 minutes under the "steam" function.
4. Naturally release the steam and uncover the lid after the beep.
5. Transfer the rest of the ingredients to the cooker to sauté for 10 minutes.
6. Puree the cooked mixture using an immersion blender.
7. Mix in the steamed potatoes to serve while hot.
8. Enjoy.

Nutritional Information:
Calories: 176, Carbs: 26.4g, Protein: 3.7g, Fat: 7.9g, Sugar: 5.2g, Sodium: 181mg

Mixed Vegetable with Noodles

Servings: 2, Prep + Cook time: 31 minutes

Ingredients

- Oriental seasoning, 1 tbsp.
- Garlic paste, ½ tsp.
- Chopped celery sticks, 2.
- Worcester sauce, ½ tbsp.
- Diced large carrots, 2.
- Ginger paste, ½ tbsp.
- Chopped small leek, ½.
- Salt.
- Soy sauce, 1½ tbsps.
- Coriander, ½ tsp.

- Water, 2 cups.
- Chinese five spice, 1 tbsp.
- Noodles, 1lb.
- Chopped large onion, ½.
- Olive oil, 1 tbsp.
- Parsley, ½ tsp.
- Pepper.

Directions
1. Sauté ginger, oil, garlic paste and onion for 5 minutes in the instant pot.

2. Mix in the rest of vegetables to stir fry for 3 minutes.
3. Let them cook at high pressure for 13 minutes under the "manual" function.
4. Naturally release the steam and open the lid after the beep.
5. Stir well before serving warm.
6. Enjoy.

Nutritional Information:
Calories: 392, Carbs: 65.1g, Protein: 9.9g, Fat: 10.8g, Sugar: 7.4g, Sodium: 780mg

Spicy Ratatouille

Servings: 4, **Prep + Cook time:** 16 minutes

Ingredients
- Balsamic vinegar, 2 tbsps.
- Chopped garlic cloves, 4.
- Sliced medium tomatoes, 4.
- Black pepper, 1 tsp.
- Sliced medium eggplants, 2.
- Olive oil, 4 tbsps.
- Sea salt, 2 tbsps.
- Sliced small red onions, 2.
- Water, 2 cups.
- Sliced large zucchinis, 2.
- Thyme leaves, 2 tbsps.

Directions
1. Line the foil on the spring form pan then put chopped garlic at the bottom.

2. In circles, alternately arrange the vegetable slices.
3. Rub the vegetables with salt, thyme and pepper topped with vinegar and oil.
4. In the instant pot, pour 1 cup of water before putting the trivet inside.
5. Cover the lid to cook at high pressure for 6 minutes under the "Manual" function.
6. Naturally release the pressure and uncover the lid.
7. Serve and enjoy.

Nutritional Information:
Calories: 250, Carbs: 29.2g, Protein: 6g, Fat: 15.1g, Sugar: 14.5g, Sodium: 970mg

Potato and Carrot Stew

Servings: 4, **Prep + Cook time:** 25 minutes

Ingredients
- Peeled and sliced potatoes, ½ lb.
- Smoked paprika, ½ tsp.
- Homemade tomato sauce, 1 cup.
- Peeled and sliced carrots, ½ lb.
- Chopped fresh cilantro, ¼ cup.
- Vegetable broth, 1 cup.
- Minced garlic clove, ½.
- Olive oil, 1½ tbsps.
- Sliced large onion, 1.

Directions
1. Sauté all the vegetables and oil for 5 minutes in the instant pot.

2. Mix in tomato sauce, paprika, and broth and cover the lid.
3. Let the mixture cook at high pressure for 10 minutes under the "manual" setting.
4. Naturally release the steam and uncover the lid after the beep.
5. Stir well before serving with fresh cilantro topping.
6. Enjoy.

Nutritional Information:
Calories: 169, Carbs: 21.5g, Protein: 3.6g, Fat: 8g, Sugar: 7.3g, Sodium: 410mg

Mixed Vegetables with Potatoes

Servings: 3, **Prep + Cook time:** 28 minutes

Ingredients

- Water, 3 cups.
- Sliced fresh portabella mushrooms, 4 oz.
- Minced small onion, ½.
- Red wine, ¼ cup.
- Minced celery stalk, ½.
- Crushed dried sage, ½ tsp.
- Peeled and minced carrot, ½.
- Freshly ground black pepper
- Crushed dried rosemary, ½ tsp.
- Trimmed and chopped fresh green beans, ¾ cup.
- Tomato paste, ½ cup.
- Frozen peas, 2 oz.
- Chopped tomatoes, 1 cup.
- Sliced fresh white mushrooms, 4 oz.
- Salt.
- Minced garlic clove, 1.
- Olive oil, 1 tbsp.
- Peeled and diced Yukon gold potato, 1.
- Balsamic vinegar, ½ tbsp.
- Lemon juice, ½.
- Fresh cilantro, 2 tbsps.

Directions

1. Sauté tomatoes, oil, celery and onions for 5 minutes in the instant pot.
2. Mix in garlic and herbs to cook for 1 minute.
3. Add mushrooms then sauté for 5 minutes and stir in wine to cook for 2 more minutes.
4. Mix in diced potatoes and cover the lid to cook for 3 minutes.
5. Add tomato paste, green beans, peas, carrots, vinegar, water and seasonings.
6. Cover the lid to cook for 8 minutes at high pressure on "Manual" function with the pressure valve sealed.
7. Perform a quick release and uncover the pot to stir in veggies then add cilantro and lemon juice.
8. Serve with rice and enjoy.

Nutritional Information:

Calories: 183, Carbs: 28.1g, Protein: 6.7g, Fat: 5.3g, Sugar: 11g, Sodium: 80mg

Mushroom Tacos with Adobo Sauce

Servings: 3, **Prep + Cook time:** 23 minutes

Ingredients

- Vegetable broth, ¾ cup.
- Ground cumin, 2 tsps.
- Bay leaves, 2.
- Salt.
- Garlic cloves, 2.
- Ground cinnamon, ½ tsp.
- Chipotle chilies in adobo sauce, 2.
- Sliced large onions, 2.
- Tacos.
- Smoked hot paprika, 1 tsp.
- Lime juice, 3 tsps.
- Dried oregano, 1 tsp.
- Chopped mushrooms, 8 oz.
- Large guajillo chilies, 4.
- Oil, 2 tsps.
- Apple cider vinegar, 1 tsp.
- Sugar, ¼ tsp.

Directions

1. Sauté bay leaves, garlic, oil, onion and salt in the instant pot for 5 minutes.
2. Blend all the chilies and spices with half of the mixture.
3. Add the rest of onions and mushrooms then sauté for 3 minutes.
4. Transfer the blended mixture into the pot and cover the lid.
5. Cook for 5 minutes at high pressure on the "manual" function.
6. Quickly release the steam and uncover the lid once everything is done.
7. Stir well before serving with tacos.
8. Enjoy.

Nutritional Information:

Calories: 160, Carbs: 22.9g, Protein: 4.1g, Fat: 6.7g, Sugar: 8.2g, Sodium: 519mg

Egg Plant with Chili

Servings: 4, Prep + Cook time: 32 minutes

Ingredients

- Baby spinach leaves, 1 cup.
- Turmeric, ¼ tsp.
- Chopped onion, ½.
- Olive oil, 1 tsp.
- Chopped tomatoes, 2.
- Ground cumin, ½ tsp.
- Chopped garlic cloves, 4.
- Cubed sweet potatoes, 1 cup.
- Chopped hot green chili, 1.
- Salt, ¾ tsp.
- Chopped eggplant, 1 cup.
- Lemon.
- Pepper flakes.
- Water, 2 cups.
- Soaked and rinsed lentils, ¾ cup.
- Chopped ginger, 1 tsp.
- Cayenne.

Directions

1. Sauté ginger, oil, salt, garlic and chili for 3 minutes in the instant pot.
2. Mix in all spices and the tomatoes to cook for 5 minutes.
3. Add the rest of ingredients with the exception of spinach then garnish.
4. Cover the lid to cook at high pressure for 12 minutes on the "manual" function.
5. Naturally release the pressure and open the lid after the beep.
6. Stir in spinach leaves to cook on low heat for 2 minutes.
7. Add a pepper flakes garnishing to serve while warm.
8. Enjoy.

Nutritional Information:
Calories: 212, Carbs: 38.7g, Protein: 11.2g, Fat: 1.9g, Sugar: 3.8g, Sodium: 458mg

Jack Fruit with Nigella Seeds Stew

Servings: 4, Prep + Cook time: 15 minutes

Ingredients

- Chopped ginger, 2 inch.
- Mustard seeds, 1 tsp.
- Dried red chilies, 4.
- Chopped garlic cloves, 5.
- Bay leaves, 2.
- Water, 3 cups.
- Coriander powder, 2 tsps.
- Nigella seeds, 1 tsp.
- Chopped small onions, 2.
- Salt.
- Turmeric, 2 tsps.
- Tomato puree, 3 cups.
- Cumin seeds, 1 tsp.
- Oil, 2 tsps.
- Black pepper, ½ tsp.
- Drained and rinsed green Jackfruit, 20 oz.

Directions

1. Set up the instant pot to add ginger, oil, bay leaves, onions, red chilies, salt and garlic.
2. Let the mixture sauté cook for 2 minutes then stir in the rest of ingredients.
3. Cover the lid to cook at high pressure for 8 minutes on "manual".
4. Naturally release the steam and open the lid after the beep.
5. Stir in to serve while hot.
6. Enjoy.

Nutritional Information:
Calories: 319, Carbs: 70.2g, Protein: 5.4g, Fat: 4.8g, Sugar: 1.8g, Sodium: 49mg

Sweet Potato with Paprika

Servings: 8, **Prep + Cook time:** 13 minutes

Ingredients

- Diced sweet potato, 2 lbs.
- Chopped cilantro, 4 tbsps.
- Paprika, 2 tsps.
- Water, 2 cups.
- Salt, 4 tsps.
- Ground coriander, 2 tsps.
- Diced large garlic cloves, 4.
- Olive oil, 4 tbsps.
- Cilantro.
- Vegetable stock, 2 cups.
- Ground cumin, 4 tsps.
- Lemon juice.
- Finely diced large brown onions, 2.
- Sliced red chili, 1.
- Chopped tinned tomatoes, 4 cups.

Directions

1. Sauté onions and oil for 5 minutes in the instant pot.
2. Add the rest of ingredients and stir well then cover the lid.
3. Let it cook at high pressure for 3 minutes on "manual" function.
4. Quickly release the steam and uncover the lid once done.
5. Add a cilantro and lemon juice garnishing.
6. Serve and enjoy.

Nutritional Information:
Calories: 203, Carbs: 32g, Protein: 4g, Fat: 7.8g, Sugar: 11.6g, Sodium: 1027mg

Potato, Tomatoes and Scallion Stew

Servings: 8, **Prep + Cook time:** 13 minutes

Ingredients

- Diced medium potatoes, 2 lbs.
- Chopped medium scallions, 4.
- Ground turmeric, ½ tsp.
- Chopped tinned tomatoes, 4 cups.
- Salt, 4 tsps.
- Sliced large garlic cloves, 4.
- Lemon juice.
- Ground cumin, 4 tsps.
- Vegetable stock, 2 cups.
- Olive oil, 4 tbsps.
- Water, 3 cups.
- Finely diced large brown onions, 2.
- Paprika, 2 tsps.
- Cilantro.

Directions

1. Sauté onions and oil for 5 minutes in the instant pot.
2. Add the remaining ingredients and stir then cover the lid.
3. Let them cook at high pressure for 3 minutes on the 'manual' function.
4. Quickly release the steam and open the lid once it beeps.
5. Add lemon juice and cilantro to garnish.
6. Serve and enjoy.

Nutritional Information:
Calories: 496, Carbs: 99.9g, Protein: 9.4g, Fat: 7.6g, Sugar: 4.4g, Sodium: 1249mg

Sweet Potato with Ginger and Cilantro

Servings: 8, **Prep + Cook time:** 23 minutes

Ingredients

- Cubed medium sweet potatoes, 2.
- Ground cumin, 2 tsps.
- Tomatoes, 4.
- Turmeric, 1 tsp.
- Chopped ginger, 2-inch.
- Diced small cauliflowers, 2.
- Olive oil, 2 tsps.
- Salt.
- Paprika, 1 tsp.
- Small onion, 1.
- Chopped garlic cloves, 4.
- Chopped fresh cilantro, 2 tbsps.

Directions

1. In a blender, blend ginger, tomatoes, onion and garlic.
2. Sauté cumin and oil for 1 minute in the instant pot.
3. Stir in the rest of spices and the blended mixture.
4. Add sweet potatoes to cook for 5 minutes on 'sauté'.
5. Put cauliflower chunks in the pot and cover the lid.
6. Let it cook at high pressure for 2 minutes on 'manual' function.
7. Quickly release the steam and uncover the lid once done.
8. Stir to serve with a cilantro topping.
9. Enjoy.

Nutritional Information:
Calories: 118, Carbs: 24.3g, Protein: 4.1g, Fat: 1.7g, Sugar: 6.7g, Sodium: 51mg

Spicy Eggplants

Servings: 4, **Prep + Cook time:** 24 minutes

Ingredients

- Baby eggplants, 4.
- Coconut shreds, 2 tbsps.
- Chopped hot green chili, 1.
- Cumin seeds, ½ tsp.
- Chickpea flour, 3 tbsps.
- Mustard seeds, ½ tsp.
- Chopped garlic cloves, 2.
- Coriander seeds, 1 tbsp.
- Water.
- Cinnamon, ¼ tsp.
- Chopped peanuts, 2 tbsps.
- Lemon juice, 1 tsp.
- Cayenne, ½ tsp.
- Salt, ¾ tsp.
- Turmeric, ½ tsp.
- Chopped ginger.
- Ground cardamom, ½ tsp.
- Raw sugar, ½ tsp.
- Fresh cilantro.

Directions

1. In the instant pot, add mustard seeds, cumin and coriander.
2. Let it roast for 2 minutes on 'sauté' function.
3. Add coconut shred, chickpea flour and nuts to the pot to roast for 2 minutes.
4. Blend the mixture and put it in a medium sized bowl.
5. In a blender, roughly blend raw sugar, ginger, all spices, garlic, raw sugar and chili.
6. Add lemon juice and water and make a paste then combine with dry flour mixture.
7. Cut the eggplants on one side to fill with spice mixture.
8. Add a cup of water then put the filled eggplants inside.
9. Season with salt and cover the lid.
10. Let it cook at high pressure for 5 minutes on the 'manual' function then release the steam.
11. Open the lid to garnish with fresh cilantro.
12. Serve while hot and enjoy.

Nutritional Information:
Calories: 316, Carbs: 64.4g, Protein: 11.1g, Fat: 5.7g, Sugar: 34.4g, Sodium: 312mg

Sesame with Mixed Vegetables

Servings: 4, **Prep + Cook time:** 28 minutes

Ingredients

- Sesame oil, ½ tbsp.
- Peeled and diced white potatoes, 1 lb.
- Diced medium carrots, 1½.
- Sesame seeds, 2 tsps.
- Diced medium portabella mushroom, 1.
- Chopped celery ribs, 1½.
- Tomato paste, ¼ cup.
- Peas, ¾ cups.
- Water, 2 cups.
- Fresh rosemary, 1 tsp.
- Paprika, ½ tbsp.
- Chopped garlic, ¾ tbsp.

- Chopped large yellow onion, ¾.
- Chopped fresh parsley, ¼ cup.

Directions
1. Sauté all the vegetables, sesame seeds and oil for 5 minutes in the instant pot.
2. Stir in the rest of the ingredients and cover the lid.
3. Let it cook at high pressure on for 13 minutes on the 'manual' function.
4. Naturally release the steam and open the lid after the beep.
5. Add a fresh parsley garnishing to serve while hot.
6. Enjoy.

Nutritional Information:
Calories: 202, Carbs: 34.5g, Protein: 6.2g, Fat: 5.3g, Sugar: 9.2g, Sodium: 49mg

Cauliflower, Potatoes and Beans

Servings: 8, Prep + Cook time: 23 minutes

Ingredients
- Cooked black beans, ½ cup.
- Turmeric, 1 tsp.
- Tomatoes, 4.
- Olive oil, 2 tsps.
- Minced garlic cloves, 4.
- Paprika, 1 tsp.
- Fresh cilantro, 2 tbsps.
- Cubed medium potatoes, 4.
- Ground cumin, 2 tsps.
- Small onion, 1.
- Chopped ginger, 2-inch
- Salt.
- Diced small cauliflowers, 2.

Directions
1. In a blender, blend ginger, tomatoes, onion and garlic.
2. Sauté cumin and oil for 1 minute in the instant pot.
3. Stir in the rest of the spices and the blended mixture.
4. Put the potatoes in the pot to cook for 5 minutes on sauté.
5. Add chunks of cauliflower and close the lid.
6. Let them cook at high pressure for 2 minutes on the 'manual'.
7. Quickly release the steam and open the lid once everything is done.
8. Stir in beans to serve with a cilantro topping.
9. Enjoy.

Nutritional Information:
Calories: 153, Carbs: 30.5g, Protein: 6.6g, Fat: 1.8g, Sugar: 4.5g, Sodium: 53mg

Green Beans with Celery & Potatoes

Servings: 4, Prep + Cook time: 28 minutes

Ingredients
- Sliced green beans, 1 cup.
- Peeled and diced white potatoes, 1 lb.
- Fresh rosemary, 1 tsp.
- Chopped garlic, ¾ tbsp.
- Paprika, ½ tbsp.
- Chopped celery ribs, 1½.
- Peas, ¾ cups.
- Water, 2½ cups.
- Chopped large yellow onion, ¾.
- Tomato paste, ¼ cup.
- Chopped fresh parsley, ¼ cup.

Directions
1. Add all the vegetables in the instant pot to sauté for 5 minutes.
2. Stir in the rest of ingredients and cover the lid.
3. Let them cook at high pressure for 13 minutes on the 'manual' function.
4. Naturally release the steam and open the lid after the beep.
5. Add fresh parsley to garnish then serve while hot.
6. Enjoy.

Nutritional Information:
Calories: 167, Carbs: 32.6g, Protein: 5.6g, Fat: 2.5g, Sugar: 8.1g, Sodium: 34mg

Potato with Peas

Servings: 4, Prep + Cook time: 28 minutes

Ingredients

- Fresh rosemary, 1 tsp.
- Peeled and diced white potatoes, 1 lb.
- Chopped celery ribs, 1½
- Peas, ¾ cup.
- Corn kernels, ¼ cup.
- Diced carrots, ¼ cup.
- Paprika, ½ tbsp.
- Chopped fresh cilantro, ¼ cup.
- Water, 2½ cups.
- Chopped garlic, ¼ cup.
- Tomato paste, ¼ cup.
- Chopped large yellow onion, ¾.

Directions

1. Sauté al the vegetables and oil for 5minutes in the instant pot.
2. Stir in the rest of the ingredients and cover the lid.
3. Allow them to cook at high pressure for 13 minutes on 'manual' function.
4. Naturally release the steam and open the lid after the beep.
5. Add fresh cilantro to garnish and serve while hot.
6. Enjoy.

Nutritional Information:
Calories: 170, Carbs: 33.2g, Protein: 5.4g, Fat: 2.6g, Sugar: 8.3g, Sodium: 39mg

Celery Mixed Pasta

Servings: 6, Prep + Cook time: 21 minutes

Ingredients

- Worcester sauce, ½ tbsp.
- Chopped large onion, ½.
- Olive oil, 1 tbsp.
- Green bell pepper, ½ cup.
- Diced large carrots, 2.
- Ginger paste, ½ tbsp.
- Chopped celery sticks, 2.
- Water, 1 cup.
- Soy sauce, 1½ tbsps.
- Pepper.
- Coriander, ½ tsp.
- Chopped small leek, ½.
- Cooked penne pasta, 1lb.
- Garlic paste, ½ tsp.
- Chopped parsley, ½ tsp.
- Salt.

Directions

1. Sauté ginger, onion, garlic paste and oil for 5 minutes in the instant pot.
2. Stir in the rest of the vegetables then stir fry for 3 minutes.
3. Add the rest of the ingredients with exception of pasta and close the lid.
4. Let it cook at high pressure for 3 minutes on the 'manual' function.
5. Naturally release the steam and open the lid after the beep.
6. Stir in cooked pasta to serve while warm.
7. Enjoy.

Nutritional Information:
Calories: 368, Carbs: 67.4g, Protein: 13.1g, Fat: 4.9g, Sugar: 2.8g, Sodium: 284mg

Coriander Carrots with Rice

Servings: 4, Prep + Cook time: 23 minutes

Ingredients

- Chopped parsley, ½ tsp.
- Ginger paste, ½ tbsp.
- Chopped celery sticks, 2.
- Soaked chickpeas, ½ cup.
- Worcester sauce, ½ tbsp.
- Diced large carrots, 2.
- Chopped large onion, ½.
- Pepper.
- Olive oil, 1 tbsp.
- Chopped coriander, ½ tsp.
- Water, 2½ cups.
- Long-grain white rice, 1 cup.
- Chopped small leek, ½.
- Garlic paste, ½ tsp.
- Salt.

Directions

1. Sauté ginger, oil, garlic paste and onion for 5 minutes in the instant pot.
2. Mix in the rest of vegetables then stir fry for 3 minutes.
3. Add the rest of ingredients and cover the lid.
4. Let them cook at high pressure for 5minutes on 'manual' function.
5. Naturally release the steam and remove the lid after the beep.
6. Stir and serve while still warm.
7. Enjoy.

Nutritional Information:

Calories: 341, Carbs: 64.1g, Protein: 9.1g, Fat: 5.5g, Sugar: 6g, Sodium: 57mg

Carrots with Pepper and Chili

Servings: 3, Prep + Cook time: 25 minutes

Ingredients

- Crushed and dried oregano, ½ tbsp.
- Sugar-free tomato paste, 1 oz.
- Diced tomatoes, 15 oz.
- Chopped small yellow onion, 1.
- Peas, ¼ cup.
- Worcestershire sauce, 1 tbsp.
- Chopped green bell pepper, ½ cup.
- Freshly ground black pepper.
- Red chili powder, 2 tbsps.
- Chopped scallions, ½ cup.
- Green chilies with liquid, 4 oz.
- Ground cumin, 1 tbsp.
- Olive oil, ½ tbsps.
- Minced garlic cloves, 4.
- Diced carrots, ½ cup.
- Salt.

Directions

1. Set the instant pot to sauté, add garlic, onion and oil and stir for 5 minutes.
2. Mix in the rest of the vegetables then stir fry for 3 minutes.
3. Let them cook at high pressure for 2 minutes on the manual function.
4. Release the steam naturally and open the lid after the beep.
5. Stir well before serving it warm.
6. Enjoy.

Nutritional Information:

Calories: 144, Carbs: 26.2g, Protein: 4.6g, Fat: 3.9g, Sugar: 12g, Sodium: 219mg

Chapter 8 Stew and Soup

Homemade Chicken Stock

Serves:8, **Prep Time + Cook Time:** 66 minutes

Ingredients

- Fresh parsley - 1 sprig
- Whole black peppercorns – ½ tsp.
- Water – 10 cups
- Celery stalk - 1 chopped into thirds
- Chicken carcass – 2 ½ lbs.,
- dried bay leaf - 1 tsp.
- small onion - 1 unpeeled and halved
- Kosher salt – 1 tsp.

Directions

1. Empty all of the water into the instant pot.
2. Include all of your ingredients in the instant pot.
3. Close the pot lid and ensure it is tightly locked. Set the pressure release handle to the 'sealed' position.
4. Click on the 'manual' function of your instant pot then set to high pressure and reset the time to 60 minutes.
5. Do a 'Natural release' immediately after the beep for 10 minutes and remove the lid.
6. Get a mesh strainer and Strain the cooked stock through it and throw away all the solids.
7. Scrub off all of the fats on the surface
8. Serve hot

Nutrition Values Per Serving
Calories: 306, Carbohydrate: 1g, Protein: 25.2g, Fat: 21.3g ,Sugar: o.4g, Sodium: 408mg

Homemade Chicken Vegetable Stock

Serves: 8, Prep Time + Cook Time: 66 minutes

Ingredients

- chicken bones only - 2½ lbs
- carrots chopped - ¼ cup
- Salt and black pepper to taste
- fresh parsley - 1 sprig
- green bell pepper chopped - ¼ cup
- small onion - 1 unpeeled and halved
- water - 8 cups
- celery stalk - 1 chopped into thirds
- green onions -¼ cup chopped

Directions

1. Empty all of the water into the instant pot.
2. Include all of your ingredients in the instant pot.
3. Close the pot lid and ensure it is tightly locked. Set the pressure release handle to the 'sealed' position.
4. Click on the 'manual' function of your instant pot then set to high pressure and reset the time to 60 minutes.
5. Do a 'Natural release' immediately after the beep for 10 minutes and remove the lid.
6. Get a mesh strainer and Strain the cooked stock through it and throw away all the solids.
7. Scrub off all of the fats on the surface
8. Serve hot.

Nutrition Values Per Serving
Calories: 224, Carbohydrate: 2.2g, Protein: 41.5g, Fat: 4.3g, Sugar: 1g, Sodium: 101mg

Creamy Chicken Mushroom Stock

Servings: 8, **Prep Time + Cook Time:** 70 minutes

Ingredients

- cremini mushrooms - 1 cup diced
- leek - 1 finely chopped
- water – 8 cups
- Dried bay leaf - 1 tsp.
- chicken bones only - 2½ lbs
- Kosher salt - 1 tsp.
- Whole black peppercorns - ½ tsp.
- small onion - 1 unpeeled and halved
- white pepper - ½ tsp.

Directions

1. Empty all of the water into the instant pot.
2. Include all of your ingredients in the instant pot.
3. Close the pot lid and ensure it is tightly locked. Set the pressure release handle to the 'sealed' position.
4. Click on the 'manual' function of your instant pot then set to high pressure and reset the time to 60 minutes.
5. Do a 'Natural release' immediately after the beep for 10 minutes and remove the lid.
6. Get a mesh strainer and Strain the cooked stock through it and throw away all the solids.
7. Scrub off all of the fats on the surface
8. Serve hot.

Nutrition Values Per Serving

Calories: 228, Carbohydrate: 3.1g, Protein: 41.6g, Fat: 4.4g, Sugar: 1g, Sodium: 390mg

Homemade Chicken with Herbs Stock

Serves: 8, **Prep Time + Cook Time: 70** minutes

Ingredients

- sea salt - 1 tsp.
- oregano - ¼ tsp.
- chicken bones only - 2½ lbs.
- dried bay leaf - 1 tsp.
- fresh parsley - 1 sprig
- dried basil - ¼ tsp.
- whole black peppercorns - ½ tsp
- small onion - 1 unpeeled and halved
- water – 8 cups

Directions

1. Empty all of the water into the instant pot.
2. Include all of your ingredients in the instant pot.
3. Close the pot lid and ensure it is tightly locked. Set the pressure release handle to the 'sealed' position.
4. 04. Click on the 'manual' function of your instant pot then set to high pressure and reset the time to 60 minutes.
5. Do a 'Natural release' immediately after the beep for 10 minutes and remove the lid.
6. Get a mesh strainer and Strain the cooked stock through it and throw away all the solids.
7. Scrub off all of the fats on the surface
8. Serve hot.

Nutrition Values Per Serving

Calories: 221, Carbohydrate: 3.3g, Protein: 41.2g, Fat: 4.6g, Sugar: 0.1g, Sodium: 378mg

Braised Kale Stock

Serves: 8, Prep Time + Cook Time: 70 minutes

Ingredients
- Salt and black pepper to taste
- small onion - 1 unpeeled and halved
- Dried bay leaf - 1 tsp.
- chicken bones only - 2½ lbs
- fresh kale - 1 sprig
- celery stalk - 1 chopped into thirds
- water – 8 cups

Directions
1. Empty all of the water into the instant pot.
2. Include all of your ingredients in the instant pot.
3. Close the pot lid and ensure it is tightly locked. Set the pressure release handle to the 'sealed' position.
4. Click on the 'manual' function of your instant pot then set to high pressure and reset the time to 60 minutes.
5. Do a 'Natural release' immediately after the beep for 10 minutes and remove the lid.
6. Get a mesh strainer and Strain the cooked stock through it and throw away all the solids.
7. Scrub off all of the fats on the surface
8. Serve hot.

Nutrition Values Per Serving
Calories: 218, Carbohydrate: 2.5g, Protein: 42.1g, Fat: 3.9g, Sugar: 1g, Sodium: 387mg

"Brown" Beef Stock

Serves: 10, Prep Time + Cook Time: 2 Hours 30 minutes

Ingredients
- garlic cloves - 2 chopped
- Beef stock bones - 4 lbs.
- small onion - 1 unpeeled and halved
- Kosher salt - 1 tsp.
- Olive oil - 2 tbsps.
- Apple cider vinegar - 1 tbsp.
- celery stalk - 1 chopped into thirds
- fresh parsley - 1 sprig
- Water as needed
- dried bay leaf - 1 tsp.
- whole black peppercorns - ½ tsp.

Directions
1. Use olive oil to grease your baking tray and then place your beef bones on it.
2. Preheat your oven 420o F then introduce the bones and cook for 30 minutes; Flip the bones to the other side and roast again for another 20 minutes3. Pour water up to the level of one inch below the 'max line' of your Instant Pot.
3. Introduce all of your ingredients, plus the roasted beef bones, to the water in your pot.
4. Close the pot lid and ensure it is tightly locked. Set the pressure release handle to the 'sealed' position.
5. Click on the 'manual' function of your instant pot then set to high pressure and reset the time to 75 minutes.
6. Do a 'Natural release' immediately after the beep for 10 minutes and remove the lid.
7. Get a mesh strainer and Strain the cooked stock through it and throw away all the solids.
8. Scrub off all of the fats on the surface and serve hot

Nutrition Values Per Serving
Calories: 388, Carbohydrate: 1g, Protein: 49.8g ,Fat: 19.1g ,Sugar: 0.3g,Sodium: 363mg

Beef Vegetable Soup

Serves: 10, Prep Time + Cook Time: 2 Hours 15 minutes

Ingredients

- Cabbage - ¼ chopped
- beef stock bones - 4 lbs.
- small onion - 1 unpeeled and halved
- apple cider vinegar - 1 tbsp.
- carrots - 1 cup chopped
- bell peppers - ½ cup sliced
- garlic cloves - 1, chopped
- celery stalk - 1, chopped into thirds
- olive oil - 2 tbsp.
- whole black peppercorns - ½ tsp.
- fresh parsley - 1 sprig

Directions

1. Use olive oil to grease your baking tray and then place your beef bones on it.
2. Preheat your oven 420o F then introduce the bones and cook for 30 minutes; Flip the bones to the other side and roast again for another 20 minutes3. Pour water up to the level of one inch below the 'max line' of your Instant Pot.
3. Introduce all of your ingredients, plus the roasted beef bones, to the water in your pot.
4. Close the pot lid and ensure it is tightly locked. Set the pressure release handle to the 'sealed' position.
5. Click on the 'manual' function of your instant pot then set to high pressure and reset the time to 75 minutes.
6. Do a 'Natural release' immediately after the beep for 10 minutes and remove the lid.
7. Get a mesh strainer and Strain the cooked stock through it and throw away all the solids.
8. Scrub off all of the fats on the surface and serve hot

Nutrition Values Per Serving
Calories: 396, Carbohydrate: 1.3g,Protein: 48.4g,Fat: 18.9g,Sugar: 0.4g,Sodium: 365mg

Grilled Beef Mushroom Stock

Serves: 10, Prep Time + Cook Time: 2 Hours 15 minutes

Ingredients

- cremini mushrooms - 1 cup, sliced
- olive oil - 2 tbsp.
- white pepper - ½ tsp.
- black pepper ground - 1 tsp.
- small onion - 1, unpeeled and halved
- garlic cloves - 2, chopped
- kosher salt - 1 tsp.
- celery stalk - 1, chopped into thirds
- apple cider vinegar - 1 tbsp.
- beef stock bones - 4 lbs.
- Water as needed

Directions

1. Use olive oil to grease your baking tray and then place your beef bones on it.
2. Preheat your oven 420o F then introduce the bones and cook for 30 minutes; Flip the bones to the other side and roast again for another 20 minutes3. Pour water up to the level of one inch below the 'max line' of your Instant Pot.
3. Introduce all of your ingredients, plus the roasted beef bones, to the water in your pot.
4. Close the pot lid and ensure it is tightly locked. Set the pressure release handle to the 'sealed' position.
5. Click on the 'manual' function of your instant pot then set to high pressure and reset the time to 75 minutes.
6. Do a 'Natural release' immediately after the beep for 10 minutes and remove the lid.
7. Get a mesh strainer and Strain the cooked stock through it and throw away all the solids.
8. Scrub off all of the fats on the surface and serve hot

Nutrition Values Per Serving
Calories: 393,Carbohydrate: 1.2g,Protein: 47.4g ,Fat: 20g,Sugar: 0.4g,Sodium: 365mg

Quick Mixed Vegetable Stock

Serves: 8, Prep Time + Cook Time: 25 minutes

Ingredients

- Carrots - 1 cup, diced
- celery stalk - 1, chopped into thirds
- small onion - 1, unpeeled and halved
- kosher salt - 1 tsp.
- green onions - ½ cup, chopped
- ginger - 1 tbsp., grated
- dried bay leaf - 1 tsp.
- whole black peppercorns - ½ tsp.
- potatoes - 1 cup, diced
- ground turmeric - ½ tsp.
- fresh parsley - 1 sprig
- bell peppers - ½ cup, chopped
- water - 8 cups

Directions

1. Empty all of the water into the instant pot.
2. Include all of your ingredients in the instant pot
3. Close the pot lid and ensure it is tightly locked; Set the pressure release handle to the 'sealed' position.
4. Click on the 'manual' function of your instant pot then set to high pressure and reset the time to 15 minutes.
5. Do a 'Natural release' immediately after the beep for 10 minutes and remove the lid.
6. Get a mesh strainer and Strain the cooked stock through it and throw away all the solids.
7. Serve hot.

Nutrition Values Per Serving
Calories: 30,Carbohydrate: 6.9g,Protein: 0.8g,Fat: 0.1g,Sugar: 1.9g,Sodium: 312mg

Corn and Mushroom Soup

Serves: 8, Prep time: 5 minutes **Cooking time**: 15 minutes

Ingredients

- small onion - 1, unpeeled and halved
- turmeric ground - ½ tsp.
- celery stalk -1, chopped into thirds
- whole black peppercorns - ½ tsp.
- water - 8 cups
- dried bay leaf - 1 tsp.
- grated ginger - 1 tsp.
- fresh sprig parsley - 1
- kosher salt-1 tsp.
- diced large mushrooms – 4.
- corns - 2 cobs

Directions

1. Empty all of the water into the instant pot.
2. Include all of your ingredients in the instant pot
3. Close the pot lid and ensure it is tightly locked; Set the pressure release handle to the 'sealed' position.
4. Click on the 'manual' function of your instant pot then set to high pressure and reset the time to 15 minutes.
5. Do a 'Natural release' immediately after the beep for 10 minutes and remove the lid.
6. Get a mesh strainer and Strain the cooked stock through it and throw away all the solids.
7. Serve hot.

Nutrition Values Per Serving
Calories: 47, Carbohydrate: 9.6g, Protein: 1.6g, Fat: 0.9g, Sugar: 0.6g, Sodium: 308mg

Classic Fish Anchovy Stock

Serves: 8, **Prep Time + Cook Time: 25** minutes

Ingredients

- whole black peppercorns - ½ tsp.
- celery stalk - 1, chopped into thirds
- dried anchovies - 2 oz.
- kosher salt - 1 tsp.
- kombu* a brown seaweed used by the Japanese for cooking - 6 small pieces'
- water - 8 cups

Directions

1. Empty all of the water into the instant pot.
2. Include all of your ingredients in the instant pot
3. Close the pot lid and ensure it is tightly locked; Set the pressure release handle to the 'sealed' position.
4. Click on the 'manual' function of your instant pot then set to high pressure and reset the time to 20 minutes.
5. Do a 'Natural release' immediately after the beep for 10 minutes and remove the lid.

6. Get a mesh strainer and Strain the cooked stock through it and throw away all the solids.
7. Serve hot.

Nutrition Values Per Serving
Calories: 20, Carbohydrate: 0.9g, Protein: 2.3g, Fat: 0.7g, Sugar: 0g, Sodium: 638mg

Note: Kombu* - a brown seaweed used in Japanese cooking, especially as a base for stock.

Tunisian Chickpea Soup Lablabi

Serves: 8, Prep Time + Cook Time: 30 minutes

Ingredients

- Chickpeas - 2 cups, rinsed and drained
- green onions - ½ cup, chopped
- thyme leaves - 1 tbsp.
- carrots - 1 cup, diced
- dried bay leaf - 1 tsp.
- apple cider vinegar - ½ tsp.
- kosher salt - 1 tsp.
- red pepper flakes - ½ tsp.
- water - 8 cups

Directions

1. Empty all of the water into the instant pot.
2. Include all of your ingredients in the instant pot

3. Close the pot lid and ensure it is tightly locked; Set the pressure release handle to the 'sealed' position.
4. Click on the 'manual' function of your instant pot then set to high pressure and reset the time to 15 minutes.
5. Do a 'Natural release' immediately after the beep for 10 minutes and remove the lid.
6. Get a mesh strainer and Strain the cooked stock through it and throw away all the solids.
7. Serve hot.

Nutrition Values Per Serving
Calories: 191, Carbohydrate: 32.4g, Protein: 9.9g, Fat: 3.1g, Sugar: 6.2g, Sodium: 321mg

Crabmeat and Rustic Tomato Stock

Serves: 8, Prep Time + Cook Time: 1 Hour 30 minutes

Ingredients

- Carrots - 1 cup, rough chop
- olive oil - 3 tbsps.
- crab shells - 2 lbs.
- onion - 1, rough chop skin on
- garlic - 4 cloves
- black peppercorns - 1 tsps.
- parsley flakes - 1 tsps.
- bay leaves - 2
- fresh thyme - 4 sprigs
- tomato paste - 2 tbsps.
- celery - 2 stalks, rough chop
- water - 10 cups

Directions

1. Include the oil, garlic, onion, crab shells, and vegetables into the instant pot and cook in sauté mode for 5 minutes.
2. Empty all of the water into the instant pot.
3. Include all of the remaining ingredients in the instant pot
4. Close the pot lid and ensure it is tightly locked; Set the pressure release handle to the 'sealed' position.
5. Click on the 'manual' function of your instant pot then set to high pressure and reset the time to 80 minutes.
6. Do a 'Natural release' immediately after the beep for 10 minutes and remove the lid.

7. Get a mesh strainer and Strain the cooked stock through it and throw away all the solids.
8. Serve.

Nutrition Values Per Serving
Calories: 156, Carbohydrate: 5.2g, Protein: 27.4g, Fat: 1.5g, Sugar: 1.9g,Sodium: 468mg

Homemade Salmon Balls with Fish Stock

Serves: 6, Prep Time + Cook Time: 60 minutes

Ingredients
- small onion-1, quartered
- peppercorns- 5
- sprigs fresh thyme-3
- Garlic-2 cloves minced
- olive oil- 2 tbsps.
- Carrot-1 diced
- bay leaf-1
- cold water -6 cups
- salmon heads-2 to 2½ lbs
- dry white wine- 1 cup

Directions
1. Include the oil, garlic, onion, crab shells, and vegetables into the instant pot and cook in sauté mode for 5 minutes.
2. Empty all of the water into the instant pot.
3. Include all of the remaining ingredients in the instant pot
4. Close the pot lid and ensure it is tightly locked; Set the pressure release handle to the 'sealed' position.
5. Click on the 'manual' function of your instant pot then set to high pressure and reset the time to 80 minutes.
6. Do a 'Natural release' immediately after the beep for 10 minutes and remove the lid.
7. Get a mesh strainer and Strain the cooked stock through it and throw away all the solids.
8. Serve.

Nutrition Values Per Serving
Calories: 123, Carbohydrate: 3.9g, Protein: 11.9g ,Fat: 3.7g, Sugar: 1.3g,Sodium: 43mg

Fantastic Seafood Gumbo Stock

Serves: 6, Prep Time + Cook Time: 60 minutes

Ingredients
- crab shells - ½ lb.
- carrot - 1, diced
- salmon head - 1
- small onion - 1, quartered
- cloves garlic - 2, minced
- peppercorns - 5
- cold water - 6 cups
- dry white wine - 1 cup
- tablespoons olive oil - 3
- shrimp shells - ½ lb.
- bay leaf - 1
- fresh thyme - 3 sprigs

Directions
1. Include the oil, garlic, onion, crab shells, and vegetables into the instant pot and cook in sauté mode fat for 5 minutes.
2. Empty all of the water into the instant pot.
3. Include all of the remaining ingredients in the instant pot
4. Close the pot lid and ensure it is tightly locked; Set the pressure release handle to the 'sealed' position.
5. Click on the 'manual' function of your instant pot then set to high pressure and reset the time to 48 minutes.
6. Do a 'Natural release' immediately after the beep for 10 minutes and remove the lid.
7. Get a mesh strainer and Strain the cooked stock through it and throw away all the solids.
8. Serve.

Nutrition Values Per Serving
Calories: 126,Carbohydrate: 3.4g, Protein: 16.8g, Fat: 2.4g, Sugar: 1g, Sodium: 171mg

Turkey Bone Soup

Serves: 8, Prep Time + Cook Time: 70 minutes

Ingredients

- whole black peppercorns - ½ tsp.
- turkey carcass - 1
- small onion - 1, unpeeled and halved
- dried bay leaf – 1 tsp.
- celery stalk - 1, chopped into thirds
- kosher salt - 1 tsp.
- fresh parsley - 1 sprig
- water - 10 cups

Directions

1. Empty all of the water into the instant pot.
2. Include all of your ingredients in the instant pot.
3. Close the pot lid and ensure it is tightly locked. Set the pressure release handle to the 'sealed' position.
4. Click on the 'manual' function of your instant pot then set to high pressure and reset the time to 60 minutes.
5. Do a 'Natural release' immediately after the beep for 10 minutes and remove the lid.
6. Get a mesh strainer and Strain the cooked stock through it and throw away all the solids.
7. Scrub off all of the fats on the surface
8. Serve hot.

Nutrition Values Per Serving

Calories: 39, Carbohydrate: 1g, Protein: 5g, Fat: 1.4g, Sugar: 0.4g, Sodium: 312mg

Pork Bone Stock

Serves: 8, Prep Time + Cook Time: 45 minutes

Ingredients

- celery stalk - 1, chopped into thirds
- dried bay leaf - 1 tsp.
- water - 8 cups
- fresh parsley - 1 sprig
- small onion - 1, unpeeled and halved
- kosher salt-1 tsp.
- whole black peppercorns - ½ tsp.
- pastured pork bones - 3 lbs.

Directions

1. Empty all of the water into the instant pot.
2. Include all of your ingredients in the instant pot.
3. Close the pot lid and ensure it is tightly locked. Set the pressure release handle to the 'sealed' position.
4. Click on the 'manual' function of your instant pot then set to high pressure and reset the time to 60 minutes.
5. Do a 'Natural release' immediately after the beep for 10 minutes and remove the lid.
6. Get a mesh strainer and Strain the cooked stock through it and throw away all the solids.
7. Scrub off all of the fats on the surface
8. Serve hot.

Nutrition Values Per Serving

Calories: 445, Carbohydrate: 7g, Protein: 22.1g, Fat: 36g, Sugar: 0.4g, Sodium: 1601mg

Pork and Veggie Soup

Serves: 8, Prep Time + Cook Time: 55 minutes

Ingredients

- pastured pork bones-2 lbs.
- bell peppers-½ cup
- carrots-½ cup, chopped
- green onions-½ cup chopped
- small onion-1, unpeeled and halved
- dried bay leaf-1 tsp.
- celery stalk-1, chopped into thirds
- sprig fresh parsley-1
- kosher salt-1 tsp.
- whole black peppercorns-½ tsp.
- water-8 cups

Directions

1. Empty all of the water into the instant pot.
2. Include all of your ingredients in the instant pot.
3. Close the pot lid and ensure it is tightly locked. Set the pressure release handle to the 'sealed' position.
4. Click on the 'manual' function of your instant pot then set to high pressure and reset the time to 45 minutes.
5. Do a 'Natural release' immediately after the beep for 10 minutes and remove the lid.
6. Get a mesh strainer and Strain the cooked stock through it and throw away all the solids.
7. Scrub off all of the fats on the surface
8. Serve hot.

Nutrition Values Per Serving

Calories: 443, Carbohydrate: 7.1g, Protein: 25.1g, Fat: 32g, Sugar: 0.4g, Sodium: 1611mg

Chicken Green Beans Stock

Serves: 8, Prep Time + Cook Time: 70 minutes

Ingredients

- whole black peppercorns - ½ tsp.
- fresh parsley - 1 sprig
- green beans - 1 cup, sliced
- water - 8 cups
- celery stalk - 1, chopped into thirds
- chicken bones only - 2½ lbs.
- small onion - 1, unpeeled and halved
- dried bay leaf - 1 tsp.
- kosher salt - 1 tsp.

Directions

1. Empty all of the water into the instant pot.
2. Include all of your ingredients in the instant pot.
3. Close the pot lid and ensure it is tightly locked. Set the pressure release handle to the 'sealed' position.
4. Click on the 'manual' function of your instant pot then set to high pressure and reset the time to 60 minutes.
5. Do a 'Natural release' immediately after the beep for 10 minutes and remove the lid.
6. Get a mesh strainer and Strain the cooked stock through it and throw away all the solids.
7. Scrub off all of the fats on the surface
8. Serve hot.

Nutrition Values Per Serving

Calories: 480, Carbohydrate: 2g, Protein: 30.8g, Fat: 9.5g, Sugar: 0.6g, Sodium: 495mg

Spicy Red Hot Sauce

Serves: 4, Prep Time + Cook Time: 10 minutes

Ingredients

- garlic cloves - 6, peeled and smashed
- carrot - ¼ cup, shredded
- roasted red pepper - 1, chopped
- sea salt - 1 tbsp.
- white vinegar - 1 cup
- Fresno peppers - 1 lb.
- apple cider vinegar - ¼ cup
- water - ½ cup

Directions

1. Include all of the remaining ingredients in the instant pot
2. Close the pot lid and ensure it is tightly locked; Set the pressure release handle to the 'sealed' position.
3. Click on the 'manual' function of your instant pot then set to high pressure and reset the time to 2 minutes.
4. Do a 'quick release' immediately after the beep and remove the lid.5. Pour the entire sauce into your blender and blend until it is smooth
5. Store in a bottle or use instantly.

Nutrition Values Per Serving
Calories: 43, Carbohydrate: 9.5g, Protein: 0.5g, Fat: 0.1g, Sugar: 1.4g, Sodium: 457mg

Simple Chicken Soup

Servings: 4 , Prep + Cooking Time: 45 minutes

Ingredients:

- Water – 2 cups
- Salt and black pepper
- Frozen Boneless chicken breast – 2
- Chicken stock – 2 cups
- Diced big onion – ½
- Peeled and cut into chunks carrots – 3
- Cut into chunks medium-sized potatoes – 4

Directions:

1. Get an Instant Pot and combine the carrots, potatoes, stock, onion, pepper, stock, salt and water
2. Close and lock the lid, select MANUAL and cook at HIGH pressure for 25 minutes
3. Once the timer goes off, allow it to release for 10 minutes naturally
4. Release the remaining pressure manually
5. Uncover the pot and serve

Buffalo Chicken Soup Recipe

Servings: 4 , Prep + Cooking Time: 35 minutes

Ingredients:

- Butter – 2 tbsp
- Diced onion – ¼ cup
- Ranch dressing mix – 1 tbsp
- Hot sauce – 1/3 cup
- Chopped garlic clove – 1
- Butter – 2 tbsp
- Boneless, skinless and frozen chicken breast
- Shredded cheddar cheese – 2 cups
- Heavy cream – 1 cup
- Chicken broth – 3 cups

Directions:

1. Get an Instant Pot, add in the chicken, garlic, onion, chicken breast, butter, celery, hot sauce, broth and ranch dressing mix
2. Close and lock the lid, select MANUAL and cook at HIGH pressure for 10 minutes
3. Once the cooking is complete, allow the pressure to release naturally for 10 minutes
4. Release the remaining pressure with the manual process and uncover the pot
5. Arrange the chicken to a plate and shred the meat, and return to the pot
6. Put the cheese and heavy cream, stir well and leave for 5 minutes before you serve

Stew Beef and Rice

Servings: 4-6 ,Prep + Cooking Time: 30 minutes

Ingredients:
- Thinly sliced carrots – 2
- Cubed potato – 1
- Frozen peas – ½ cup
- Canned beef stock – 28 oz
- Canned crushed tomatoes – 14 oz
- Rinsed canned garbanzo beans – 15 oz
- Ground beef meat – 1 lb
- Frozen peas – ½ cup
- Salt and pepper
- Spicy V8 juice – 12 oz
- Minced clove garlic – 3
- Chopped yellow onion – 1
- White rice – ½ cup
- Canned beef stock – 28 0z

Directions:
1. Give your instant pot prior heating and select SAUTE
2. Put the ground beef and cook, stir for 5 minutes until it is browned
3. Arrange the meat to a bowl, put the onion, celery and the oil and cook for 5 minutes
4. Add the garlic and cook for another 1 minute
5. Put the potatoes, rice beans, stock, spicy juice, salt, pepper, browned beef and carrots, stir thoroughly, press the CANCEL key to stop the SAUTE function
6. Close and lock the lid, select MANUAL and cook at high pressure for 5 minutes
7. Once the timer beeps, make use of a quick release. Carefully unlock the lid
8. Pour the peas to the pot and stir, release carefully and unlock the lid
9. Add the peas to the pot and stir, leave for 5 minutes and serve.

Nutritious Beef Borscht Soup

Servings: 6 ,Prep + Cooking Time: 40 minutes

Ingredients:
- Diced large carrots – 2
- Beef stock – 6 cups
- Thyme – ½ tbsp
- Salt and black pepper
- Ground beef – 2 lbs
- Bay leaf – 1
- Diced garlic cloves – 2
- Peeled and diced beets – 3
- Shredded cabbage – 3 cups
- Diced stalks of celery - 3
- Diced onion – 1

Directions:
1. Give the Instant Pot prior heating by selecting SAUTE
2. Put the ground beef and cook, stir for 5 minutes until it becomes brown
3. Mix in all the remaining ingredients to the Instant Pot
4. Mix evenly, close and lock the lid, select the CANCEL button to stop the SAUTE function
5. Select the MANUAL setting and cook for 15 minutes at a HIGH pressure
6. Once the timer goes off, give room to enable Natural Release for 10 minutes
7. Uncover the pot and leave it for 10 minutes. Serve and enjoy

Beef Barley Soup with Fish Sauce

Servings: 6-8 ,Prep + Cooking Time: 1hr 10 minutes

Ingredients:
- Fish sauce – 1 tbsp
- Chopped onions – 2
- Olive oil – 2 tbsp
- Chicken stock – 8 cups
- Rinsed pearl barley – 1 cup
- Salt and black pepper
- Chopped large carrots – 4
- Beef chuck roast – 2 lbs
- Sliced cloves of garlic – 4
- The chopped stalk of celery – 1

- Chopped large carrots – 4

Directions:
1. Get an Instant Pot and select the SAUTE setting and heat the oil
2. Sprinkle the beef with salt and pepper, add in the salt and brown for 5 minutes turn and brown the other side as well
3. Take off the meat from the pot, put in the carrots, garlic, celery and carrots. Stir and cook for 7 minutes
4. Put the beef back to the pot, add in the bay leaf, chicken stock, pearl barley and fish sauce
5. Close and lock lid, press the CANCEL button to reset the cooking program
6. Press the MANUAL button and set the cooking time to 30 minutes at a HIGH pressure
7. Once the cooking is complete, allow the pressure to Release Naturally for 15 minutes
8. Release the remaining steam manually and uncover the pot
9. Remove the cloves garlic, large vegetables chunks and bay leaf
10. Add salt to give it a suitable taste

Homemade Cabbage and Beef Soup

Servings: 4-6 ,Prep + Cooking Time: 35 minutes

Ingredients:
- Diced onion – 1
- Water – 4 cups
- Salt and black pepper
- Chopped cabbage – 1 head
- Ground beef – 1 lb
- Coconut oil – 2 tbsp
- Undrained, diced can tomatoes – 14 oz
- Minced clove garlic – 1

Directions:
1. Get an Instant Pot and give it prior heating buy selecting SAUTE
2. Put the garlic and onion and SAUTE for 3 minutes
3. Put the beef and cook, stir for 3 minutes until it's lightly brown
4. Slowly pour the water and add the tomatoes, add salt and pepper and stir well
5. Press the CANCEL key to stop the SAUTE function
6. Close the locking lid, select MANUAL and cook at high pressure for 15 minutes
7. Once the timer goes off, use a quick release
8. Add the cabbage, select SAUTE and cook for 5 minutes
9. Serve and enjoy

Tantalizing Egg Roll Soup

Servings: 6 ,Prep + Cooking Time: 50 minutes

Ingredients:
- Onion powder – 1 tsp
- Olive oil – 1 tbsp
- Salt and black pepper
- Chopped head cabbage – ½
- Cubed onion – 1
- Chicken broth – 4 cups
- Soy sauce or coconut aminos – 2/3 cups
- Ground beef – 1 lb
- Garlic powder – 1 tsp
- Shredded carrots – 2 cups
- Ground ginger – 1 tsp

Directions:
1. Get an Instant Pot, add some oil and select SAUTE
2. Put the onion and ground beef, stir on occasional base until all the meat is brown
3. Put the cabbage, garlic, carrots, coconut aminos, ginger, coconut aminos and broth, ensure you stir thoroughly, add salt and pepper and stir
4. Close and lock the lid, press the CANCEL button to stop the SAUTE function
5. Then you can select the soup setting and cook for 25 minutes
6. Once the timer goes off, use a quick release and carefully unlock the lid
7. Leave the soup for 10 minutes and serve

Delicious Pork Shank Soup

Servings: 4-6 ,Prep + Cooking Time: 1hr 40 minutes

Ingredients:

- Water – 4½ cups
- Cut into chunks; carrots – 2
- Sea salt
- Dried jujubes – 2
- Pork shank – 1½ lbs
- Cut into chunks, large green radish – 1
- Thinly sliced, ginger – 1
- Small piece of oragne peel, dry

Directions:

1. Get cold water and soak in the orange peel for 20 minutes
2. Get an Instant Pot and mix in all the ingredients
3. Close and lock the lid, select MANUAL and cook at HIGH pressure for 35 minutes
4. When the cooking is complete, allow the pressure to Release Naturally for 20 minute
5. Release the remaining steam manually, select SAUTE, bring the soup to a boil and cook another 20 minutes
6. Taste for seasoning and enjoy

Yummy Chicken Noodle Soup

Servings: 6 ,Prep + Cooking Time: 30 minutes

Ingredients:

- Oregano – 1 tsp
- Dried thyme – 1 tsp
- Dried basil – 1 tsp
- Chopped spinach – 2 cups
- Salt and black pepper
- Minced cloves garlic – 5
- Butter - 3 tbsp
- Chopped spinach – 2 cups
- Chicken broth or vegetable broth – 8 cups
- Spaghetti noodles – 8 oz
- Skinless and boneless chicken breast – 2 cups
- Diced celery stalks – 3
- Diced large carrots – 2

Directions:

1. Get an Instant Pot and give it a prior heating, once it is hot, put the butter until it melts
2. Put the onion, carrot, celery and a big pinch of salt, stir thoroughly and cook for 5 minutes until it's soft
3. Put in the garlic, thyme, oregano and basil, stir well and cook for an additional 1 minute
4. Put the chicken broth and noodles, close and lock the lid
5. Press the CANCEL button to reset the cooking program
6. Press the MANUAL button and set the cooking time to 4 minutes at a HIGH pressure
7. Once the timer beeps, make a quick release and gently unlock the lid
8. Put the spinach and add salt and pepper
9. Stir thoroughly and mix

Homemade Chicken Barley Soup

Servings: 6 ,Prep + Cooking Time: 35 minutes

Ingredients:

- Bay leaf – 1
- Salt and black pepper
- Rinsed and drained pearl barley – ½ cup
- Diced carrots – 2 cups
- Sliced chicken breast – 2 cups
- Chicken stock – 3 cups
- Water – 2 cups
- Celery – ¾ cup
- Oregano – 1 tbsp
- Diced onion – 1 cup
- Peeled and diced red potatoes – 1 cup

Directions:

1. Get an Instant Pot and add all the ingredients, stir thoroughly
2. Close and lock the lid, select MANUAL and cook at a HIGH pressure for 20 minutes
3. Once the cooking is complete, select CANCEL and let it Naturally for 5 minutes
4. Release other remaining steam using the manual process

Moringa Chicken Soup

Servings: 6-8 ,Prep + Cooking Time: 45 minutes

Ingredients:
- Water – 5 cups
- Minced garlic cloves – 2
- Thumb-size ginger – 1
- Chicken breast – 1½ lbs
- Salt and black pepper
- Chopped tomatoes – 1 cup
- Moringa or Kale leaves – 2 cups
- Chopped onion – 1

Directions:
1. Get an Instant Pot and combine all the ingredients except the Moringa leaves
2. Stir to mix evenly and close the locking lid, press POULTRY button and set the cooking time for 15 minutes
3. Once the timer beeps, let the pressure release Naturally for 15 minutes
4. Release other remaining steam manually and open the lid
5. Put the moringa leaves and stir thoroughly, select SAUTE and cook for 3 minutes
6. Taste the seasoning and add more salt if needed. Serve and enjoy

Chicken and Wild Rice Soup

Servings: 4-6 ,Prep + Cooking Time: 30 minutes

Ingredients:
- Wild Rice – 6 oz
- Red pepper flakes – A pinch
- Half and a half – 1 cup
- Cornstarch mixed with water – 2 tbsp each
- Cubed cream cheese – 4 oz
- Butter – 2 tbsp
- Chopped yellow onion – 1 cup
- Chopped celery – 1 cup
- Dried parsley – 1 tbsp
- Milk – 1 cup
- Chicken stock – 28 oz
- Chopped carrots – 1 cup
- Cubed cream cheese
- Skinless, boneless and chopped chicken breast – 2

Directions:
1. Get an Instant Pot and give it prior heating by selecting SAUTE, once it's hot, add the butter and melt it
2. Add the onion, carrot and celery, stir and cook for 5 minutes
3. Add the rice, red pepper, black pepper, salt and chicken breast and stir well
4. Close and lock the lid, press the CANCEL button to stop the SAUTE function
5. Select the MANUAL setting, set the cooking time for 5 minutes at a HIGH pressure
6. Once the timer beeps, make a quick release and carefully unlock the lid
7. Put the cornstarch and mix with water, stir thoroughly
8. Put cheese, half and half, milk and stir thoroughly, select SAUTE and cook for 3 minutes
9. Serve and Enjoy

Easy Turkey Cabbage Soup

Servings: 4-6 , Prep + Cooking Time: 35 minutes

Ingredients:
- Water – 2 cups
- Chicken broth – 4 cups
- Marinara sauce – 1 jar
- Cauliflower florets – 1 pack
- Minced garlic cloves – 2
- Chopped head cabbage – 1
- Salt and black pepper
- Cubed frozen onion – 1 pack
- Chopped cabbage head – 1
- Ground turkey – 1 lb

Directions:

1. Get an Instant Pot and heat the oil by selecting SAUTE
2. Put the ground turkey and garlic and SAUTE
3. Stir occasionally for 6 minutes until the meat turns brown
4. Arrange the brown turkey to a bowl, press the CANCEL key to stop the SAUTE function
5. Put the marinara sauce, broth, cabbage, cauliflower, water to the top and stir
6. Close and lock the lid, select MANUAL and cook at HIGH pressure for 6 minutes
7. Once the timer beeps, use a Natural Release for 10 minutes and uncover the pot
8. Return the meat to the pot and stir well
9. Add salt and pepper

Smoked Garlic Turkey Soup

Servings: 8 , Prep + Cooking Time: 1hr 20 minutes

Ingredients:

- Pressed clove garlic – 3
- Chopped medium-size onion – 1
- Olive oil – ½ tbsp
- Chopped parsley – ½ cup
- Salt – 1 tsp
- Bay leaves – 2
- Dried black beans – 2 cups
- Water – 6 cups
- Smoked turkey drumstick – 12 oz
- Bay leaves – 2
- Chopped large carrot – 1
- Dried black beans – 2 cups

Directions:

1. Get an Instant Pot and give it prior heating by selecting SAUTE
2. Slowly pour the oil and heat. Add the onion, carrots, parsley and celery to the pot
3. Sauté for 10 minutes until the veggies are softened, put the garlic and sauté for an additional 1 minute
4. Slowly pour the water, put in the beans, pepper, salt and bay leaves, bring to a boil and close the locking lid
5. Press the CANCEL button to reset the cooking program
6. Press the MANUAL button and set the cooking time for 30 minutes at a HIGH pressure
7. Once the cooking is complete, select CANCEL and let it Naturally Release for 10 minutes
8. Release the other remaining steam using the manual process
9. Take off the bay leaves. Transfer the turkey drumstick to a plate
10. Get an immersion blender, blend the soup to your desired texture
11. Return the meat to the pot and stir thoroughly
12. Serve and enjoy

Ultimate Fish Soup

Servings: 4-6 , Prep + Cooking Time: 20 minutes

Ingredients:

- Chopped carrot – 1
- Heavy cream -2 cups
- Chopped bacon – 1 cup
- Boneless, skinless and cubed white fish fillets – 1 lb
- Chicken Stock – 4 cups

Directions:

1. Get an Instant Pot and combine the carrot, fish, bacon and stock
2. Stir well and close the locking lid, select MANUAL and cook for 5 minutes at a high pressure
3. Once the timer goes off, use a quick release and carefully open the lid
4. Put the heavy cream and stir, select SAUTE and cook the soup for 3 minutes
5. Serve and enjoy

Tasty Meatball Soup

Servings: 4-6 , Prep + Cooking Time: 35 minutes

Ingredients:

- Oregano – 1 tbsp
- Minced garlic cloves – 2
- Salt and ground black pepper
- Chopped carrots – 1 cup finely
- Cumin – ½ tsp
- Prepared meatballs – 1 package
- Olive Oil – 1 tbsp
- Beaten egg – 1
- Chopped green bell pepper – 1
- Chopped onion – 1
- Diced tomatoes – 1

Directions:

1. Get an Instant Pot and select SAUTE to heat the oil, put the onions and garlic and SAUTE for 2 minutes
2. Put the meatballs for 5 minutes until the meat has browned all over
3. Put the carrots, bell pepper, potatoes, oregano, tomatoes, salt and black pepper
4. Close and lock the lid, press the CANCEL button to stop the SAUTE
5. Select the SOUP setting and set the cooking time for 15 minutes at a high pressure
6. Once the timer beeps, use a quick release and carefully unlock the lid
7. Return to SAUTE, pour them and cook for 4 minutes
8. Serve and enjoy

Super Toscana Soup

Servings: 4-6 , Prep + Cooking Time: 40 minutes

Ingredients:

- Diced onion – 1
- Water – ¼ cup
- Chopped kale – 2 cups
- Chopped Italian sausage – 1 lb
- Salt and black pepper
- Heavy cream – ¾ cup
- Chicken broth – 6 cups
- Chicken broth – 6 cups
- Unpeeled and thickly sliced, large russet potatoes – 3
- Olive oil – 2 tbsp

Directions:

1. Get an Instant Pot and put it in a SAUTE mode
2. Put the onion, Italian sausage, and garlic, stir and SAUTE for 5 minutes until the sausages have turned light brown
3. Put the water, potatoes and chicken broth and stir, add salt and pepper
4. Close and lock the lid, select MANUAL and cook at high pressure for 20 minutes
5. Once the timer goes off, use a quick release and carefully open the lid
6. Set your Instant Pot on SAUTE mode, add kale and heavy cream and cook for 4 minutes
7. Press the CANCEL key and let it sit for 5 minutes
8. Serve and Enjoy

Delicious Ham and Potato Soup

Servings: 4-6 , Prep + Cooking Time: 40 minutes

Ingredients:

- Diced onion – 1
- Salt and black pepper
- Butter – 2 tbsp
- Cayenne pepper – A dash
- Grated cheddar cheese – ½ cup
- Cut into small chunks, Yukon Gold potatoes – 2 lbs
- Fried bacon bits – 2 tbsp
- Minced cloves garlic – 8
- Diced cooked ham – 1 cup
- Chicken broth – 4 cups

Directions:

1. Get an Instant Pot and give it a prior heating, once it's hot, add the butter and melt it
2. Put the onion and garlic and SAUTE for 2 minutes
3. Put the potatoes and SAUTE for 3 minutes
4. Put the cayenne pepper, cheese and cooked ham, pour in the broth and stir well
5. Add Salt and Pepper, press the CANCEL button to reset the cooking program
6. Press the MANUAL button and set the cooking time for 25 minutes at a high pressure
7. Once the timer goes off, use a quick release, and carefully unlock the lid
8. Put bacon bits on top. Serve and enjoy

Simple Sweet Potato Soup

Servings: 4 , Prep + Cooking Time: 45 minutes

Ingredients:

- Thyme – ½ Tsp
- Butter – 2 tbsp
- Salt and black pepper
- Peeled and diced – 6 carrots
- Chopped whole onion – 1
- Chopped cloves garlic – 4
- Peeled and diced large red sweet tomatoes – 4
- Ground sage – ½ Tsp
- Quart vegetarian broth – 1

Directions:

1. Get an Instant Pot and give it prior heating by selecting SAUTE, add the butter and melt it
2. Put the garlic, onion, carrots and SAUTE for 8 minutes until the onion is translucent
3. Put the sweet potatoes, sage, broth and thyme, add salt and pepper, stir well, close and lock the lid, press the CANCEL button to stop the SAUTE function
4. Select the MANUAL setting and set the cooking time to for 20 minutes at a HIGH pressure
5. Once the timer goes off, use a quick release
6. Using an immersion blender, blend the soup to your desired texture
7. Enjoy and serve

Healthy Bean and Chicken Soup

Servings: 6 , Prep + Cooking Time: 1hr 5 minutes

Ingredients:

- Chopped Jalapeno Pepper – 1
- Water – 7 cups
- Salsa – 4 tbsp
- White Sliced onion – 1
- Soy sauce – 1 tsp
- Ground black pepper – 1 tsp
- Cannellini beans – 1 cup
- Chopped fresh dill – 1 cup
- Chicken fillet – 1 lb
- Kosher salt – 2 tbsp
- Cup cream – 1/3
- Red bell pepper – 1

Directions:

1. Get an Instant Pot and add the Cannellini beans and chicken, pour in the water and stir thoroughly
2. Close and lock the lid, select Manual and cook at high pressure for 30 minutes
3. Once the timer beeps, use a quick release, carefully unlock the lid
4. Put in the onion, bell pepper, onion, dill and jalapeno pepper
5. Close and lock the lid, select the SOUP setting and cook for 15 minutes
6. Once the timer goes off, make a quick release and carefully open the lid
7. Put the cream, salsa, salt, black pepper and soy sauce
8. Stir thoroughly, close the lid and let the soup sit for 10 minutes

Basic Bean and Ham Soup

Servings: 6-8 , Prep + Cooking Time: 1hr 10 minutes

Ingredients:

- Diced onion – 1
- Rinsed white beans – 1 lb
- Chilli powder – 1 tsp
- Leftover ham bone with meat – 1
- Juiced lemon – 1
- Minced garlic cloves -1
- Diced tomatoes – 1 can
- Chicken broth – 8 cups

Directions:

1. Get an Instant and mix in all the ingredients and stir
2. Close and lock the lid, select the BEAN/CHILI setting and set the cooking time for 50 minutes
3. Once the timer beeps, use a quick release, leave the soup for 10 minutes and carefully unlock the lid
4. Serve and enjoy

Spicy Black Beans Soup

Servings: 6 , Prep + Cooking Time: 1hr 10 minutes

Ingredients:

- Chopped onion – 1
- Olive oil – 2 tbsp
- Ground cumin – 1 tsp
- Water – 4 cups
- Sherry vinegar – 2 tbsp
- Salt and black pepper
- Red – ½ cup
- Chopped red bell pepper – 1
- Bay leaf- 1
- Ground oregano – 2 tbsp
- Dried black beans - - 1 lb
- Water – 4 cups

Directions:

1. Get an Instant Pot and give prior heating by selecting SAUTE
2. Heat the oil, add garlic and onion and SAUTE for 2 minutes
3. Put the oregano, bay leaf, bell pepper, cumin, stir and SAUTE for 1 minute
4. Add the beans, wine, water, vinegar, salt and pepper
5. Close and lock the lid, press CANCEL button to stop the SAUTE function
6. Press BEAN/CHILI setting and set the cooking time for 45 minutes
7. Once the timer beeps, use a quick release
8. Enjoy and serve

Sweet Potato, Orange and Chickpea Soup

Servings: 6 , Prep + Cooking Time: 45 minutes

Ingredients:

- Orange juice – 8 oz
- Salt and black pepper
- Olive oil – ½ tbsp
- Diced sweet potatoes 1 lb
- Vegetable broth – 4 cups
- Sliced onions – 2
- Canned chicken peas – 30 oz

Directions:

1. Get an Instant Pot and select the SAUTE button, add the onion and sauté for 5 minutes
2. Put the chickpeas, broth, potatoes and orange juice. Stir well
3. Select the CANCEL key to stopping the SAUTE function
4. Close and lock the lid, press MANUAL and cook for 5 minutes at a high pressure
5. Once the cooking is done, allow the pressure to release Naturally for 10 minutes
6. Release other remaining steam manually and uncover the pot
7. Add the salt and pepper to taste and enjoy

Navy Bean, Bacon and Spinach Soup

Servings: 6 , Prep + Cooking Time: 50 minutes

Ingredients:
- Bay leaves – 2
- Baby spinach – 3 cups
- Tomato paste – 2 tbsp
- Salt and black pepper
- Large Chopped carrots – 1
- Baby spinach – 3 cups
- Water – 1 cup
- Sprig fresh rosemary – 1
- Rinsed and drained navy beans – 3 cans
- Chopped bacon – 4 slices
- Chopped large Celery stalk – 1
- Chicken broth – 4 cups

Directions:
1. Mix 1 can of beans with a cup of water, get an immersion blender and blend the mixture
2. Get your Instant Pot and put it on SAUTE mode, put the and sauté until it crisp
3. Arrange the bacon to a plate lined with a paper towel
4. Add the onion, celery, carrot and SAUTE for 5 minutes until it softened
5. Put the tomato paste and stir, put the bay leaves, 2 cans beans, pureed beans, broth and rosemary
6. Close and lock the lid, press the CANCEL key to stop the SAUTE function
7. Once the cooking is complete, allow the pressure to Release Naturally for 10 minutes
8. Remove the bay leaves and rosemary, add the spinach season with salt and pepper
9. Allow the dish to sit for 5 minutes and serve

Slow-Cooker Multi-Bean Soup

Servings: 8-10 , Prep + Cooking Time: 55 minutes

Ingredients:
- Chopped stalks celery – 2
- Vegetable stock – 8 cups
- Minced garlic cloves – 3
- Sprigs fresh thyme – 3
- Chopped onion – 1
- Salt and black pepper
- Olive oil – 1 tbsp
- Crushed tomatoes – 1 can
- 15-bean soup blend – 1 bag
- Peeled and chopped carrots – 2
- Chopped red bell – pepper
- Olive oil – 1 tbsp

Directions:
1. Get an Instant Pot and put on a SAUTE mode, add the oil and heat it up
2. Put the onion and garlic, SAUTE for 6 minutes
3. Put the beans, thyme, tomatoes, bay leaf and stock. Stir until it's evenly combined
4. Add salt and pepper, close and lock the lid, press the CANCEL button to reset the cooking program
5. Press the MANUAL button and set the cooking time for 30 minutes at a HiGH pressure
6. Once the cooking is done, select CANCEL and let it Naturally Release for 10 minutes
7. Release any remaining steam manually and uncover the pot
8. Stir and serve

Tasty Lentil Serve

Servings: 6 , Prep + Cooking Time: 35 minutes

Ingredients:
- Minced garlic cloves – 3
- Olive oil – 2 tbsp
- Smoked paprika – 1½ tsp
- Water – 8 cups
- Salt and black pepper
- Rinsed brown lentils – 1 cup
- Chopped rainbow chard or spinach – 1 bunch
- Smoked Paprika – 1½ tsp
- Red bliss Yukon gold potatoes – 1
- Diced celery stalks – 2

- Chopped medium onion – 1
- Cumin – ½ tsp
- Rinsed red lentils – 1 cup

Directions:
1. Get an Instant Pot and select SAUTE to heat the oil
2. Put in the garlic, onion, celery, cumin, paprika, potatoes and carrot, cook for 5 minutes
3. Add the lentils and water, stir well and close and close the lid
4. Press the CANCEL button to stop the SAUTE function, select MANUAL setting and set the cooking time for 3 minutes at a HIGH pressure
5. Once a timer beeps, use a NATURAL release for 10 minutes and uncover the pot
6. Put the chard and sprinkle salt and pepper, leave the soup for 5 minutes and stir

Lentil Soup with Sweet Potato and Spinach

Servings: 6 , Prep + Cooking Time: 40 minutes

Ingredients:
- Paprika – 1 tsp
- Green lentils – 1 cup
- Water – 1 cup
- Ground cumin – 1 tsp
- Minced cloves – garlic
- Diced large celery stalk – 1
- Peeled sweet potato – ¾ lb
- Petite diced tomatoes – 1 can
- Olive oil – 2 Tsp
- Red pepper flakes – ½ tsp
- Spinach leaves – 4 oz
- Vegetable broth – 3½ cups
- Salt and black pepper
- Chopped yellow onion – ½

Directions:

1. Get an Instant Pot, select SAUTE and heat the oil
2. Put the onion, celery and SAUTE for 5 minutes until it's soft
3. Put the Paprika, red pepper flakes and paprika and SAUTE for 1 minute
4. Add the sweet potatoes, tomatoes, broth, lentil and water, stir thoroughly
5. Add salt and pepper, select the CANCEL key to stopping the SAUTE function
6. Close and lock the lid, select MANUAL and cook for 12 minutes at a high pressure
7. Once the timer goes off, use a quick release and carefully unlock the lid
8. Put the spinach and stir

Delicious Split pea soup

Servings: 6 , Prep + Cooking Time: 55 minutes

Ingredients:
- Minced garlic cloves – 2
- Bay leaf – 1
- Salt and fresh pepper
- Sliced stalks celery – 3
- Olive oil – 2 tbsp
- Diced yellow onion – 1
- Vegetable broth – 6 cups
- Split peas – 1 lb
- Smoked paprika – ½ tbsp
- Diced yellow onion – 1
- Sliced carrots – 3

Directions:

1. Get an Instant Pot and select the SAUTE function to heat the oil
2. Put the onion, celery, carrot, garlic and stir for 6 minutes until it's evenly combined
3. Add the salt and pepper and lock the lid
4. Select the CANCEL button to reset the cooking program
5. Press the MANUAL button and set the cooking time for 15 minutes at a HIGH pressure
6. Once the cooking is complete, use a Natural Release for 10 minutes and open the lid
7. Add salt, serve and enjoy

Vegetarian Green Split Pea Soup

Servings: 6 , Prep + Cooking Time: 50 minutes

Ingredients:

- Chopped onion – 1 cup
- Salt and black pepper
- Olive oil – 1 tbsp
- Chopped celery – 1 cup
- Chopped carrots – 1 cup
- Beef broths – 6 cups
- Minced clove garlic – 1
- Chopped leftover hem – 1 cup
- Split green peas – 1 lb

Directions:

1. Get an Instant Pot by selecting SAUTE to the heat
2. Put the onion, carrot, garlic and celery, stir and SAUTE for 6 minutes
3. Add salt and pepper. Close and lock the lid, Select the CANCEL button and stop the SAUTE function
4. Press the BEAN and leave it on the default
5. Once the timer goes off, allow the pressure to release Naturally for 10 minutes
6. Release remaining steam using a manual process

Turkish Red Lentil Soup

Servings: 4 , Prep + Cooking Time: 40 minutes

Ingredients:

- Chopped onion – 1
- Chopped carrot – 1
- Red lentils – 1 cup
- Coriander – ½ Tsp
- Salt
- Celery – ½ cup
- Rice – 1 tbsp
- Paprika – ½ tsp
- Minced garlic cloves – 3
- Chopped potato – 1
- Olive oil – 3 Tsp
- Coriander – ½ Tsp

Directions:

1. Get an Instant Pot and select the SAUTE setting to the oil
2. Put the onion. Garlic and sauté for 3 minutes
3. Put the rice and lentils and stir well to combine
4. Put the celery, paprika, potato, carrot, water and coriander, stir well
5. Close and lock the lid, select the CANCEL button to reset the cooking program
6. Select MANUAL button and cook for 10 minutes at a high pressure
7. Once the timer beeps, allow it to release naturally for 5 minutes
8. Add salt and stir, allow the mixture to sit for 10 minutes

Potato Broccoli and Cheese Soup

Servings: 6 , Prep + Cooking Time: 40 minutes

Ingredients:

- Crushed cloves garlic – 2
- Half and a half – 1 cup
- Butter – 2 tbsp
- Shredded cheddar cheese – 1 cup
- Salt and black pepper
- Broken into large florets, medium-sized broccoli head – 1
- Chopped green onion
- Yukon gold potatoes – 2 lbs
- Vegetable broths – 4 cups

Directions:

1. Get an instant pot and give it prior heating by selecting SAUTE, once it gets hot, add the butter to melt, put the garlic and cook for 3 minutes until it gets brown
2. Put the broccoli, broth, potato, pepper and salt and stir thoroughly
3. Select the CANCEL button to stop the SAUTE function
4. Close and lock the lid, press MANUAL and cook for 5 minutes at a high pressure

5. Once the timer goes off, allow the pressure to release Naturally for 10 minutes
6. Release the remaining steam manually, open the lid
7. Put the half and half and the ½ cup cheese

8. Make use of an immersion blender and blend until it's smooth
9. Add more seasoning if needed, serve warm and top with cheese and green onion

Classic Minestrone Soup

Servings: 6 , Prep + Cooking Time: 40 minutes

Ingredients:
- Minced garlic cloves – 3
- Dried basil – 1 tsp
- Dried oregano – 1 tsp
- Bay leaf – 1
- Salt and black pepper
- Diced celery stalks – 2
- Elbow pasta – 1 cup
- Vegetable broths – 4 cups
- Diced tomatoes – 28 oz can
- Chopped fresh spinach – ½ cup
- Cannellini beans – 15 oz
- Olive oil – 2 tbsp
- Diced large carrots – 1
- Diced large onion – 1

Directions:
1. Get an Instant Pot and preheat by selecting SAUTE
2. Put the garlic, onion, carrot and celery, Stir and SAUTE for 6 minutes
3. Put the spinach, broth, bay leaf, tomatoes and pasta, stir to combine evenly
4. Select the CANCEL key to stopping the SAUTE function
5. Close and lock the lid, press MANUAL and cook at HIGH pressure for 6 minutes
6. Once the timer beeps, allow it to sit for 2 minutes and use a quick release
7. Carefully unlock the lid, put the kidney beans and stir

Homemade Tomato and Basil Soup

Servings: 8 , Prep + Cooking Time: 20 minutes

Ingredients:
- Chopped fresh basil leaves – ½ cup
- Whole Roma tomatoes – 2 cans
- Heavy cream – ¾ cup
- salt and black pepper
- chopped fresh basil leaves – ½ cup

Directions:
1. Get an Instant Pot and mix in all the Ingredients excluding the heavy cream
2. Close and lock the lid, press MANUAL and cook it for 8 minutes at a HIGH pressure
3. Once the timer beeps, use a quick release
4. Carefully unlock the lid, press the SAUTE setting on the Instant Pot
5. Put the heavy cream and stir, cook for 2 minutes
6. Select the CANCEL key to stopping the SAUTE function

Easy Beet Soup

Servings: 4 , Prep + Cooking Time: 60 minutes

Ingredients:
- Chopped onion- 1
- Chopped fresh basil leaves – ¼ cup
- Chicken broth – 4 cups
- Salt and black pepper
- Chopped and peeled beets – ¾ lb

Directions:
1. Get an Instant Pot and mix in all the ingredients, mix evenly
2. Close and lock the lid, select SOUP setting and cook for 35 minutes
3. Once the timer goes off, allow the pressure to Release Naturally for 1o minutes
4. Release remaining steam manually and open the lid
5. Get an immersion blender, blend until the soup is smooth
6. Taste for salt and add seasoning

Creamy Pomodoro Soup

Servings: 8 , Prep + Cooking Time: 30 minutes

Ingredients:
- Vegetable broth – 3½ cups
- Vegan butter – 3 tbsp
- Diced onion – 1
- Coconut cream - 1 cup
- Peeled and quartered tomatoes – 3 lbs

Directions:
1. Get an Instant Pot and give prior heating by selecting SAUTE
2. Put the butter and melt it, put the onion and sauté for 5 minutes
3. Add the tomatoes and sauté for 3 minutes
4. Add in the broth, stir and close the lock the lid
5. Select the CANCEL button to reset the cooking program
6. Select the SOUP button and set the cooking time for 6 minutes
7. Once the timer beeps, make a quick release
8. Add the coconut cream and stir, press the SAUTE again and cook for 2 minutes
9. Using an immersion blender, blend the soup to your desired texture
10. Serve and enjoy

Tasty Cauliflower Soup

Servings: 4 , Prep + Cooking Time: 25 minutes

Ingredients:
- Chopped large onion
- Salt and ground black pepper
- Chicken broth – 3 cups
- Chopped cauliflower – 1 medium
- Butter – 1 tbsp

Directions:
1. Get an Instant Pot by selecting SAUTE, once it's hot, add the butter and melt it
2. Put the onion and SAUTE for 5 minutes until softened
3. Put the cauliflower, pepper, broth and salt, mix well and close the lid
4. Select the CANCEL button and stop the SAUTE function
5. Select the manual setting and cook for 5 minutes at a HIGH pressure
6. Once the timer goes off, use a quick release
7. Get an immersion blender, blend the soup to your desired texture
8. Serve and enjoy

Easy Broccoli Cheddar Cheese

Servings: 4 , Prep + Cooking Time: 25 minutes

Ingredients:
- Chicken broth – 4 cups
- Heavy cream – ¼ cups
- Chopped broccoli – 6 cups
- Chopped carrots – 2
- Olive oil - 1 tbsp
- Grated cheddar cheese – 1½ cups
- Chopped onion – ½
- Garlic salt – ½ tsp

Directions:
1. Get an Instant Pot and give prior heating by selecting SAUTE, put the oil and heat
2. Put the onion and sauté for 4 minutes until translucent
3. Put the broccoli and carrots and sauté for 2 minutes
4. Pour in the broth, press CANCEL key to stop the SAUTE function
5. Close and lock the lid, press MANUAL and cook for 5 minutes at a HIGH pressure
6. Once the timer beeps, use a quick release. Carefully unlock the lid
7. Allow the dish chill for a while, get an immersion blender, and blend to soup to your desired texture
8. Add salt, cheese and heavy cream, stir well for 2 minutes until the cheese melts
9. Serve and enjoy

Classic Garden Harvest Soup

Servings: 8 , Prep + Cooking Time: 30 minutes

Ingredients:

- Thyme – 1 tsp
- Bone broth – 6 cups
- Parsley – 1 tsp
- Salt and black pepper
- Crushed tomatoes – 1 can
- Rosemary – 1 tsp
- Packaged vegetable – 10 cups
- Basil – 1 tsp

Directions:

1. Get an Instant Pot and mix in all the ingredients
2. Close and lock the lid, select MANUAL and cook for 10 minutes at a HIGH pressure
3. Once the cooking is complete, select CANCEL and let it Naturally Release for 10 minutes
4. Release the remaining steam manually and uncover the pot, taste for seasoning
5. Serve and enjoy

Cheesy Veggie Soup

Servings: 6 , Prep + Cooking Time: 30 minutes

Ingredients:

- Cheese sauce – 1 jar
- Shredded mozzarella cheese
- Frozen vegetables – 1 package
- Salt and black pepper
- Cheese sauce – 1 jar

Directions:

1. Get an Instant Pot and add the vegetables, add in the cheese sauce and mushroom sauce, ensure you stir well, add salt and pepper and stir
2. Top with Mozzarella cheese, close and lock the lid
3. Select MANUAL and cook for 7 minutes at a HIGH pressure
4. When the timer goes off, allow to Naturally Release for 10 minutes
5. Release other remaining pressure manually
6. Uncover the pot and serve

Pumpkin Soup with Coconut Milk

Servings: 4 , Prep + Cooking Time: 35 minutes

Ingredients:

- Chicken stock – 1½ cup
- Bay leaves – 2
- Chopped brown onion – ½
- Curry powder – a pinch
- Coconut milk – 1 cup
- Butter ½ tbsp
- Diced red potatoes or radishes – ½
- Chunks butternut pumpkin – ½
- Salt and black pepper
- Peeled, cored and grated apple – ½

Directions:

1. Get an Instant Pot and select SAUTE, add the butter to melt
2. Put the onion, potato, pumpkin and curry powder, stir and SAUTE for 9 minutes until the onion is browned
3. Put the apple, salt, bay leaves and black pepper, close and lock the lid
4. Select the CANCEL button to reset the cooking program
5. Select the MANUAL button and set the cooking time for 5 minutes at a HIGH pressure
6. Once the cooking is done, select CANCEL and use a Natural Release for 10 minutes
7. Take off the bay leaves, add milk and stir thoroughly
8. Get an immersion blender, blend the soup until it suits your desired taste
9. Add seasoning

Rich and Simple French Onion Soup

Servings: 6 , Prep + Cooking Time: 40 minutes

Ingredients:
- Butter – 6 tbsp
- Bay leaf – 1
- Toasted slices bread – 8
- Chopped onion – 3 lbs
- Dry sherry - ½ cup
- Apple cider vinegar – 1 tsp
- Fish sauce – 1 tsp
- Sprigs thyme – 2
- Chives for garnish – 1 tbsp
- Chicken stock – 3 cups
- Grated cheese – 1 lb
- Salt and ground black pepper

Directions:
1. Give your Instant Pot prior heating by selecting SAUTE, once it's hot, add the butter and melt it
2. Put the onion and SAUTE for until caramelized, stirring occasionally
3. Put the vinegar, dry sherry, cheese, bay leaf, fish sauce and stock
4. Add salt and pepper and stir, put the bread slices on top
5. Select CANCEL key to stopping the SAUTE function
6. Close and lock the lid, select MANUAL and cook at a HIGH pressure for 10 minutes
7. Once the cooking is done, allow the pressure to release Naturally for 10 minutes
8. Release the remaining steam manually, uncover the pot and remove the sprigs thyme
9. Top with chives and serve

Curried Butternut Squash Soup

Servings: 4 , Prep + Cooking Time: 50 minutes

Ingredients:
- Minced clove garlic – 2
- Coconut milk – ½ cup
- Water – 3 cups
- Chopped large onion – 1
- Olive oil – 1 tsp
- Butternut squash – 1
- Salt – 1½ tsp
- Curry powder – 1 tbsp

Directions:
1. Get an Instant Pot and give prior heating by selecting SAUTE
2. Put the oil and heat, put the onion and SAUTE for 5 minutes until it softened, put the garlic and cook for 1 minute
3. Select the CANCEL button and stop the SAUTE function
4. Pour in the water and add the squash, sprinkle with salt and curry powder and stir well, press SOUP setting and cook for 30 minutes
5. Once the timer beeps, make a quick release, carefully unlock the lid
6. Get an immersion blender, and blend the soup to your desired texture
7. Add in the coconut milk and mix well
8. Serve with pumpkin seeds and dried cranberries

Miso Soup with Tofu and Carrots

Servings: 4 , Prep + Cooking Time: 20 minutes

Ingredients:
- Tamari sauce – 1 tbsp
- Salt to taste
- Chopped celery stalks – 2
- Miso paste – 2 tbsp
- Cubed silken tofu – 1 cup
- Water – 4 cups
- Chopped carrot – 1
- Chopped carrot – 1

Directions:
1. Get an Instant Pot and add in all the ingredients except miso and salt

2. Close and lock the lid, select the POULTRY setting and cook for 7 minutes
3. Once the timer goes off, use a quick release, carefully open the lid

4. Whisk the miso soup together with some soup, add the mixture in the soup and stir
5. Add salt and serve

Easy Keto Low-Carb Soup

Servings: 6 , Prep + Cooking Time: 35 minutes

Ingredients:
- Onion powder – 1 tbsp
- Half and a half- 1 cup
- Diced large yellow onion – 1
- Dijon mustard – 1 tbsp
- Chicken stock – 32 oz
- Olive oil - 1tbsp
- Chopped green bell pepper
- Coarsely chopped cauliflower – 1
- Hot pepper sauce – 4 dashes
- Diced cooked turkey bacon – 6 slices
- Olive oil – 1 tbsp
- Shredded cheddar cheese – 2 cups
- Salt and ground black pepper

Directions:
1. Get an Instant Pot and select SAUTE to heat the oil
2. Put the garlic and onion and select SAUTE for 4 minutes
3. Put the onion powder, stock, bell pepper and cauliflower, add salt and pepper and stir well
4. Close and lock the lid, select the CANCEL button to stop the SAUTE function
5. Select the SOUP setting and cook for 15 minutes once the timer beeps, allow a quick release
6. Wait for 5 minutes and carefully unlock the lid
7. Put the Dijon mustard, turkey bacon, half and half, hot sauce and cheddar cheese
8. Stir thoroughly, then select SAUTE and cook the soup for 5 minutes
9. Serve and enjoy

Corn Chowder Recipe

Servings: 4 , Prep + Cooking Time: 30 minutes

Ingredients:
- Chopped onion – 1
- Butter – 3 tbsp
- Diced red bell pepper - 1 green
- Corn kernels – 4 cups
- Cubed potatoes – 3
- Flour 1 tbsp mixed with milk 1 cup
- Diced green bell pepper – 1
- Salt and black pepper
- Cubed potatoes – 3
- Chicken broth – 4 cups

Directions:
1. Get an Instant Pot and give it prior heating by selecting SAUTE, add the oil and heat
2. Put the onion and cook for 3 minutes until fragrant
3. Put the potatoes, bell peppers and corn kernels, sprinkle salt and pepper
4. Add the chicken broth and stir, close and lock the lid
5. Select the CANCEL button to reset the cooking program
6. Select the MANUAL button and cook for 6 minutes at a high pressure
7. Once the timer beeps, make a quick release, carefully unlock the lid
8. Whisk together the flour and milk, press SAUTE and pour the mixture in the pot
9. Put the butter and cook for 3 minutes
10. String occasionally and cook until chowder has thickened

Salted Italian Potatoes

Servings: 2, Prep + Cook time: 30 minutes

Ingredients:

- Potatoes – 4 pieces (washed and peeled)
- Water – enough to cover the potatoes on the pot
- Italian Seasoning – 1 tbsp.
- Chives – 1 cup
- Butter or bacon fat – 1 tbsp.
- Seasoning – salt and pepper to taste

Directions:

1. Put the potatoes in the Instant Pot then pour enough water to cover the potatoes and securely close the lid.
2. Set to manual and high pressure then cook the potatoes for 10 minutes. After cooking the potatoes, press cancel. Have the Instant Pot naturally release for 10 minutes then open up the pot and transfer the potatoes in a bowl.
3. Mash the potatoes using a fork going back to the Instant Pot, press Sauté and put your butter or bacon fat.
4. When the pot is already heated by the butter or bacon fat, return the potatoes on the pot then sprinkle the Italian seasoning, pepper, and salt.
5. Securely close the lid then press the manual setting and let the potatoes cook at high pressure for 1 minute. After cooking the potatoes, press quick release. Open up the lid and gently stir the mashed potatoes then top up with chives and serve hot.

Spiced Sweet Potato Hash

Servings: 4, Prep + Cook time: 20 minutes

Ingredients:

- Garlic – 2 cloves, minced
- Medium sized onions – 2 pieces chopped
- Large potato – diced into ½ inch
- Large sweet potato – diced into 1 inch
- Olive oil – 2 tbsp.
- Black pepper – ½ tsp.
- Cumin – 1 ½ tsp.
- Water – 1 cup
- Cayenne pepper – ¼ tsp.
- Bell peppers – 4 pieces chopped
- Paprika – 1 ½ tsp.
- Kosher salt – 1 tsp.

Directions:

1. Grab your Instant Pot and put all the following Ingredients: garlic, potato, sweet potato, oil, bell pepper, and onion. Sprinkle with cayenne pepper, cumin, paprika, pepper, and salt.
2. Pour the water and then close the lid tightly then press the manual setting and for 1 minute, cook at high pressure. After cooking, press the quick release and gently open up the lid. Press sauté and cook the potato mixture for 7 minutes.
3. When the potatoes already turned brown, press cancel.
4. Serve hot and enjoy!

Salted Baked Potatoes

Servings: 8, Prep + Cook time: 30 minutes

Ingredients:

- Potatoes – 5 lbs. peeled and cut into half
- Seasoning – salt to taste
- Water – 1 ½ cup

Directions:

1. Set up your Instant Pot by putting the steamer basket inside then add the water. Put the potatoes in the basket and close the lid tightly.
2. Press the manual setting and cook the potatoes for 10 minutes at high pressure. After cooking the potatoes, let your Instant Pot naturally release for 15 minutes.
3. Gently open up the lid then sprinkle salt on top of the potatoes.
4. Serve hot.

Cheesy Potato Hash

Servings: 4 - 6, **Prep + Cook time:** 25 minutes

Ingredients:

- Medium sized potato – 5 pieces, peeled and chopped
- Eggs – 5 pieces, whisked
- Cheddar cheese – 1 cup, shredded
- Ham – 1 cup, chopped
- Water – ¼ cup
- Seasoning – salt and pepper to taste
- Olive oil – 1 tbsp.

Directions:

1. On your Instant Pot, press sauté and heat up the olive oil. Place potatoes and sauté for 3-4 minutes then wait for the potatoes to turn brown before adding the cheese, ham, eggs, salt, and pepper.
2. Close the lid tightly then select cancel and press the manual setting.
3. For 5 minutes cook the potatoes at high pressure. After cooking, press cancel and quick release then gently open up the lid.
4. Serve the potatoes hot.

Pierced Baked Potatoes

Servings: 4 – 6, **Prep + Cook time:** 25 minutes

Ingredients:

- Medium sized Russet potatoes –8 pieces
- Ground black pepper – ½ tsp.
- Kosher salt – ½ tsp.
- Olive oil – 2 tbsp.
- Water – 1 cup
- Butter (Optional)

Directions:

1. Wash the potatoes and let it dry. Put holes in the middle of each potatoes using a fork.
2. Mix the salt, pepper, and oil inside a separate bowl. Place the potatoes in the bowl and make sure the potatoes are well coated by the salt, pepper, and oil mixture.
3. Prepare your Instant Pot by placing the steam rack inside and adding the water then put the potatoes on the steam rack.
4. Close the lid tightly then press manual setting and for 10 minutes cook the potatoes at high pressure.
5. After cooking the potatoes, press quick release and gently open up the lid after that place the cooked potatoes in a serving plate or bowl.
6. Serve with butter if you want.

Crunchy Potatoes

Servings: 4, **Prep + Cook time:** 50 minutes

Ingredients:

- Butter – 2 tbsp.
- Olive oil – 2 tbsp.
- Sea salt – 1 tsp.
- Ground black pepper – 1 tsp.
- Water – ½ cup
- Yukon gold potatoes – 1 ½ lb. cut in half

Directions:

1. Press sauté on your Instant Pot and heat the olive oil. Add the butter in the Instant Pot and let it melt then place the potatoes in the pot and sauté for 10 minutes.
2. When the halves turned golden, sprinkle with salt and pepper. Add the water and securely close the lid. Select cancel then press manual setting.
3. Cook the potatoes at high pressure for 6 minutes. Once cooking is finished, press cancel again then release the steam naturally from the pot for 20 minutes.
4. Gently open up the lid.
5. Serve hot.

Organic Roasted Potatoes

Servings: 4, **Prep + Cook time:** 30 minutes

Ingredients:

- Small sized Yukon or red potatoes – 2 lbs.
- Dried marjoram – ½ Tsp.
- Dried oregano – ½ tsp.
- Dried rosemary – ¼ Tsp.
- Dried thyme- ½ tsp.
- Ground black pepper – ½ tsp.
- Chicken broth – ½ cup
- Sea salt – 1tsp.
- Garlic powder – ½ tsp.

Directions:

1. Wash the potatoes and let it dry then press sauté on the Instant Pot then add the oil to heat.
2. Sauté the potatoes on the Instant Pot for 7 minutes after that set aside the potatoes when they already turned light brown.
3. In a separate bowl, mix the marjoram, garlic powder, thyme, rosemary, oregano, salt, and pepper, add this mixture on the Instant Pot and mix well.
4. Add the water to the Instant Pot and tightly close the lid. Select cancel to end sautéing the potatoes.
5. Press manual and for 7 minutes cook the potatoes at high pressure. After cooking the potatoes, press quick release and then gently open up the lid.
6. Serve hot and enjoy!

Creamy Mashed Potatoes

Servings: 4 – 6, **Prep+ Cook time:** 35 minutes

Ingredients:

- Potatoes – 2 lbs. peeled and quartered
- Milk – 1 cup
- Water – 1 cup
- Butter 3 tbsp.
- Seasoning – salt and pepper to taste

Directions:

1. Grab your Instant Pot then add the water. Place the steamer basket inside the pot while place the potatoes in the steamer basket.
2. Close the lid of the pot. Press manual on the Instant Pot and for 15 minutes cook the potatoes at high pressure. After cooking the potatoes, let the steam naturally release from the pot for 15 minutes.
3. Gently open up the lid then place the potatoes in a bowl. Pour down the water and milk.
4. Mash the potato until it reaches a creamy texture then sprinkle with salt and pepper.
5. Serve and enjoy!

Buttered Mashed Potatoes with Parsnips

Servings: 4 – 6, **Prep + Cook time:** 20 minutes

Ingredients:

- Yukon gold potatoes – 2 lbs. peeled and cubed
- Water – 2 cups
- Sea salt – 1 tsp.
- Ground black pepper – 1 tsp.
- Parsnips – ¾ lb. sliced into 1 inch thick
- Butter – 2 tbsp. melted
- Mixed milk and cream – 5 tbsp.

Directions:

1. Add the water in the Instant Pot. Place the steamer basket inside. Also, place the potatoes and parsnips in the steamer basket.
2. Close the lid tightly. Press manual and for 7 minutes cook the potatoes and parsnips in high pressure. After cooking, press quick release.
3. Gently open up the lid and transfer the potatoes and parsnips in a bowl then sprinkle salt and pepper then mix well.
4. Mash the potatoes. While mashing, slowly add and mix the mixture of milk and cream and butter.
5. When it reaches a creamy and smooth texture, you can now serve and enjoy your mashed potato.

Rosemary and Garlic Mashed Potatoes

Servings: 4 -6, **Prep + Cook time:** 25 minutes

Ingredients:
- Garlic cloves – 3 pieces
- Large potatoes – 6 pieces, peeled and cubed
- Rosemary – 1 sprig
- Chicken broth – 1 cup
- Butter – 2 tbsp.
- Milk – ¼ cup
- Seasoning – salt to taste

Directions:
1. Mix well the potatoes, garlic, rosemary, and broth in the Instant Pot. Close the lid tightly.
2. Press manual and for 15 minutes and cook the potato mixture for 15 minutes. After cooking the potatoes. Press quick release and gently open up the lid.
3. Remove the broth from the potatoes.
4. In a bowl, add the potatoes and mash it using an electric beater. Add the butter and milk while mixing the potatoes.
5. When the mixture is already creamy and smooth in texture, you can now serve it.

Sour Cream Potatoes

Servings: 2 – 4, **Prep + Cook time:** 25 minutes

Ingredients:
- Medium sized potatoes -6 pieces, peeled and thinly sliced
- Chives – 1 tbsp.
- Kosher salt – ½ tsp.
- Chicken broth – 1 cup
- Sour cream - ⅓ cup
- Milk – ⅓ cup
- Paprika – ¼ Tsp.
- Potato starch – 2 tbsp.
- Ground black pepper – ¼ tsp.

Directions:
1. Place the potatoes, salt, pepper, and chives in the Instant Pot. Pour down the broth and mix well.
2. Cover the lid tightly. Press manual and cook the potatoes for 5 minutes at high pressure.
3. After cooking the potatoes, press cancel and quick release. Gently open up the lid.
4. Put the potatoes on a baking sheet then preheat the oven to broil.
5. Going back to the Instant Pot. Add the milk, potato starch, and sour cream on the broth where you cooked the potatoes. Cook the mixture for 1 minute using the sauté function of the Instant Pot.
6. After cooking the mixture, pour it down on the potatoes. Add paprika on top and broil it in the oven for 5 minutes.
7. Serve after broiling.

Roasted Garlic Potatoes

Servings: 4 – 6, **Prep + Cook time:** 30 minutes

Ingredients:
- Vegetable oil – 5 tbsp.
- Garlic cloves – 5 pieces
- Rosemary – 1 sprig
- Stock – ½ cup
- Seasoning – salt and black pepper to taste
- Baby potatoes – 2 lbs.

Directions:
1. Press sauté on the Instant Pot and heat the oil then add the rosemary, baby potatoes and garlic.
2. Cook the potatoes for 10 minutes until they turn brown. After that, pour down the stock and sprinkle with salt and pepper.
3. Select cancel and close the lid tightly. Press manual and cook the potatoes for 7 minutes at high pressure. After cooking the potatoes, press quick release and then gently open up the lid.
4. Serve and enjoy!

Potato Salad

Servings: 4 – 6, Prep + Cook time: 25 minutes

Ingredients:

- Eggs – 4 pieces
- Medium sized potatoes – 6 pieces peeled and cut into ½ inch cubes each piece
- Dill pickle juice – 1 tbsp.
- Mayonnaise – 1 cup
- Mustard – 1 tbsp.
- Seasoning – salt and pepper to taste
- Parsley – 2 tbsp. finely chopped
- Onion – ¼ finely chopped
- Water – 1 ½ cup

Directions:

1. Pour down the water inside the Instant Pot then place the steamer basket inside.
2. Put the potatoes and eggs in the steamer basket. Next, press manual and cook the potatoes and egg for 5 minutes at high pressure.
3. After cooking the eggs and potatoes, press quick release and then gently open the lid.
4. Let the eggs cool down in a bowl with cold water. So, in a separate bowl, mix the mayonnaise, parsley, mustard, onion and dill pickle juice.
5. Get the potatoes from the Instant Pot then mix it with the dill pickle juice mixture. Afterward, peel off the eggs and slice them in half.
6. Place the eggs in the salad then sprinkle with salt and pepper.
7. Serve fresh.

Salted Bacon and Potato Salad

Servings: 6 – 8, Prep + Cook time: 25 minutes

Ingredients:

- Eggs – 6 pieces
- Potatoes – 3 lbs. peeled and cut into ½ inch cubes each piece
- Water – 1 ½ cups
- Mayonnaise – 2 cups
- Cooked bacon – ½ lb. sliced into 1 inch each
- Green onions – 1 bunch
- Celery Stalk – 2 pieces, chopped
- Seasoning – salt and pepper

Directions:

1. Pour down the water in your Instant Pot then place the steamer basket inside.
2. Put the potatoes and eggs in the steamer basket next press manual and cook the potatoes and eggs for 5 minutes at high pressure.
3. After cooking the eggs and potatoes, press quick release and then gently open up the lid then get the eggs and put them in a bowl with cold water.
4. In a separate bowl, mix the bacon, mayonnaise, cooked potatoes, celery, and green onion then peel the eggs and slice them.
5. Put the eggs in the salad and mix well then sprinkle with salt and pepper.
6. Serve fresh.

Butter Coconut Potatoes

Servings: 2, Prep + Cook time: 20 minutes

Ingredients:

- Water – 2/3 cup
- Potatoes – 1 lb.
- Garlic cloves – 2 pieces, diced
- Coconut butter – 3 tbsp.
- Seasoning – salt and pepper

Directions:

1. Add water in your Instant Pot then place the steamer basket inside the pot.
2. Put the potatoes in the steamer basket. Next, add the coconut butter and garlic.
3. Sprinkle with salt and pepper and secure the lid.
4. Press manual and cook the potatoes for 4 minutes in high pressure. After cooking the potatoes, switch off the pot and let it sit for 5 minutes. Press quick release.
5. Grab the potatoes from the pot and serve hot.

Cheesy Red Potatoes

Servings: 2 – 4, **Prep + Cook time:** 60 minutes

Ingredients:
- Butter – 1 tbsp.
- Chicken broth – 1 cup
- Dried rosemary – 1 tsp.
- Dried oregano – 1 tsp.
- Dried parsley – 1 tsp.
- Salt – ¼ tsp.
- Parmesan cheese – ½ cup, shredded
- Red potatoes – 1 lb. cut into 1-inch cubes

Directions:
1. Press sauté in the Instant Pot then add the butter. Next, add the potatoes when the butter already melts.
2. Mix the potatoes and butter well then sauté for 5 minutes and then add the dried herbs and the broth.
3. Close the lid tightly then select cancel to finish sautéing.
4. Press manual and cook the potatoes for 5 minutes at high pressure. After cooking the potatoes, let the pot naturally release the steam for 10 minutes then gently remove the lid and sprinkle with salt and cheese.
5. Serve fresh and hot.

Cheesy Bacon Potatoes

Servings: 4 – 6, **Prep + Cook time:** 25 minutes

Ingredients:
- Bacon strips – 3 pieces, cut into small pieces
- Water – 3 tbsp.
- Red potatoes – 2 lbs. quartered
- Garlic powder – 1 tsp.
- Dried parsley – 2 tsp.
- Kosher salt – 1 tsp.
- Ranch dressing – ⅓ cup
- Cheddar cheese – 5 oz. shredded

Directions:
1. Mix the potatoes, bacon, and water in the Instant Pot then sprinkle with parsley, salt and, garlic powder. Mix well.
2. Secure the lid. Press manual and cook the potatoes and bacon for 7 minutes. After cooking the bacon and potatoes, press quick release.
3. Gently open up the lid then drizzle the ranch dressing and sprinkle the cheese.
4. Mix well then serve fresh and hot.

Cheesy Potato Sticks

Servings: 4, **Prep + Cook time:** 25 minutes

Ingredients:
- Water – 1 ¼ cups
- Medium sized potatoes – 8 pieces, peeled and cut into ½ inch sticks
- Seasoning – salt and cheese powder
- Olive oil – 4 tbsp.
- Baking soda – ¼ tsp.

Directions:
1. Mix the baking powder, water, and salt in the Instant Pot. Afterward, place the steam rack inside the pot.
2. Put the potato sticks in the steam rack. Secure the lid. Press manual and cook the potato sticks for 3 minutes at high pressure.
3. After cooking the potato sticks, press quick release. Gently open up the lid. Set aside the potato sticks in a serving bowl to dry.
4. Remove the water from the Instant Pot (make sure that it is dry). Press sauté on high heat. Add oil and heat it.
5. Return the potato sticks to the Instant Pot and sauté until it turns golden brown. After sautéing, sprinkle with salt and cheese powder. Mix well until the potato sticks are well coated.
6. Serve hot and enjoy.

Cheesy Potato Pie

Servings: 4, **Prep + Cook time:** 40 minutes

Ingredients:

- Water – 1 ½ cups
- Butter – 2 tbsp.
- Potato – 1 ½ piece, peeled and thinly sliced
- Cheddar cheese – 1 cup, grated
- Seasoning – salt and pepper
- Chives – 2 tbsp. chopped
- Salad (optional)
- Onions – 1 lb. sliced

Directions:

1. Pour down the water in the Instant Pot then place the steam rack inside the pot.
2. Prepare a baking pan by spreading butter on it after that place the bottom side of the potatoes in the baking pan.
3. Then top up the potatoes with onion and cheese. Next, cover it with another layer of sliced potato, then again add cheese and sprinkle it with salt and pepper.
4. Cover the pan with aluminum foil then carefully place the baking pan on the steam rack.
5. Secure the pot's cover. Press manual and cook the potatoes for 20 minutes at high pressure. After cooking the potatoes, press quick release. Gently remove the lid and sprinkle it with chives.
6. Serve with the optional salad.

Spicy Ranch Potatoes

Servings: 2 – 4, **Prep + Cook time:** 25 minutes

Ingredients:

- Large yellow potatoes – 3 pieces, sliced to cubes
- Ranch dressing – 2 tbsp.
- Water – ½ cup
- Seasoning – salt and pepper
- Butter – 2 tbsp.
- Chili Sauce – depends on the amount you want to put

Directions:

1. Press sauté in the Instant Pot. When the pot is hot already, add the butter to melt. Once the butter melts, add the potatoes.
2. Add the ranch dressing and mix well then pour down the water and secure the lid.
3. Select Cancel to stop sautéing after that press manual and cook the potatoes for 6 minutes at high pressure.
4. After cooking the potatoes, press quick release. Next, gently remove the lid then sprinkle with salt and pepper then drizzle with hot sauce.
5. Serve and enjoy hot.

Potatoes with Bread Crumbs

Servings: 4 – 6, **Prep + Cook time:** 35 minutes

Ingredients:

- Yellow onion- ½ cup, chopped
- Butter – 2 tbsp.
- Chicken stock – 1 cup
- Potatoes – 6 pieces, peeled and sliced
- Sour cream – ½ cup
- Monterey jack cheese – 1 cup, shredded
- Seasoning – salt and black pepper
- Bread crumbs – 1 cup
- Melted butter – 3 tbsp.

Directions:

1. Press sauté in your Instant Pot. When the pot is hot already add the butter, onion and sauté for 5 minutes then pour down the chicken stock.
2. Place the steam rack in the pot after that put the potatoes in the steam rack then secure the lid.
3. Select Cancel to stop sautéing. Press manual and cook the potatoes for 5 minutes in high

pressure. After that grab a bowl and mix the bread crumbs with the melted butter.

4. After cooking the potatoes in the pot, press quick release then gently open up the lid. Set aside the potatoes in a separate bowl from the steam rack. After that, mix the cheese and sour cream inside the pot.

5. Bring back the potatoes to the pot and mix it well with the cheese and sour cream mixture. Get your oven and preheat it to boil then place the mixture of potatoes in a baking tray and top it up with the bread crumbs mixture. Lastly, Broil the potatoes for 7 minutes.

6. Serve hot and fresh.

Original Sweet Potato

Servings: 4 – 6, **Prep + Cook time:** 20 minutes

Ingredients:
- Water – 2 cups
- Medium sized sweet potatoes – 6 pieces

Directions:
1. Pour down the water in your Instant Pot and place the steam rack inside the pot.
2. Wash the sweet potatoes then put it in the steam rack. Secure the lid of the pot.
3. Press manual and cook the sweet potatoes for 12 minutes at high pressure. After cooking the sweet potatoes, press quick release.
4. Gently open up the lid and serve fresh and hot.

Creamy Sweet Potatoes

Servings: 4 -6, **Prep + Cook time:** 30 minutes

Ingredients:
- Water – 1 cup
- Sweet potatoes – 1 lb. peeled and cubed
- Garlic cloves – 2 pieces
- Dried thyme – ¼ tsp.
- Dried sage – ¼ Tsp.
- Dried rosemary – ¼ Tsp.
- Dried parsley – ½ tsp.
- Milk – ¼ cup
- Butter – 2 tbsp.
- Parmesan cheese – ½ cup, grated
- Seasoning – salt and pepper

Directions:
1. Add water in your Instant Pot. Place the steamer basket inside the pot then place the potatoes and garlic cloves in the steamer basket.
2. Secure the lid. Press manual and cook the potatoes for 15 minutes at high pressure. After cooking the potatoes, press cancel and quick release.
3. Gently open the lid and put the potatoes in a bowl.
4. Add the dried herbs and mix well then mash the potatoes with an electric beater or manually.
5. While mashing, slowly add the milk and butter. When it reaches a creamy and smooth texture, add the cheese then sprinkle salt and pepper on top.
6. Serve fresh.

Sweet and Spicy Potatoes

Servings: 4, **Prep + Cook time:** 35 minutes

Ingredients:

- Large sweet potatoes – 3 pieces, peeled
- Water – 1 cup
- Vegetable oil – 2 tbsp.
- Kosher salt – ½ tsp.
- Paprika – 1 tsp.
- Dry mango powder – 1 tbsp.

Directions:

1. Cut the potatoes in wedges and pour down water to your Instant Pot then place the steam rack inside the pot. Add the sweet potatoes in the rack then secure the lid of the pot.
2. Press manual and cook the potatoes for 15 minutes at high pressure. After cooking the potatoes, press quick release then gently open up the lid.
3. Remove the water from the pot and then preheat the pot by pressing sauté. Add the oil to heat.
4. Add the potatoes and sauté for 5 minutes. When they turn brown in color, sprinkle with salt, mango powder, and paprika.
5. Serve hot and enjoy.

Sparkle Potatoes

Servings: 4 – 6, **Prep + Cook time:** 30 minutes

Ingredients:

- Brown sugar – ½ cup
- Lemon zest – 1 tbsp.
- Sea salt -1/2 tsp.
- Water – 1 ¼ cup
- Large sweet potatoes – 4 pieces, peeled and sliced
- Butter – ¼ cup
- Maple syrup – ¼ cup
- Cornstarch – 1 tbsp.
- Pecans – 1 cup, chopped

Directions:

1. Mix the sugar, water, salt and lemon zest inside your Instant Pot.
2. Add the sweet potatoes and secure the lid of the pot.
3. Press manual and cook the sweet potatoes for 15 minutes at high pressure. After cooking the potatoes, press quick release.
4. Gently open up the lid and set aside the potatoes in a bowl.
5. Press sauté and add the butter to melt. Add the cornstarch, maple syrup, and pecans then sauté them for 2 minutes.
6. Serve right after cooking.

Chapter 9 Desserts

Instant Raspberry Curd

Serves: 4 , Prep + Cooking Time: 25 minutes

Ingredients:
- Raspberries-12 oz.
- Lemon juice-2 tbsp.
- Butter-2 tbsp.
- Sugar-1 cup
- 2 Egg yolks

Directions:
1. Place some raspberries in your already cleaned instant pot.
2. Put lemon juice and sugar; then still until it is well mixed. Cover the instant pot with its lid and allow it to cook at High for about 2 minutes.
3. Allow the pot to cool by reducing pressure for 5 minutes then carefully open the lid; strain the raspberries and pour away the seed
4. Mix egg yolks with the raspberries in a clean bowl, then stir thoroughly.
5. Transfer the above mixture back to your instant pot, put it on the Sauté mode and allow it to simmer for about 2 minutes then add some butter, stir again and turn it into a clean container. Ensure to serve it cold.

Quick Pot Baked Apples

Serves: 6 , Prep + Cooking Time: 20 minutes

Ingredients:
- Red wine-1 cup
- Raw sugar-1/2 cup
- Cinnamon powder-1 tbsp.
- Raisins-1/4 cup
- 6 apples, cored

Directions:
1. In a clean instant pot, place the apples.
2. Add cinnamon, raisins, sugar, and wine, cover the pot with its lid and allow to cook at High for about 10 minutes.
3. Allow the pressure to reduce naturally, then open the lid carefully; turn the apples and their cooking juice into plates, then serve.

Pineapple and Ginger Risotto

Serves: 4 , Prep + Cooking Time: 22 minutes

Ingredients:
- Candied ginger; chopped-1/4 cup.
- risotto rice-1 ¾ cups
- Canned pineapple; chopped-20 oz.
- Milk-4 cups
- Coconut, shredded. - 1/2 cup

Directions:
1. In an already cleaned instant pot, combine milk with ginger, pineapple, coconut, and rice and stir thoroughly. Cover the pot with its lid and allow it to cook at High for about 12 minutes.
2. Allow the pressure to reduce naturally, then open the lid carefully; your dessert can now be served

Pudding of Tapioca

Serves: 6 , Prep + Cooking Time: 18 minutes

Ingredients:
- Tapioca pearls, rinsed-1/3 cup
- Sugar-1/2 cup
- Milk-1 ¼ cups
- Water-1 cup
- Cup water-1/2
- Zest from 1/2 lemon

Directions:
1. Using a clean heat resistant bowl, mix milk with tapioca, lemon zest, sugar, and 1/2 cup water, then stir thoroughly.
2. Place the above mixture in the steamer basket compartment of your instant pot, add 1 cup water and cover the pot with the lid and allow to cook at High for about 8 minutes.
3. Release the pressure quickly and put it aside for about 5 minutes more, open the lid carefully; remove the pudding and serve when warm

Apple-made Bread

Serves: 6 , Prep + Cooking Time: 1 hour and 20 minutes

Ingredients:
- Sugar-1 cup
- Eggs-2
- Apples, cored and cubed-3 cups
- 1 stick butter
- Vanilla-1 tbsp.
- Water-1 cup
- Waking powder-1 tbsp.
- Apple pie spice-1 tbsp.
- White flour-2 cups

Directions:
1. Using a clean bowl, mix the egg with apple pie spice,1 butter stick, and sugar and stir with your mixer.
2. To the above, add apples and stir thoroughly again.
3. Using another clean bowl, mix flour and baking powder then stir.
4. Merge the two mixtures, stir and transfer into a pan of the springform.
5. Put in the steamer basket compartment of your instant pot then add a cup of water to the instant pot, cover the instant pot with the lid and allow to cook at High for about 1 hour and 10 minutes.
6. Release the pressure quickly, allow the bread to stand bread to a cooler temperature, cut it and serve.

Quick Pot Sweet Carrots

Serves: 4 , Prep + Cooking Time: 25 minutes

Ingredients:
- 2 cups baby carrots
- Water-1/2 cup
- Butter-1/2 tbsp.
- Brown sugar-1 tbsp.
- A pinch of salt

Directions:
1. Melt butter using your instant pot by setting it on Sauté mode.
2. Add salt, water, and sugar, stir and allow to cook for about 1 minute.
3. Add carrots then toss it to coat, cover the instant pot lid and cook at High for about 15 minutes. Release the pressure quickly and open the lid carefully;
4. Put carrots in plates then serve

Banana-made Bread

Serves: 6 , **Prep + Cooking Time:** 40 minutes

Ingredients:

- 2 bananas, mashed
- Coconut sugar-3/4 cup
- Ghee, soft-1/3 cup
- Vanilla-1 tbsp.
- Baking soda-1/2 tbsp.
- Cashew milk-1/3 cup
- One egg
- Cream of tartar-1 ½ tbsp.
- Water-2 cups
- Baking powder-1 tbsp.
- Cups flour-1 ½
- A pinch of salt
- Cooking spray

Directions:

1. Using a clean bowl, combine cream of tartar and milk then stir well.
2. Add ghee, egg, sugar, bananas, and vanilla and stir everything.
3. Using another clean bowl, mix baking powder with flour, soda, and salt
4. Mix the 2 mixtures above and stir well, pour the mixture into an already greased cake pan then arrange pan in the steamer basket compartment of your instant pot
5. Pour some water into your instant pot, cover the instant pot lid and cook at High for about 30 minutes
6. Quick-release the pressure to enable easy opening of the lid; remove the bread and leave to stand in order to cool, slice and serve.

Recipe for Pears Jam

Serves: 12 , **Prep + Cooking Time:** 15 minutes

Ingredients:

- Apple juice-1/4 cup
- 8 pears, cored and cut into quarters
- 2 apples, peeled, cored and cut into quarters
- Cinnamon, ground. - 1 tbsp.

Directions:

1. In an already cleaned instant pot, mix apples with cinnamon, pears and apple juice; then stir thoroughly. cover the instant pot with the lid and cook at High for about 4 minutes.
2. Allow the pressure to release naturally, then open the lid carefully;
3. Blend the mixture with the use of an immersion blender, divide jam into portions and put into jars, keep in a cold place until you are ready to serve it

Tasty Apple Crisp

Serves: 4 , **Prep + Cooking Time:** 18 minutes

Ingredients:

- 5 apples, cored and cut into chunks
- Cinnamon-2 tbsp.
- Nutmeg-1/2 tbsp.
- Brown sugar-1/4 cup
- Flour-1/4 cup
- Old fashioned rolled oats-3/4 cup
- Water-1/2 cup
- Maple syrup-1 tbsp.
- Butter-4 tbsp.
- A pinch of salt

Directions:

1. In a clean instant pot, Put the apples gently.
2. Put the maple syrup, cinnamon, nutmeg, and water.
3. Using a clean bowl, mix butter with salt, flour, oats, and sugar then stir well.
4. Use spoonful of the oats mix to top the apples, close the pot with a lid and cook at High for about 8 minutes.
5. Release the pressure quickly and serve while warm

Crème Brule Recipe

Serves: 6 , **Prep + Cooking Time: 1 hour 15** minutes

Ingredients:

- White sugar-5 tbsp.
- Cinnamon powder-1 tbsp.
- 6 egg yolks
- A pinch of nutmeg for serving
- Fresh cream-2 cups
- Water-2 cups
- Raw sugar-4 tbsp.
- Zest from 1 orange

Directions:

1. Using a clean pan, mix cinnamon with orange zest and cream, stir and allow to a boil over a moderate-high heat.
2. Remove the pan from heat and place it aside for about 30 minutes.
3. Using a clean bowl, mix egg yolks and white sugar then whisk thoroughly. Combine the mixture with the cooled cream and whisk thoroughly once again.
4. Strain the mix then apportion into ramekins
5. Carefully cover the ramekins with foil and put them in the steamer basket of instant pot, pour 2 cups water into the instant pot then cover it with lid and allow to cook at Low for about 10 minutes.
6. Release the pressure naturally and carefully open the lid; remove ramekins and arrange them aside for about 30 minutes.
7. Top each of the ramekins with nutmeg and raw sugar then melt with a culinary torch. Serve immediately.

Wine-Glazed Apples Rings

Serves: 4 , **Prep Cook time**: 15 minutes

Ingredients

- Apples, cored - 4
- Red wine - ¾ cup
- Demerara sugar - 1/3 cup
- Raisins - ¼ cup
- Ground cinnamon - ¾ tsp.
- Cooking oil for topping

Directions

1. Combine all the ingredients to the Instant Pot.
2. Click on the 'manual' function of your instant pot then set to high pressure and reset the time to 10 minutes
3. Do a 'quick release' immediately after the beep and remove the lid
4. Top the apples with some cooking oil and serve.

Nutrition Values Per Serving

Calories: 227, Carbohydrate: 51.4g, Protein: 0.9g, Fat: 0.5g, Sugar: 40.6g, Sodium: 9mg

Fastest Brown Fudge Cake

Servings: 3 , **Prep + Cook time:** 12 minutes

Ingredients

- Milk - ¼ cup
- Extra-virgin olive oil - 2 tsps.
- Egg - 1
- Unbleached all-purpose flour - ¼ cup
- Brown sugar - ¼ cup
- Cocoa powder 1 tsp.
- Baking powder ½ tsp.
- Fresh orange zest, grated finely 2 tsps.
- Water - 1 cup
- Powdered sugar, as required
- Ramekins - 3

Directions

1. Combine all the ingredients to a large bowl except the powdered sugar.
2. Whisk all the ingredients well to prepare a smooth mixture.
3. Grease the three ramekins and pour the prepared mixture into the ramekins.
4. Empty a cup of water into the Instant Pot and Place the steamer trivet inside.
5. Place the ramekins on top the trivet.

6. Click on the 'manual' function of your instant pot then set to high pressure and reset the time to 6 minutes
7. Do a 'quick release' immediately after the beep and remove the lid

8. Let the ramekins cool. Sprinkle powdered sugar on top of each cake.
9. Serve.

Nutrition Values Per Serving
Calories: 166, Carbohydrate: 21.2g, Protein: 3g, Fat: 8.7g, Sugar: 13.9g, Sodium: 24mg

Delicious Chocolate Cheesecake

Serves: 3,Prep Time + Cook Time: 28 minutes.

Ingredients
- Cream cheese softened - 8 oz.
- Ramekins, greased - 3
- Swerve brown sugar Sweetener - ¼ cup
- Cocoa powder - 3/4 tsp.
- Eggs - 2
- Water as needed
- Powdered peanut butter - 1 tsp.
- Pure vanilla extract - ½ tsp

Directions
1. Pour the eggs and cream cheese in a blender and blend well to form a smooth mixture.
2. Include the brown sugar, peanut butter, and vanilla extract to the egg mixture and blend thoroughly.
3. Put the entire mix in a greased ramekin.
4. Empty the water into the Instant Pot and arrange the trivet inside.
5. Place the ramekins on top the trivet.
6. Click on the 'manual' function of your instant pot then set to high pressure and reset the time to 18 minutes
7. Do a 'quick release' immediately after the beep and remove the lid
8. Set the ramekins aside to cool then top it with cocoa powder; Refrigerate for 8 hours.
9. Serve.

Nutrition Values Per Serving
Calories: 223, Carbohydrate: 17.8g, Protein: 6.5g, Fat: 21.2g, Sugar: 15.4g, Sodium: 195mg

Silky Maple-Glazed Flan

Serves: 4 , Prep + Cook time: 19 minutes

Ingredients
- Large eggs -2
- Milk - ½ cup
- Sweeten condensed milk - ½ can
- Cup water - ¼
- Vanilla extract - ½ tsp.
- A pinch of salt
- Maple syrup - ¼ cup
- Cherries for topping - ¼ cup

Directions
1. mix the eggs in a large bowl and stir in the remaining ingredients minus the maple syrup and cherry
2. Slightly Glaze a ramekin with maple syrup and put the vanilla mix into it.
3. Empty a cup of water into the Instant Pot and set the trivet inside.
4. Place the ramekin in an ordered manner over the trivet.
5. Click on the 'manual' function of your instant pot then set to high pressure and reset the time to 10 minutes
6. Do a 'quick release' immediately after the beep and remove the lid
7. Set the ramekins aside to cool off and refrigerate flan for 3 hours.
8. Add at the top of the flan additional maple glaze and cherries then serve.

Nutrition Values Per Serving
Calories: 227, Carbohydrate: 35.8g, Protein: 7.2g, Fat: 6.5g, Sugar: 34.2g, Sodium: 139mg

Luscious Almond Cheesecake

Serves: 3, **Prep time:** 10 minutes **Cooking time**: 18 minutes

Ingredients

- 1Cream cheese softened - 8 oz.
- Eggs - 2
- Ramekins, greased 3
- Powdered brown sugar - ¼ cup
- Almonds, thinly sliced - ¼ cup
- Powdered peanut butter - 1 tsp.
- Pure vanilla extract - ½ tsp.
- Water - 1 cup

Directions

1. Pour the eggs and cream cheese in a blender and blend properly to form a smooth mixture.
2. Include the brown sugar, peanut butter, and vanilla extract to the egg mix and blend.
3. Pour the mix into a greased ramekin.
4. Empty the water 1 cup into the Instant Pot and place the trivet inside.
5. Set the ramekins over the top of the trivet.
6. Close the pot lid and ensure it is tightly locked and Click on the 'manual' function of your instant pot then set to high pressure and reset the time to 10 minutes
7. Do a 'quick release' immediately after the beep and remove the lid
8. Set the ramekins aside to cool then top it with almonds.
9. Refrigerate cake for 8 hours.
10. Serve cold.

Nutrition Values Per Serving

Calories: 248, Carbohydrate: 11g, Protein: 7.6g, Fat: 24g, Sugar: 8g, Sodium: 195mg

Chocolate Crème Brûlée

Servings: 4 , **Prep + Cook time:** 23 minutes

Ingredients

- Ramekins - 4
- Egg yolks - 5
- Heavy cream - 2 cups
- Vanilla extract 1 tsp. extract
- Cocoa powder - ½ tbsp.
- Sugar - ½ cup
- Water - 1 cup

Directions

1. Pour the egg yolks, cream, vanilla extract, and sugar in a bowl and mix properly.
2. Split the entire mix into 4 ramekins.
3. Empty water 1 cup into the Instant Pot and place the trivet inside.
4. Arrange the ramekins over the trivet.
5. Close the pot lid and ensure it is tightly locked and Click on the 'manual' function of your instant pot then set to high pressure and reset the time to 10 minutes
6. Do a 'quick release' immediately after the beep and remove the lid
7. Set the ramekin aside to cool and refrigerate for about 4 hours.
8. Top with superfine sugar and serve.

Nutrition Values Per Serving

Calories: 377, Carbohydrate: 27.8g, Protein: 4.6g, Fat: 27.8g, Sugar: 25.6g, Sodium: 33mg

Apple Crisp

Serves: 4 , **Prep + Cook time:** 17 minutes

Ingredients

- peeled, cored and diced medium apples-4
- ground cinnamon-1 tsp.
- ground nutmeg-¼ sp.
- pure maple syrup or honey-2 tbsps.
- water-1 cup

For topping:

- old-fashioned rolled oats-2/3 cup
- Flour-1/3 cup
- brown sugar-¼ cup
- melted unsalted butter-¼ cup
- Nutmeg-¼ tbsp.
- Cinnamon-½ tbsp.
- A pinch of salt

Directions

1. Mix in a large bowl the diced apples, nutmeg, maple syrup, and cinnamon, and toss until well coated.
2. Pour the mix into the ramekins.

3. Pour the topping spices in the same bowl and mix them properly,
4. Pour the entire mix over the apples till they are entirely covered with the mixture.
5. Add a cup of water into the pot and add trivet and stack the ramekins on the trivet.
6. Close the pot lid and ensure it is tightly locked; Set the pressure release handle to the 'sealed' position.

7. Click on the 'manual' function of your instant pot then set to high pressure and reset the time to 10 minutes
8. Do a 'quick release' immediately after the beep and remove the lid
9. Set aside for a while to cool and serve.

Nutrition Values Per Serving
Calories: 383, Carbohydrate: 67.8g, Protein: 3.7g, Fat: 13.2g, Sugar: 41g, Sodium: 128mg

Dark Chocolate Crème Brûlée

Servings: 4 , **Prep + Cook time:** 23 minutes

Ingredients
- Ramekins - 4
- Egg yolks - 5
- Heavy cream - 2 cups
- Vanilla extract 1 tsp. extract
- Cocoa powder - ½ tbsp.
- Sugar - ½ cup
- Water - 1 cup
- Superfine sugar - ¼ cup
- Grated chocolate - ½ tbsp.

Directions
1. Mix the egg yolks, cream, cocoa powder, vanilla extract and sugar in a large skillet.
2. Split the mix into 4 ramekins.
3. Empty a cup of water into the Instant Pot and put the trivet inside.

4. Place the ramekins on top of the trivet.
5. Close the pot lid and ensure it is tightly locked and Click on the 'manual' function of your instant pot then set to high pressure and reset the time to 10 minutes
6. Do a 'quick release' immediately after the beep and remove the lid.
7. Set the ramekin aside and allow to cool
8. Refrigerate for 4 hours.
9. Spread superfine sugar grounded chocolate over the top and serve.

Nutrition Values Per Serving
Calories: 386, Carbohydrate: 29g, Protein: 4.8g, Fat: 28.3g, Sugar: 26.3g, Sodium: 34mg

Classic Tapioca Pudding

Serving: 4 , **Prep + Cook time:** 14 minutes

Ingredients
- Water -1½ cups
- Small pearl tapioca - ½ cup
- Sugar - ½ cup
- A pinch of salt
- Milk - ½ cup
- egg yolks - 2
- vanilla extract - ½ tsp.
- fresh raspberries - ¼ cup

Directions
1. Start by putting water and tapioca into the Instant Pot and mix them well.
2. Set your Instant pot to manual; cover the pot with the lid and cook for 6 minutes at high pressure.

3. Do a quick release immediately after the beep.
4. Use a beater to mix the egg, sugar, salt, and milk in a bowl then add this mixture into the pot.
5. Reset your instant pot to saute and cook for 3 minutes then stir in the vanilla extract slowly.
6. Refrigerate for 30 minutes.
7. Top with raspberries and then serve.

Nutrition Values Per Serving
Calories: 295, Carbohydrate: 63.7g, Protein: 3.3g, Fat: 3.9g, Sugar: 35.8g, Sodium: 88mg

Blueberry Cheesecake Cookies

Serving: 6 , **Prep + Cook time:** 45 minutes
Ingredients

- Cream cheese - 8 oz.
- Ricotta cheese - 8 oz.
- Sugar - ½ cup
- Eggs - 2
- Sour cream - ¼ cup
- Vanilla extract – 1 tsp.
- Crushed Butter cookies-10
- Water-1 cup
- Unsalted butter, melted- 2 tsp.
- Powdered sugar - 2 tsp.
- Pitted Fresh blueberries, ¼ cup

Directions

1. Pour the eggs, ricotta, sugar and cream cheese in a blender then blend appropriately until they are smooth.
2. Slowly pour and mix vanilla extract and sour cream.
3. Combine your crushed cookies along with butter.
4. Layer a 7-inch springform pan with the cookies and cream cheese mixture.
5. Pour the water into the Instant Pot and place the trivet inside.
6. Place the pan on top of the trivet.
7. Close the pot lid and ensure it is tightly locked; Set the pressure release handle to the 'sealed' position.
8. Click on the 'manual' function of your instant pot then set to high pressure and reset the time to 10 minutes
9. Do a 'quick release' immediately after the beep and remove the lid
10. Set aside and allow to cool
11. Sprinkle toppings of powdered sugar and blueberries over cake.
12. Refrigerate cake for 12 hours.
13. Serve cold.

Nutrition Values Per Serving
Calories: 471, Carbohydrate: 29.4g, Protein: 9g, Fat: 35.5g, Sugar: 19.1g, Sodium: 368mg

Creamy Cherry Cheesecake

Servings: 6. **Prep Time + Cook Time:** 45 minutes

Ingredients

- Cream cheese - 8 oz.
- Ricotta cheese - 8 oz.
- Sugar - ¼ cup
- Eggs - 2
- Sour cream - ¼ cup
- Vanilla extract - 1 ts.p
- Oreo cookies, crushed - 10
- Water - 1 cup
- Unsalted butter, melted - 2 tsp.
- Powdered sugar - 2 tsp.
- Fresh cherries, pitted - ¼ cup

Directions

1. Pour the eggs, ricotta, sugar, and cream cheese in your electric blender and blend till smooth.
2. Pour your vanilla extract and sour cream into the mix and continue to stir.
3. Put your butter and crushed sugar into a pan and mix properly.
4. Get a 7-inch springform pan and layer it with the cream cheese and cookies mix.
5. Pour the 1½ cup of water into the Instant Pot and place the trivet in the pot.
6. Arrange the pan over the trivet.
7. Secure the lid and cook on manual function for 35 minutes at high pressure.9. Do a 'quick release' immediately after the beep and remove the lid; set aside and allow to cool.
8. Top cake with powdered sugar and cherries.
9. Put the cake into the fridge for 12 hours
10. Serve cold.

Nutrition Values Per Serving
Calories: 366, Carbohydrate: 21.5g, Protein: 10.3g, Fat: 26.7g, Sugar: 12.3g,Sodium: 293mg

Quick and Easy Lavender Crème Brûlée

Serves: 4 , **Prep + Cook time:** 23 minutes

Ingredients

- Ramekins - 4
- Egg yolks - 5
- Heavy cream - 2 cups
- Vanilla extract - 1 tsp.
- Sugar - ½ cup
- Water - 1 cup
- Superfine - ¼ cup sugar
- Lavender buds - ½ tbsp.

Directions

1. Pour the egg yolks, cream, vanilla extract, and sugar should be beaten in a large bowl and mix prop.
2. Divide the mixture into 4 ramekins.3. Empty a cup of water into the Instant Pot and place the trivet inside.
3. Arrange the ramekins over the trivet.
4. Secure the lid and cook on manual function for 13 minutes at high pressure.6. Do a 'quick release' immediately after the beep and remove the lid.
5. Set the ramekin aside to cool for a while
6. Refrigerate for 4 hours.
7. Sprinkle superfine sugar and lavender buds on top of the ramekins
8. serve cold.

Nutrition Values Per Serving

Calories: 377, Carbohydrate: 27.8g, Protein: 4.6g, Fat: 27.8g, Sugar: 25.6g, Sodium: 33mg

Classic Pumpkin Bundt Cake

Servings: 3 , **Prep + Cook time:** 50 minutes

Ingredients

- whole wheat flour-6 tbsps.
- unbleached all-purpose flour-6 tbsps.
- Salt-¼ tsp.
- baking soda-½ tsp.
- baking powder-½ tsp.
- pumpkin pie spice-¼ tsp.
- Sugar-6 tbsps.
- banana mashed-½ medium
- canola oil-1 tbsp.
- Greek yogurt-¼ cup
- can pumpkin puree-¼ 15 oz.
- Egg-½
- pure vanilla extract-¼ tsp.
- chocolate chips-¼ cup
- 3 mini Bundt pans tools

Directions

1. Pour every of the dry ingredients in a large bowl and set them aside for a while.
2. Put the banana, sugar, oil, yogurt, egg, vanilla and pureed pumpkin in an electric mixer and pulse until smooth.
3. Introduce all of the dry ingredients to the egg mix and mix until smooth.
4. Arrange chocolate chips into the mix and split the entire mixture into 3 mini Bundt pans.
5. Empty 1 cup of water into the Instant Pot and put the trivet inside.
6. Place the Bundt pans orderly over the trivet.
7. Close the pot lid and Click on the 'manual' function of your instant pot then set to high pressure and reset the time to 35 minutes.
8. Do a 'quick release' immediately after the beep and remove the lid
9. Now set the Bundt aside and allow to cool then remove the cake.
10. Top with fresh cream and serve cold.

Nutrition Values Per Serving

Calories: 356, Carbohydrate: 59.7g, Protein: 6.7g, Fat: 10.5g, Sugar: 36.1g, Sodium: 453mg

Cinnamon Apple Sauce

Serves: 4 , **Prep Time + Cook Time:** 22 minutes

Ingredients

- large apples, peeled, cored and roughly chopped-6
- water-1 cup
- cinnamon essential oil-1-2 drops
- lemon juice- 1 tbsp.
- organic cinnamon-1 tsp.

Directions

1. Introduce and combine all your ingredients in the Instant Pot.
2. Click on the 'manual' function of your instant pot then set to high pressure and reset the time to 10 minutes
3. Do a 'quick release' immediately after the beep and remove the lid
4. Set aside and allow to cool then pulse the entire mixture well using an immerse blender.
5. Add more cinnamon if desired and serve or You can refrigerate for up to 10 days.

Nutrition Values Per Serving
Calories: 321, Carbohydrate: 62.2g, Protein: 1.2g, Fat: 10.1g, Sugar: 46.4g, Sodium: 6mg

Apple Pie Bread Pudding

Serves: 8 , **Prep Time + Cook Time:** 35 minutes

Ingredients

- apples peeled, cored, and cubed-3
- thick slices of bread, cubed, toasted-8
- brown sugar-1 cup
- eggs-2
- vanilla extract-1 tbsp.
- cinnamon-1 tbsp.
- milk- 3 cups
- cornstarch-2/3 tbsp.
- A pinch of salt

Vanilla Sauce:

- Melt together:
- Sugar-2 tbsp.,
- brown sugar-2 tbsp.
- Milk-¼ cup,
- Butter-2 tbsp,
- Vanilla- ½ tbsp.

Directions

1. Butter a ½ quart glass dish that can fill in your instant pot. Add cubed bread.
2. Combine the milk, eggs, cinnamon, vanilla extract, and the salt.
3. Pour the entire mix all over bread and allow it sit for 10 to 20 minutes.
4. Pour the cornstarch and sugar in another bowl then introduce apples into the mixture; slowly pour over the bread cubes.
5. Wrap with aluminum foil if mixture appears to be full.
6. Empty a cup of water into the Instant Pot and put the trivet inside.
7. Position the pan on top of the trivet and close the lid.
8. Click on the 'manual' function of your instant pot then set to high pressure and reset the time to 20 minutes.
9. Do a 'quick release' immediately after the beep and remove the lid.
10. Place the ingredients for vanilla sauce on a stove of medium heat and allow to melt.
11. Slowly pour the sauce over bread pudding and serve.

Nutrition Values Per Serving
Calories: 554, Carbohydrate: 95.4g, Protein: 5.1g, Fat: 18.5g, Sugar: 67g, Sodium: 234mg

No Bake Orange Cheesecake

Serves: 3 , **Prep Time + Cook Time:** 18 minutes

Ingredients

- half pint mason jars-3
- cream cheese-8 oz.
- sugar-¼ cup
- flour-½ tsp.
- vanilla-¼ tsp.
- sour cream-2 tbsps.
- orange Juice-½ tbsp.
- zest of ¼ orange
- eggs-1 ½
- Greek yogurt-½ jar
- Raspberries-½ jar
- Water-1 cup

Directions

1. Mix the cream cheese, flour, and sugar in a large skillet.
2. Introduce the sour cream, orange juice, zest, vanilla, and eggs. Beat again.
3. Set the cheese batter and drop of yogurt as layers on top of the Mason jar.
4. Empty a cup of water into the Instant Pot and put the trivet inside.
5. Wrap the jars with tin foil and place them over the trivet.
6. Close the lid properly and cook on manual for about 8-10 minutes at high pressure.
7. Do a 'quick release' immediately after the beep and remove the lid.
8. Set the cakes aside and allow to cool for a while, then top with yogurt and raspberries..
9. Serve.

Nutrition Values Per Serving

Calories: 382, Carbohydrate: 23.3g, Protein: 9.6g, Fat: 28.8g, Sugar: 19.3g, Sodium: 241mg

Banana Chocolate Chip Bundt Cake

Serves: 10 , **Prep Time + Cook Time:** 55 minutes

Ingredients

- whole wheat flour-1 cup
- A pinch of salt
- baking soda-½ tsp.
- sugar-6 tbsp.
- medium bananas mashed-2
- nutmeg-½ tbsp.
- melted unsalted butter-1/3 cups
- Greek yogurt-1/2 cup
- Cinnamon-1 tbsp.
- Egg-1
- white chocolate chips-½ cup
- semi-sweet chocolate chips-¼ cups
- pure vanilla extract-1 tsp.

Directions

1. mix all of the spices properly in a large bowl set aside for a while.
2. Coat a 7-inch Bundt pan with, then pour the batter in evenly.
3. Empty 1 cup of water into the pot, then place the Bundt pan into the instant pot. Cook on high pressure for about 45 minutes.
4. Do a 'natural' release after the beep.
5. Set a 10-15 minutes then remove from the pan.
6. Store in a bottle or use instantly; can store for up to 1 week.

Nutrition Values Per Serving

Calories: 332, Carbohydrate: 63.2g, Protein: 7.7g, Fat: 6.5g, Sugar: 35.4g, Sodium: 427mg

Sunny Lemon Cheesecake

Serves: 3 , **Prep Time + Cook Time:** 13 minutes

Ingredients

- half pint mason jars-3
- cream cheese-8 oz.
- sugar-¼ cup
- flour-½ tsp.
- vanilla-¼ tsp.
- sour cream-2 tbsp.
- lemon juice-½ tbsp..
- zest of half lemon
- eggs-1 ½
- lemon curd-½ jar
- raspberries-3
- water-1 cup

Directions

1. Mix the cream cheese, flour, and sugar in a large skillet.
2. Introduce the sour cream, lemon juice, zest, vanilla and eggs, and then mix again.
3. Set the cheese batter and lemon curd as layers on top of the Mason jar.
4. Empty the water into the Instant Pot and put the trivet inside.
5. Wrap the jars with tin foil and place them on top of the trivet.
6. Close the pot lid and cook on the 'manual' function of your instant pot then set to high pressure and reset the time to 8 minutes.
7. Do a 'quick release' immediately after the beep and remove the lid.
8. Set the cakes aside and allow to cool then top with lemon curd and raspberries.
9. Serve.

Nutrition Values Per Serving

Calories: 385, Carbohydrate: 23.6g, Protein: 8.9g, Fat: 28.5g, Sugar: 19.3g, Sodium: 237mg

Honey Yogurt

Servings: 6 , **Prep + Cook time:** 9 hours 15 minutes

Ingredients

- Milk- 1 gallon
- vanilla extract-1 tbsp.
- Greek yogurt-1/3 cup
- Honey-¼ cup
- Cheesecloth
- Wire sieve

Directions

1. Pour the milk slowly into the Instant Pot and close the lid tightly.
2. Set your instant pot 'yogurt' function and boil for 1 hour; Remove the lid immediately after the beep.
3. Slowly mix in the Greek yogurt, honey and vanilla extract then close the lid.
4. Click on the yogurt key and reset the time to 8 hours.
5. After the beep, do a natural release then remove the lid.
6. Place the wire sieve in a bowl, layer it with cheesecloth.
7. Pour the prepared curd into the bowl and strain the excess liquid.
8. Allow curd strain for 45 minutes more, and then discard the thick yogurt.
9. Store in a bottle or use instantly.

Nutrition Values Per Serving

Calories: 383, Carbohydrate: 44.4g, Protein: 22.5g, Fat: 13.6g, Sugar: 41.6g, Sodium: 311mg

Yogurt Bowls

Serves: 6, **Cooking time + Prep Time:** 9 hours 20 minutes

Ingredients

- honey - ¼ cup
- sliced kiwi - ¼ cup
- milk - 1 gallon
- vanilla extract – 1 tbsp.
- sliced raspberries - ¼ cup
- sliced blueberries - ¼ cup
- pomegranate seeds - ¼ cup
- Greek yoghurt - 1/3 cup
- Cheesecloth
- Wire sieve

Directions

1. Pour the milk into the Instant Pot and close the lid tightly.
2. Set your instant pot 'yogurt' function and boil for 1 hour; Remove the lid immediately after the beep.
3. Slowly mix in Greek yogurt, honey and vanilla extract then close the lid.
4. Click on the 'yogurt' key and reset the time to 8 hours.
5. Do a 'natural release' immediately after the beep and remove the lid.
6. Set your wire sieve in a bowl and layer it with cheesecloth.
7. Pour the prepared curd into the bowl and strain the excess liquid.
8. Allow curd strain for 45 minutes more, and then discard the thick yogurt.
9. Split the yogurt in the serving dishes.
10. Sprinkle top with all fruits and few drops of honey then serve

Nutrition Values Per Serving

Calories: 392, Carbohydrate: 44.3g, Protein: 23.1g, Fat: 14.2g, Sugar: 42.3g, Sodium: 301mg

Classic Egg Custard

Serves: 4 , **Prep Time + Cook Time:** 22 minutes

Ingredients

- milk – 4 cups
- Eggs - 6
- water – 1 cup
- sugar - 3/4 cup
- vanilla extract – 1 tsp.
- ground cinnamon - ¼ tsp.
- A pinch of sea salt.
- A round stainless-steel skillet
- Grated Nutmeg
- diced Fresh fruits

Directions

1. Mix the milk, eggs, sugar, cinnamon, vanilla extract and salt in the bowl until they become smooth.
2. Pour the entire mixture to the steel pan.
3. Empty the water into the Instant Pot and put the trivet inside.
4. Wrap the top of the bowl with tin foil, and poke some holes in it, and then arrange it over the trivet.
5. Close the pot lid and ensure it is tightly locked and cook on the 'manual' function of your instant pot then set to high pressure and reset the time to 7 minutes
6. Do a 'quick release' immediately after the beep and remove the lid.
7. Sprinkle the custard with fresh fruits, and nutmeg then serve.

Nutrition Values Per Serving

Calories: 360, Carbohydrate: **50.3g**, Protein: 16.3g, Fat: 11.6g, Sugar: 49.1g, Sodium: 266mg

Fruity Pineapple Cheesecake

Serves: 6 , **Prep Time + Cook Time:** 50 minutes

Ingredients

- cream cheese – 8 oz.
- ricotta cheese - 8 oz.
- pineapple juice- 2 tbsp.
- powdered sugar - ¼ cup
- eggs - 2
- sour cream - ¼ cup
- extract of vanilla – 1 tbsp.
- crushed Oreo cookies - 10
- melted unsalted butter - 2 tbsp.
- pineapple slices - 1
- raspberries - ¼ cup
- water - 1 ½ cup

Directions

1. Pour the eggs, ricotta, sugar, and cream cheese in a blender and pulse well until smooth
2. Slowly mix in vanilla extract and sour cream.
3. Combine the crushed Oreos with butter.
4. Place the cookies and cream cheese mixture in layers over a 7-inch springform pan.
5. Empty the water into the Instant Pot and put the trivet inside.
6. Place the pan on top of the trivet.
7. Close the pot lid and ensure it is tightly locked and cook on the 'manual' function of your instant pot then set to high pressure and reset the time to 10 minutes
8. Do a 'quick release' immediately after the beep and remove the lid.
9. Allow it to cool and top it with the pineapple slices and raspberries
10. Refrigerate the cake for 12 hours then serve.

Nutrition Values Per Serving

Calories: 393. Carbohydrate: 31.2g, Protein: 6.4g, Fat: 27.2g, Sugar: 22.5g, Sodium: 239mg

Apple Custard and Cinnamon Trifle

Serves: 4 , **Prep Time + Cook Time:** 22 minutes

Ingredients

- milk – 4 cup
- eggs - 6
- sugar - ¾ cup
- extract vanilla-1
- A pinch of sea salt
- Ground cinnamon - ¼ tsp.
- Round form stainless-steel pan
- Sugar – 4 tbsp.
- Water – 2 tbsp.
- thinly sliced Large apple-1

Directions

1. Mix the milk, eggs, sugar, cinnamon, vanilla extract and salt in a large bowl until they become smooth.
2. Pour the entire mix into the steel pan.
3. Empty 1 cup of water into the Instant Pot and put the trivet inside.
4. Wrap the top of the bowl with tin foil, and poke some holes in it, and then arrange it over the trivet.
5. Close the pot lid and ensure it is tightly locked and cook on the 'manual' function of your instant pot then set to high pressure and reset the time to 7 minutes
6. Do a 'quick release' immediately after the beep and remove the lid.
7. Put the already prepared custard in the serving bowl and place the apple slices over the custard.
8. Pour 2 tsps. of sugar in boiling water in the bowl and allow it caramelize.
9. Top the custard apples with this mix then serve when cold.

Nutrition Values Per Serving

Calories: 375 ,Carbohydrate: 54.1g,Protein: 16.4g,Fat: 11.6g,Sugar: 52g,Sodium: 266mg

Chapter 10 Side Dishes

Buttery Grains With Parsley

Servings: 10 , Prep + Cooking Time: 15 minutes

Ingredients:

- Harvest grains blend- 16 oz.
- Parsley leaves; chopped for serving
- Butter- 2 tbsp.
- Chicken stock- 2 ½ cups
- Salt and black pepper

Directions:

1. Press 'Sauté' on the Instant Pot and add butter to melt then mix in the stock and grains.
2. Seal the lid to cook for 5 minutes on high pressure.
3. Quick release the pressure and flip the grains with a fork then season with salt and pepper.
4. Serve sprinkled with parsley.

Lemon Broccoli Dish

Servings: 6, Prep + Cooking Time: 20 minutes

Ingredients:

- Broccoli florets; separated- 31 oz.
- Lemon slices- 5
- Water- 1 cup
- Salt and black pepper

Directions:

1. Season broccoli with salt and pepper then pour the water in the Instant Pot and add the broccoli to the pot.
2. Mix in the lemon slices then seal the lid and cook at high pressure for 15 minutes.
3. Quick release the pressure and serve broccoli as side dish.
4. Serve with a meat-based main course.

Sweet Squash

Servings: 4, Prep + Cooking Time: 30 minutes

Ingredients:

- Acorn squash; cut into halves and seeded- 2
- Salt and black pepper
- Brown sugar- 2 tbsp.
- Water- ½ cup
- Baking soda- ¼ tsp.
- Butter- 2 tbsp.
- Nutmeg; grated- ½ tsp.

Directions:

1. Mix the squash with baking soda and season with salt and pepper, then put it in a steaming basket and put it in the Instant Pot.
2. Pour the water into the pot and seal the lid to cook at high pressure for 20 minutes.
3. Quickly release the pressure then remove the squash and set aside to cool.
4. Scrape the flesh from the squash then put it in a bowl.
5. Mix in the nutmeg, butter, sugar, salt and pepper then mash it with a potato masher.
6. Mix and serve.

Pureed Parsley With Sautéed Onions

Servings: 4, Prep + Cooking Time: 40 minutes

Ingredients:

- Thinly sliced yellow onion- 1
- Salt and black pepper
- Pastured lard- 4 tbsp.
- Beef stock- 1 ½ cups
- Thyme sprig- 1
- Chopped parsnips- 2 ½ Ib.

Directions:

1. Press 'Sauté' on the Instant Pot and put in 3 tablespoons of lard then add the parsnips to cook for 15 minutes.
2. Mix in the thyme and the stock to cook for 3 minutes at high pressure.
3. Release the pressure quickly then put the parsnips in a blender and season with pepper and salt and blend well.
4. Put the pot on 'Sauté' again then add the last tablespoon of lard and the onion to cook for 10 minutes.
5. Serve the pureed parsnips topped with sautéed onions on a plate.

Honey Sweet Carrot Blend

Servings: 4, Prep + Cooking Time: 10 minutes

Ingredients:

- Carrot; peeled and chopped- 1 ½ Ib.
- Brown sugar- 1 tsp.
- Salt to taste
- Water- 1 cup
- Soft butter- 1 tbsp.
- Honey- 1 tbsp.

Directions:

1. Pour water and add the carrots to the Instant Pot then seal to cook on high pressure for 4 minutes.
2. Natural release the pressure, drain the carrots and set aside in a bowl.
3. Mash the carrots then mix with honey, salt, and butter.
4. Blend and top with brown sugar.

Sour Turnips Dish

Servings: 4, Prep + Cooking Time: 15 minutes

Ingredients:

- Peeled and chopped turnips- 4
- Chicken stock- ¼ cup
- Chopped yellow onion- 1
- Sour cream- ¼ cup
- Salt and black pepper

Directions:

1. Combine the onions, turnips, and stock in the Instant Pot then seal the lid to cook at high pressure for 5 minutes.
2. Natural release the pressure and drain the turnips. Put it inside a bowl.
3. Blend the turnips in a mixer and add the sour cream, salt and pepper.
4. Blend to mix and serve.

Creamy Rice And Pumpkin Dish

Servings: 4, Prep + Cooking Time: 15 minutes

Ingredients:

- Pumpkin puree- 6 oz.
- Chicken stock- 4 cups
- Risotto rice- 12 oz.
- Minced garlic- 2 cloves
- Allspice- ½ tsp.
- Cinnamon- ½ tsp.
- Extra virgin olive oil- 2 oz.
- Chopped small yellow onion- 1
- Nutmeg- ½ tsp.
- Heavy cream- 4 oz.
- Grated ginger- ½ tsp.
- Chopped thyme- 1 tsp.

Directions:

1. Press 'Sauté' on the Instant Pot and add the oil, then mix in the garlic and onion to cook for 1-2 minutes.
2. Pour in the chicken stock, and mix in the rice, thyme, nutmeg, pumpkin puree, allspice, ginger, and cinnamon then seal the lid.
3. Cook for 10 minutes on high pressure.
4. Quick release the pressure and mix in the heavy cream.
5. Serve.

Lemony Calamari And Tomato Dish With Anchovies

Servings: 4, **Prep + Cooking Time:** 40 minutes

Ingredients:

- Washed calamari with tentacles separated and cut into strips- 1 ½ Ib.
- Crushed garlic- 1 clove
- A pinch of red pepper flakes
- Salt and black pepper to taste
- Extra virgin olive oil- 2 tbsp.
- Chopped parsley- 1 bunch
- White wine- ½ cup
- Chopped canned tomatoes- 14 oz.
- 1 lemon; juiced
- Water- 1 cup
- Anchovies- 2

Directions:

1. Press 'Sauté' on the Instant Pot then mix in the anchovies, garlic, oil and pepper flakes to cook for 3 minutes.
2. Mix in the calamari to cook for 5 minutes then add the wine and mix again to cook for 3 minutes.
3. Pour in the water, tomatoes, half of the parsley, salt and pepper then seal the lid to cook for 20 minutes at high pressure.
4. Quick release the pressure and add the remaining parsley, salt and pepper, and the lemon juice.
5. Serve with rice.

Creamy Cinnamon Rice With Saffron And Almonds

Servings: 10, **Prep + Cooking Time:** 20 minutes

Ingredients:

- Chopped almonds- 1/3 cup
- A pinch of salt
- Veggie stock- 3 ½ cups
- Arborio rice- 1 ½ cups
- Hot milk- 2 tbsp.
- Crushed saffron threads- ½ tsp.
- Dried currants- 1/3 cup
- Honey- 1 tbsp.
- Extra virgin olive oil- 2 tbsp.
- Cinnamon stick- 1
- Chopped onion- ½ cup

Directions:

1. Combine the saffron with hot milk in a bowl and set aside.
2. Press 'Sauté' on the Instant Pot and add the oil and onions to fry for 5 minutes.
3. Mix in the saffron mix, veggie stock, rice, almonds, currants, salt, and honey then seal the lid to cook for 5 minutes at high pressure.
4. Quick release the pressure, then loosen the rice with a fork and remove the cinnamon.

Citrus Cauliflowers With Capers And Anchovies

Servings: 4, **Prep + Cooking Time:** 15 minutes

Ingredients:

- Cauliflower with florets separated- 1
- Romanesco cauliflower with florets separated- 1
- A pinch of hot pepper flakes
- Salt and black pepper
- Juice and zest from one orange
- Broccoli florets; separated- 1 Ib.
- Extra virgin olive oil- 4 tbsp.
- Chopped capers- 1 tbsp.
- Anchovies- 4
- Peeled and sliced oranges- 2
- Water- 1 cup

Directions:

1. Combine pepper flakes, anchovies, orange zest and juice, capers, and salt and pepper together in a bowl and set aside.
2. Put the cauliflower florets inside a steaming rack and pour a cup of water into the Instant Pot. Place the rack above the water and seal the lid to cook for 6 minutes on low pressure.
3. Quick release the pressure and mix the steamed florets with the orange slices in a bowl.
4. Mix in the vinaigrette and make sure it coats the florets.
5. Serve with chicken.

Chapter 11 Snack and Appetizers

Blended Beet With Squash

Servings: 8 , Prep + Cook time: 30 minutes

Ingredients:

- Beets; peeled and chopped: 4
- Butternut squash; peeled and chopped: 1
- Yellow onion; chopped: 1
- Basil; chopped 1 bunch
- Bay leaves: 2
- Carrots; chopped: 8
- Olive oil: 2 tbsp.
- Celery ribs: 5
- Garlic cloves; minced: 8
- Veggie stock: 1 cup
- Lemon juice: 1/4 cup
- Salt and black pepper to the taste

Directions:

1. 'Sauté' oil, celery, carrots and onions in an instant pot and cook for 3 minutes
2. While stirring, add beets, squash, garlic, stock, lemon juice, basil, bay leaves, salt and pepper then cook for 12 minutes on high
3. 'Natural release' the steam and remove the lid
4. Discard the bay leaves, blend t remaining contents and serve

Steamed Zucchini Rolls

Servings: 24 , Prep + Cook time: 18 minutes

Ingredients:

- Zucchinis, thinly sliced: 3
- Olive oil: 2 tbsp.
- Basil leaves: 24
- Mint; chopped: 2 tbsp.
- Water: 1 ½ cups
- Ricotta cheese: 1 ⅓ cup
- Salt and black pepper to the taste
- Basil; chopped: 1/4 cup
- Tomato sauce for serving

Directions:

1. 'Sauté' zucchini and oil seasoned with salt and pepper for 2 minutes each side
2. Mix ricotta, chopped basil, mint, salt and pepper in a bowl then stir
3. Divide it into zucchini slices and roll them
4. Place water in the instant pot and zucchini rolls in the steamer, secure the lid and cook for 3 minutes on high
5. Top with tomato and serve

Saucy Shrimp

Servings: 16 , Prep + Cook time: 30 minutes

Ingredients:

- Shrimp, cooked, peeled and deveined: 10 oz.
- Prosciutto slices: 11
- Blackberries, ground: 1/3 cup
- Veggie stock: 1/3 cup
- Olive oil: 2 tbsp.
- Mint; chopped: 1 tbsp.
- Erythritol: 2 tbsp.

Directions:

1. Wrap the shrimps in prosciutto slices and drizzle oil on them
2. Mix blackberries, mint, stock and erythritol in an instant pot and simmer for 2 minutes
3. Place them in the steamer basket, secure the lid and cook for 2 minutes on high
4. Top with mint sauce and serve

Garlicky Chili

Servings: 8 , **Prep + Cook time:** 20 minutes

Ingredients:
- Ancho chilies; dried and chopped: 5
- Garlic cloves; minced: 2
- Water: 1 ½ cups
- Balsamic vinegar: 2 tbsp.
- Cumin, ground: 1/2 Tsps.
- Stevia: 1 ½ Tsps.
- Oregano; chopped: 1 tbsp.
- Salt and black pepper to the taste

Directions:
1. Mix water in an instant pot then stir, secure the lid and cook for 8 minutes on high
2. Blend them then add vinegar and stir. Simmer until it thickens
3. Top with veggie sticks and serve

Spicy Mango

Servings: 4 , **Prep + Cook time:** 23 minutes

Ingredients:
- Mangos; peeled and chopped: 2
- Shallot; chopped: 1
- Apple cider vinegar: 1 ¼
- Cinnamon powder: 1/2 Tsps.
- Red hot chilies; chopped: 2
- Coconut oil: 1 tbsp.
- Cardamom powder: 1/4 Tsps.
- Ginger; minced: 2 tbsp.
- Raisins: 1/4 cup
- Stevia: 5 tbsp.
- Apple; cored and chopped: 1

Directions:
1. 'Sauté' oil in an instant pot
2. Add shallot and ginger then stir and cook for 3 minutes
3. While stirring, add cinnamon, hot peppers, cardamom, mangos, apple, raisins, stevia and cider, secure the pot and cook for 7 minutes on high
4. Simmer for 6 minutes then serve

Seasoned Cheese

Servings: 4 , **Prep + Cook time:** 30 minutes

Ingredients:
- Cream cheese, soft: 4 oz.
- Black olives; pitted and chopped: 4
- Water: 2 cups
- Mozzarella cheese: 1/2 cup
- Coconut cream: 1/4 cup
- Mayonnaise: 1/4 cup
- Parmesan cheese, grated: 1/4 cup
- Tomato sauce: 1/2 cup
- Green bell pepper; chopped: 1 tbsp.
- Pepperoni slices; chopped: 6
- Italian seasoning: 1/2 Tsps.
- Salt and black pepper to the taste

Directions:
1. Mix cream cheese, mozzarella, coconut cream, mayo, salt and pepper in a bowl then stir and divide it into 4 ramekins
2. Top it with tomato sauce, parmesan cheese, bell pepper, pepperoni, Italian seasoning and black olives
3. Place water in an instant pot and the mixture in the steamer then secure the lid and cook for 20 minutes on high
4. Add veggies and serve

Spicy Tomatoes

Servings: 4 , Prep + Cook time: 20 minutes

Ingredients:

- Tomatoes; tops cut off and pulp scooped: 4
- Water: 1/2 cup
- Yellow onion; chopped: 1
- Ghee: 1 tbsp.
- Celery; chopped: 2 tbsp.
- Mushrooms; chopped: 1/2 cup
- Cottage cheese: 1 cup
- Caraway seeds: 1/4 Tsps.
- Salt and black pepper to the taste
- Parsley; chopped: 1 tbsp.

Directions:

1. 'Sauté' ghee, onion and celery for 3 minutes
2. Add tomato pulp, mushrooms, salt, pepper, cheese, parsley and caraway seeds then stir and cook for 3 minutes
3. Stuff tomato with the mix
4. Place water in an instant pot and the stuffed tomato on the steamer, secure the lid and cook for 4 minutes on high
5. Top with tomatoes and serve

Tasty Shrimp

Servings: 4 , Prep + Cook time: 15 minutes

Ingredients:

- Shrimp, peeled and deveined: 1 lb.
- Pineapple juice: 3/4 cup
- Coconut aminos: 2 tbsp.
- Vinegar: 3 tbsp.
- Chicken stock: 1 cup
- Stevia: 3 tbsp.

Directions:

1. Mix shrimp, pineapple juice, stock, aminos and stevia in an instant pot then stir it and secure the lid.and cook for 4 minutes on high
2. Top it with cooking juices and serve

Sautéed Okra Tomatoes

Servings: 6 , Prep + Cook time: 25 minutes

Ingredients:

- Canned tomatoes; chopped: 28 oz.
- Okra, trimmed: 1 lb.
- Scallions; chopped: 6
- Green bell peppers; chopped: 3
- Olive oil: 2 tbsp.
- Stevia: 1 Tsps.
- Salt and black pepper to the taste

Directions:

1. 'Sauté' oil, scallions and bell peppers in an instant pot for 5 minutes
2. Add okra, salt, pepper, stevia and tomatoes then stir and cook for 10 minutes
3. Serve

Delicious Mussels

Servings: 4 , Prep + Cook time: 15 minutes

Ingredients:

- Mussels, scrubbed: 2 lb.
- Chicken stock: 1/2 cup
- Red pepper flakes: 1/2 Tsps.
- Olive oil: 2 tbsp.
- Garlic; minced: 2 Tsps.
- Oregano; dried: 2 Tsps.
- Yellow onion; chopped: 1
- Tomatoes; chopped: 14 oz.

Directions:

1. 'Sauté' oil and dominos in an instant pot for 3 minutes
2. Add pepper flakes, garlic, stock, tomatoes, oregano and mussels then stir, secure the lid and cook for 3 minutes on low
3. Serve

Chapter 12 Rice

Special Lentil Rice

Servings: 4, Prep + Cook time: 55 minutes

Ingredients:
- Garlic - 2 cloves, minced
- Onion - 1/2 cup, chopped
- Oil - 1 tbsp.
- Brown rice - 1 ½ cups
- Fresh rosemary - a 2-inch sprig
- Brown lentils - 1 cup.
- Dried marjoram - 1 tbsp.
- Water - 3 ½ cups
- Rutabaga - 1 cup, peeled and diced
- Seasoning - salt and pepper

Directions:

1. Select Sauté in your instant pot and then add the oil to heat. Once the oil is hot, put the onion and cook for 5 minutes. Add the garlic and then cook for a minute.
2. Put the lentils, brown rice, rutabaga, marjoram, rosemary, and water in the pot, mix them well and then select cancel.
3. Press manual and then cook it for 23 minutes at high pressure. After cooking, do a natural release for 15 minutes. Gently open up the lid of the pot.
4. Season with salt and pepper and rosemary and marjoram if desired. Serve immediately.

Rice on Coconut Milk

Servings: 4, Prep + Cook time: 25 minutes

Ingredients:
- Thai sweet rice - 1 cup
- Full-fat coconut milk - 1/2 can
- Water - 1 ½ cups
- Sugar Dash of salt - 2 tbsp.

Directions:
1. Put the rice and water in your instant pot and then mix them. Press manual and then cook for 3 minutes at high pressure.
2. Do a natural release for 10 minutes. While releasing the pressure, you can heat the coconut milk, salt, and sugar in a pan. Once the sugar melts, remove the pan from heat.
3. After the pressure is released, mix the coconut milk mixture with the rice, mix well them well and then secure the lid. Let it sit for about 10 minutes before serving.

Spicy Rice

Servings: 8, Prep + Cook time: 15 minutes

Ingredients:
- Long grain rice - 1 cup
- Cilantro - 1/2 cup, chopped
- Avocado - ½ piece, pitted; peeled and chopped
- Green hot sauce - 1/4 cup
- Veggie stock - 1 ¼ cups
- Seasoning - salt and black pepper

Directions:
1. Place the rice inside the instant pot and then pour down the stock. Mix well and then secure the lid of the pot. Cook the rice for 4 minutes at high pressure.
2. Do a natural release for 10 minutes and let the remaining pressure to come out. Open up the lid of the put and then put the rice in a bowl.
3. In a food processor, blend the avocado, hot sauce, and cilantro. Pour over this mix at the top of the rice. Season with salt and pepper, mix well and then serve hot.

Easy Rice Breakfast Bowls

Servings: 4, Prep + Cook time: 12 minutes

Ingredients:

- Brown rice - 1 cup
- Coconut milk - 1 cup
- Water - 2 cups
- Maple syrup - 1/2 cup
- Coconut chips - 1/2 cup
- Raisins - 1/4 cup
- Almonds - 1/4 cup
- Cinnamon powder - a pinch only
- Salt - a pinch only

Ingredients:

1. Pour water in a pot and then add the rice. Put the pot on a stove and cook it like normal rice over medium-high heat. After cooking, drain the rice and then put it in the instant pot.
2. Pour over the milk and then add the almonds, raisins, salt, cinnamon, maple syrup, and coconut chips. Secure the lid of the pot and then cook for 5 minutes at high pressure.
3. Do a quick release and then serve the rice on breakfast bowls. Enjoy.

Chicken Rice Mix

Servings: 2, Prep + Cook time: 50 minutes

Ingredients:

- Chicken - 3 quarters cut into small pieces
- Carrots – 2 pieces, cut into chunks
- Yellow onion – 1 piece, sliced
- Cumin, - 1 tsp. ground
- Soy sauce - 1 tbsp.
- Peanut oil - 1 tbsp.
- Potatoes – 2 pieces, cut into quarters
- Shallot – 1 piece, sliced
- Cornstarch - 1 ½ tbsp. (with 2 tbsp. water mixed)
- Turmeric powder - 1 ½ tsp.
- Green bell pepper – 1 piece, chopped
- Coconut milk - 7 oz.
- Bay leaves – 2 pieces
- Garlic – 3 cloves, minced
- Seasoning - salt and black pepper
- Water - 1 ½ cups
- Rice - 1 ½ cups
- White wine - 1 tbsp.
- Soy sauce - 1 tbsp.
- Sugar - 1/2 tsp.
- White pepper - a pinch only

Directions:

1. Mix the chicken, sugar, white pepper, 1 tablespoon soy sauce and 1 tablespoon white wine in a bowl and then refrigerate it for 20 minutes.
2. Select Sauté in your instant pot and then put the peanut oil to heat. Add the shallot and onion, mix well and then cook for 3 minutes. Put the garlic, pepper, and salt. Mix well and then cook for another 2 minutes.
3. Put the cumin and the turmeric, mix well and then cook for a minute. Add the bay leaves, potatoes, carrots, bell pepper, coconut milk, and 1 tablespoon soy sauce.
4. Put a steamer basket inside the pot and then put the rice in a bowl. Put the bowl on the steamer basket and then pour 1 ½ cups water on the bowl. Secure the lid of the pot and then cook the rice for 4 minutes at high pressure.
5. Do a natural release and then serve the rice on separate plates with the chicken.

Standard Pink Rice

Servings: 8, Prep + Cook time: 15 minutes

Ingredients:
- Pink rice - 2 cups
- Water - 2 ½ cups
- Salt - 1 tsp.

Directions:
1. Place the rice inside the instant pot and then add water and salt. Mix well and then secure the lid of the pot. Cook the rice for 5 minutes at high pressure.
2. Do a natural release for 10 minutes and then gently open up the pot's lid. Serve the rice hot.

Fried Basmati Rice on Chicken Stock

Servings: 4, Prep + Cook time: 15 minutes

Ingredients:
- Basmati rice - 1 cup, uncooked
- Peas - 1/2 cups
- Soy sauce - 1/4 cup
- Chicken stock - 1 ½ cups
- Butter - 1 tbsp.
- Medium onion – 1 piece, diced
- Garlic - 2 cloves, minced
- Egg – 1 piece

Directions:
1. Select Sauté in the instant pot to heat it and then add the oil. Put the garlic and onion and then cook them for 1 minute.
2. Put the egg and garlic, mix them well to make the egg scrambled. Cook for 2 minutes.
3. Put the rice, stock, and soy sauce in the pot. Select Cancel to stop sautéing. Secure the lid of the pot and then select Rice. Let it cook for 10 minutes.
4. After cooking, do a quick release. Gently open up the lid of the pot. Mix the peas on the rice. Serve hot and enjoy.

Wild Rice with Cherries

Servings: 12, Prep + Cook time: 45 minutes

Ingredients:
- Whole grain farro - 1 ½ cups
- Parsley and sage - 1 tbsp. finely chopped
- Hazelnuts - 1/2 cup, toasted and chopped
- Wild rice - 3/4 cup
- Shallot – 1 piece, finely chopped
- Garlic - 1 tsp. minced
- Chicken stock - 6 cups
- Cherries - 3/4 cup, dried
- Chopped chives
- Extra virgin olive oil
- Seasoning - salt and black pepper

Directions:
1. Select Sauté in your instant pot and then put the oil to heat. Add the garlic and onion and then sauté for 3 minutes.
2. Put the farro, salt, rice, pepper, stock, and 1 tablespoon mixed sage and parsley. Mix well and then secure the lid of the pot. Cook the rice for 25 minutes at high pressure.
3. While the rice is cooking, put the cherries on a pot and then pour down with hot water. Set aside for 20 minutes and then drain.
4. Do a natural release for 5 minutes and then open up the lid of the pot. Drain the liquids from the instant pot. Top up the rice with the cherries and hazelnut. Serve in separate bowls.

Creamy Rice Pudding

Servings: 6, **Prep + Cook time:** 20 minutes

Ingredients:
- Long grain rice - 7 oz.
- Butter - 1 tbsp.
- Water - 4 oz.
- Milk - 16 oz.
- Sugar - 3 oz.
- Egg – 1 piece
- Cream - 1 tbsp.
- Vanilla - 1 tsp.
- Salt - a pinch only
- Cinnamon

Directions:
1. Select Sauté in your instant pot and then add the butter to melt and heat. Once the butter melts, add the rice and then mix well.
2. Pour down milk and water, mix well. Put the salt and sugar, mix well and then secure the lid of the pot. Cook for 8 minutes at high pressure.
3. While cooking the rice, get a bowl and mix the vanilla, cream, and egg on it.
4. Do a quick release and then gently open up the lid of the pot. Pour over some of the liquids inside the pot to the mixture of the egg. Mix well.
5. Put the egg mixture in the pot. Secure the lid again and then cook for 10 minutes at high pressure. Do a quick release again and then open up the lid of the pot.
6. Put cinnamon at the top of the rice and then serve.

Plain White Rice

Servings: 4, **Prep + Cook time:** 15 minutes

Ingredients:
- White basmati rice - 1 cup
- Water - 1 cup

Directions:

1. Rinse the rice until the water becomes clear. Put the rice inside the instant pot and then add the water.
2. Press manual and cook the rice for 8 minutes at low pressure. After cooking, do a quick release. Serve the rice hot.

Chapter 13 Sauce

Tasty Green Tomato Sauce

Serving: 12 , Prep + Cook time:15 minutes

Ingredients:

- green tomatoes - 2 lb.; chopped.
- red chili peppers - 4; chopped.
- Anaheim chili pepper - 1; chopped.
- brown sugar - 3/4 cup
- white vinegar - 3/4 cup
- ginger - 2 tbsp., grated
- white onion - 1; chopped.
- Currants - 1/4 cup

Directions:

1. Mix green tomatoes with onion, currants, Anaheim pepper, chili pepper, ginger, sugar, and vinegar in your instant pot; then stir gently. Close and seal the lid of the instant pot and cook at High mode for about 10 minutes.
2. Let the pressure naturally; do this for 5 minutes then release remaining pressure by turning the valve to 'Venting' mode. After this, gently unlock the lid and open.
3. Move the sauce to the jars and serve immediately.

Seasoned Cranberry Sauce

Serving: 4 , Prep + Cook time:25 minutes

Ingredients:

- Cranberries - 12 oz.
- orange juice - 1/4 cup
- orange zest - 2 ½ tsp.
- maple syrup - 2 tbsp.
- A pinch of salt
- Sugar - 1 cup

Directions:

1. Mix orange juice with maple syrup in your instant pot and stir gently.
2. Mix the orange zest and almost all cranberries together and stir well. Seal the lid of the instant pot and cook at High mode for a time of about 2 minutes.
3. Do a quick release in order to release the pressure, then open the lid of the pot and select Sauté mode.
4. Add the remaining cranberries, as well as a pinch of salt and sugar to taste, stir gently and cook until all the sugar dissolves. Serve the dish cold.

Seasoned Ancho Chili Sauce Recipe

Serving: 8 , Prep + Cook time:20 minutes

Ingredients:

- ancho chilies - 5, dried, seedless and chopped.
- garlic cloves - 2, crushed.
- Oregano - 1/2 tsp.; dried
- Cumin - 1/2 tsp; ground.
- water - 1 ½ cups
- sugar - 1 ½ tsp.
- apple cider vinegar - 2 tbsp.
- Salt and black pepper to the taste

Directions:

1. Mix water chilies, garlic, salt, pepper, sugar, cumin and oregano in your instant pot; then stir properly. Close the instant pot by placing the lid on top and cook at High for 8 minutes.
2. Let the pressure release naturally for 5 minutes then release the rest of the pressure by turning the valve to 'Venting', and gently open the lid.
3. Open the instant pot lid and transfer the sauce to a blender
4. Then add vinegar to the blender, pulse well move all of it to a bowl

Seasoned Marinara Sauce

Serving: 8 , Prep + Cook time:30 minutes

Ingredients:

- canned tomatoes - 55 oz., crushed.
- water - 1 ½ cups
- garlic cloves - 3; minced.
- red lentils - 1/2 cup
- sweet potato - 1 cup; finely chopped
- Salt and black pepper to the taste

Directions:

1. Put your instant pot on Sauté mode; then add lentils, sweet potatoes, garlic as well as salt and pepper stir and cook the ingredients for 2 minutes
2. Then add water and tomatoes; stir well. Close the lid of the pot and cook at High mode for almost 15 minutes.
3. Do a quick release of the pressure, then gently open the lid; puree everything with the use of an immersion blender. Finally, add more salt and pepper if it is required, then put the instant pot on Simmer mode and cook the sauce for another 4 minutes.

Celery Sauce Recipe

Serving: 8 , Prep + Cook time:30 minutes

Ingredients:

- yellow onion - 1; chopped.
- butternut squash - 1; chopped.
- garlic cloves - 8; minced.
- bay leaves - 2
- olive oil - 2 tbsp.
- veggie stock - 1 cup
- lemon juice - 1/4 cup
- basil - 1 bunch; chopped.
- celery ribs - 5
- carrots - 8; chopped
- beets - 4; chopped
- Salt and black pepper to the taste

Directions:

1. Put the instant pot on Sauté mode; then add oil and turn on the heat.
2. Add celery, onion and carrots, stir gently and cook for 4 minutes.
3. Then add beets, squash, garlic, stock, lemon juice, basil, bay leaves, salt and pepper and stir gently. Close the lid and cook for about 15 minutes at High mode.
4. Do a quick release of the pressure, then gently open the lid; and remove the bay leaves, puree the sauce with the help of an immersion blender, move to a clean bowl and serve right away.

Tasty Apricot Sauce

Serving: 6 , Prep + Cook time:30 minutes

Ingredients:

- Apricots - 3 oz.; dried and cut into halves
- water - 2 cups
- vanilla extract - 1 tsp.
- sugar - 2/3 cup

Directions:

1. Mix apricots with water, sugar and vanilla in your instant pot; then stir gently. Close the instant pot lid tightly and cook on Medium mode for 20 minutes
2. Do a quick release of the pressure, and gently open the lid. Move the sauce to your blender; ensure to pulse well.
3. Divide into different jars and serve with a poultry dish as a side dish.

Tasty Sriracha Sauce

Serving: 6 , Prep + Cook time:25 minutes

Ingredients:
- red chilies - 4 oz., seeded and chopped.
- palm sugar - 3 tbsp.
- bird's eye chilies - 3 oz.
- garlic cloves - 12; minced.
- distilled vinegar - 5 oz.
- water - 5 oz.

Directions:
1. Mix water with palm sugar in your instant pot and stir gently.
2. Add all chilies and garlic to the pot and stir well. Close the instant pot lid and cook at High mode for a little above 5 minutes
3. Do a quick release of the pressure, gently open the lid; pulse the sauce with an immersion blender, then add vinegar and stir well.
4. Put the pot on Simmer mode and cook; set the cooking time at 10 minutes
5. Serve the dish immediately it is wanted

Yummy Onion Sauce

Serving: 8 , Prep + Cook time:40 minutes

Ingredients:
- Butter - 6 tbsp.
- yellow onion - 3 lb., thinly chopped
- baking soda - 1/2 tsp.
- Salt and black pepper to the taste

Directions:
1. Put your instant pot on Sauté mode and add butter to it; heat up the pot.
2. Also, add onions and soda, stir gently and cook for close to 5 minutes.
3. Place the lid on the pot and close it; then cook at High for 20 minutes
4. Do a quick release of the pressure, then gently open the lid and set it on Sauté mode again. Cook for another 5 minutes and stir frequently.
5. Serve when the dish is wanted.

Tasty Clementine Sauce Recipe

Serving: 4 , Prep + Cook time:16 minutes

Ingredients:
- Cranberries - 12 oz.
- Juice and peel from 1 clementine
- water - 1 cup
- sugar - 1 cup

Directions:
1. Mix cranberries with clementine juice and peel, water and sugar; then stir properly. Place the lid on top and cover it, then cook at High for 6 minutes.
2. Do a quick release of the pressure, open the instant pot lid and serve your clementine sauce on demand.

Sweet Tabasco Sauce Recipe

Serving: 6 , Prep + Cook time:12 minutes

Ingredients:
- hot peppers - 12 oz.; chopped.
- salt - 2 tsp.
- apple cider vinegar - 1 ¼ cups

Directions:
1. Introduce the peppers to your instant pot
2. Then add vinegar and salt to the pot; stir gently. Seal the lid of the instant pot and cook at High mode for about 2 minutes.
3. Let the pressure release naturally for 15 minutes then release the rest of the pressure by turning the valve to 'Venting'. Open the pot lid and puree everything with the help of your immersion blender.
4. Move to the jars and serve immediately the dish is needed.

Appendix: Measurement Conversion Chart

Volume Equivalents(Liquid)

US STANDARD	US STANDARD(OUNCES)	METRIC(APPROXIMATE)
2 TABLESPOONS	1 fl.oz.	30 mL
1/4 CUP	2 fl.oz.	60 mL
1/2 CUP	4 fl.oz.	120 mL
1 CUP	8 fl.oz.	240 mL
1 1/2 CUP	12 fl.oz.	355 mL
2 CUPS OR 1 PINT	16 fl.oz.	475 mL
4 CUPS OR 1 QUART	32 fl.oz.	1 L
1 GALLON	128 fl.oz.	4 L

Volume Equivalents (DRY)

US STANDARD	METRIC (APPROXIMATE)
1/8 TEASPOON	0.5 mL
1/4 TEASPOON	1 mL
1/2 TEASPOON	2 mL
3/4 TEASPOON	4 mL
1 TEASPOON	5 mL
1 TABLESPOON	15 mL
1/4 CUP	59 mL
1/2 CUP	118 mL
3/4 CUP	177 mL
1 CUP	235 mL
2 CUPS	475 mL
3 CUPS	700 mL
4 CUPS	1 L

Weight Equivalents

US STANDARD	METRIC (APPROXIMATE)
1/2 OUNCE	15g
1 OUNCE	30g
2 OUNCE	60g
4 OUNCE	115g
8 OUNCE	225g
12 OUNCE	340g
16 OUNCES OR 1 POUND	455g

Temperatures Equivalents

FAHRENHEIT (F)	CELSIUS(C) (APPROXIMATE)
250	121
300	149
325	163
350	177
375	190
400	205
425	218
450	232

Made in the USA
Columbia, SC
26 December 2019

85799204R10100